99

Radical!

Radical!

A PRACTICAL GUIDE TO FRENCH GRAMMAR

IAN MAUN

Cartoons by *G. Mathieu*

A member of the Hodder Headline Group
LONDON

First published in Great Britain in 2000 by
Arnold, a member of the Hodder Headline Group,
338 Euston Road, London NW1 3BH

http://www.arnoldpublishers.com

British Library Cataloguing in Publication Data
A catalogue record for this book is available from the British Library

ISBN 0 340 71977 X

1 2 3 4 5 6 7 8 9 10

Production Editor: Julie Delf
Production Controller: Sarah Kett
Cover Design: T. Griffiths

Typeset in 11/15pt Minion by Saxon Graphics Ltd, Derby
Printed and bound in Great Britain by J W Arrowsmith Ltd, Bristol

What do you think about this book? Or any other Arnold title?
Please send your comments to feedback.arnold@hodder.co.uk

Contents

Acknowledgements

The author and publishers would like to thank the following for permission to use copyright material in the book:

Gérard Mathieu and Éditions Ellipses for the cartoons from 'Mathieu de A à Z'; Librairie Plon for Pierre Jakez Helias, 'Le Cheval d'orgueil'; Éditions Gallimard for Henri Bosco, 'L'Enfant et la rivière', Eve Curie, 'Madame Curie', Jules Romains, 'Knock ou le triomphe de la médecine', André Malraux, 'La Condition humaine', Raymond Queneau, «Portrait» and «Passé indéfini» from 'Exercices de style', and André Gide, 'La Symphonice pastorale'; Mercure de France for André Gide, 'La Porte étroite'; Mme Jacqueline Pagnol and Les Éditions de la Treille for Marcel Pagnol, 'Topaze', 'La Gloire de mon père' and 'Le Château de ma mère'. Maurice Druon for 'Le Roi de fer', 'La louve de France', 'Le Lis et le lion', 'La Loi des mâles'.

How to use this book

A grammar isn't quite like a recipe book, but it has certain similarities to one. You usually consult a recipe book if you're uncertain how to prepare a particular dish. You may know most of the ingredients, or the cooking time, but one little piece of information eludes your memory. Looking up the recipe can help you to fill in that missing piece of information. So it is with a grammar. You may know most of the rules for, say, the formation of the perfect tense, but a glance at the relevant section in the book can complete your knowledge.

Alternatively, you may know nothing about puddings, so you open the relevant section of the recipe book and read through it, exploring a field of knowledge that's completely new to you. When you've finished reading, you'll have a good idea of how puddings are made and how many varieties there are. So it is with a grammar. You may know nothing about the subjunctive mood, but you may decide to find out about it by reading the whole section on it.

Either way, you'll probably feel hungry from reading your recipe book, and it is to be hoped that you'll be hungry for more knowledge of French when you've dipped into this book or you've read whole sections to widen your knowledge.

The book is divided into sections, each dealing with a particular area of grammar.

Terminology

As the terminology of grammar is at least as difficult as that of cookery or computer software, a list of **grammatical definitions** has been included (see pages 1–6) before the grammar itself. This can either be read through first, or can be consulted when you meet a term that you don't understand.

Example:

Adjective *l'adjectif*	A word which modifies (i.e. makes more precise) a **noun** or **noun phrase**

Grammar sections

Each grammar section is numbered, and references within the text may take you to other numbered sections, rather like a hyper-text on the Internet. The rules of French grammar are explained in as brief and concise a way as possible, and each rule is illustrated with a simple example, e.g.

4.27 Relative pronouns

Relative pronouns stand at the head of a clause referring to a noun, i.e. a clause which tells us more about that noun. The relative pronouns are *qui, que, dont, où, quoi* and *lequel* – in its various forms (see 4.29).

Rule	Example
When the relative pronoun is the **subject** of its clause, *qui* is used	*Marcel Proust – un auteur **qui** était obsédé par le temps **qui** passe* – Marcel Proust, an author **who** was obsessed by the passing of time

If there are exceptions to the rule given, these are marked 'Exception'.

Quotations

To reinforce these examples, quotations from French literature and from newspapers, magazines and other contemporary sources are given. Most of the literary quotations are from twentieth-century sources. Cartoons also illustrate grammatical points.

> **Phil** plia les fauteuils de bois, retourna la table en rotin. **Il** ne souriait pas, en passant, à sa petite amie.
>
> Colette, *Le Blé en herbe*
>
> Ne gardez pas **les champignons** frais plus de deux jours au refrigérateur: au delà, **ils** sèchent ou **ils** moisissent.
>
> *Avantages*

Exercises

At the end of the sections explaining and illustrating grammatical points you will find exercises to help you to practise what you've learned. Some exercises simply require a gap to be filled, while others are more open-ended. Some exercises consist of sentences which have to be transformed in some way, others require you to use information given in order to formulate an answer.

EXERCICES

A Complément d'objet direct ou indirect? Complétez les phrases suivantes avec **le**, **la**, **les**, **lui** ou **leur**.

1 J'ai vu André et Marianne en ville et je _____ ai demandé de venir à la boum.

2 Je comprends bien l'anglais, mais je ne ___ parle pas très bien.

3 J'ai une nouvelle voisine. Je ___ connais de vue, mais je ne ___ ai pas encore parlé.

4 Il y a de très beaux rideaux dans le nouveau catalogue, mais je ne vais pas ___ acheter parce qu'ils sont trop chers.

5 J'ai un manuel pour mon ordinateur, mais je ne ___ comprends pas.

So a whole page looks like this:

Grammar explained

Quotations

Exercises

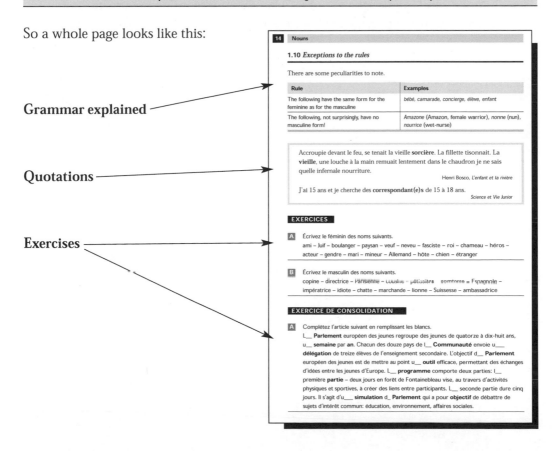

When we use language, we never concentrate on a single grammatical point for sentence after sentence. To enable you to co-ordinate a number of things that you have learned, occasional exercises require you to bring together a number of grammatical points at once. Look back to the references given to refresh your memory.

The ability to put together a sentence is very important, and there is a section to show you the most important rules in formulating well-structured sentences. Some important indications are given about word order and the rhythm of the French sentence.

Irregular verb tables

The verb is, of course, an extremely important area of grammar, and for this reason the main irregular verbs in French are each given a separate page in the verb tables at the end of the book. A summary of other irregular verbs is also appended.

A grammar is no substitute for using language – listening to it, speaking it, reading it and writing it.

It is, however, an essential tool which will enable you to understand better and to speak and write better. A grammar should be beside you just as much as a dictionary. This grammar has been designed to be as helpful and interesting as possible in its presentation. Use it like a recipe book – to dip into or to read at length.

Ian Maun

Teignmouth

May 1999

Grammatical definitions

Within these definitions, English grammatical terms are written in bold type. Each definition includes further grammatical terms. If you are uncertain of the meaning of such a term, cross-reference it with its definition elsewhere in the table, e.g. 'A word which modifies (i.e. makes more precise) the sense of a **verb**, a **phrase** or a **sentence**'. Go to '**phrase**' if you're uncertain what this means.

Adjective *l'adjectif*	A word which modifies (i.e. makes more precise) a **noun** or **noun phrase**
Adverb *l'adverbe*	A word which modifies (i.e. makes more precise) the sense of a **verb**, a **phrase** or a **sentence**
Affirmative *affirmatif*	An **affirmative** sentence is one which makes a statement that is not **negative**
Agreement *l'accord*	A **noun** which is the **subject** of a **verb** determines the form of that verb (particularly its ending) The form of a **noun** (**number** and **gender**) influences the form of any accompanying **adjective**
Apposition *l'apposition*	A noun is said to be **in apposition** with another noun when it is placed next to it to act as a definition
Article *l'article*	A word which determines whether a **noun** under discussion is **definite**, **indefinite** or **partitive**
Attributive *attributif*	**Attributive adjectives** are those which are attached directly to their noun
Auxiliary *l'auxiliaire*	The verbs *avoir* and *être* help to form **compound tenses**, and are thus known as **auxiliary** (helping) **verbs**
Clause *la proposition*	A part of a **sentence** which contains a **subject** and a **verb**. A **main clause** makes enough sense to stand on its own; a **subordinate** clause must be attached to a main clause for its sense to be clear
Command *l'impératif*	See **Imperative**

Comparative *le comparatif*	The form of the **adjective** or **adverb** which expresses a comparison between one thing and another
Complement *le complément*	An element such as an **object** which follows a **verb**
Compound noun *le nom composé*	A **noun** consisting of two parts. Both parts may be nouns, or one part may be an **adjective** or some other part of speech
Compound tense *le temps composé*	A **tense** consisting of the verbs *avoir* or *être* in some form and a **past participle**
Conditional *le conditionnel*	A **tense** which tells what *would* happen in certain circumstances
Conditional perfect *le conditionnel passé*	A **tense** which tells what *would have* happened in certain circumstances
Coordinate *coordonné*	Words, **phrases** and **clauses** which are linked by *et, mais, ou*
Declarative *déclaratif*	A **declarative sentence** makes a statement. Thus **questions** and **commands** are not declarative
Definite noun *le nom défini*	A **noun** is said to be **definite** if its identity is clear and/or known to the speaker and the listener
Demonstrative *démonstratif*	**Adjectives** and **pronouns** which are **demonstrative** point out or refer to particular **nouns**
Direct object *le complément d'objet direct*	The **direct object** of a verb is the **noun** or noun **phrase** directly affected by the action of the **verb**
Direct question *la question directe*	A **question** which is directly quoted using the original words of the speaker
Di-transitive verb *le verbe transitif double*	See **Transitive verb**
Feminine *féminin*	One of two types of **noun** in French
Finite verb *le verbe fini*	A **verb** which has indications of **tense** and **agreement**
Future *le futur*	A **tense** which tells what *will* happen in the future
Future perfect *le futur antérieur*	A **tense** which tells what *will have* happened by a certain time

Gender *le genre*	French nouns are either **masculine** or **feminine** by gender
Gerund *le gérondif*	The form of the **present participle** which is preceded by *en*
Imperative *l'impératif*	The **imperative** is the form of the verb used to give commands or instructions or to issue invitations
Imperfect *l'imparfait*	A **tense** which tells what *was* happening or what *used to* happen. It is also used in descriptions
Impersonal **pronoun** *le pronom* *impersonnel*	The **pronoun** *il*, when it is used without reference to a person or thing
Impersonal verb *le verbe* *impersonnel*	**Impersonal verbs** are those verbs which are introduced by *il*, when this *il* does not refer to anything
Indefinite **adjective** *l'adjectif indéfini*	**Indefinite adjectives** give a vague idea of quality or quantity connected with the **noun** to which they are linked
Indefinite noun *le nom indéfini*	A **noun** is said to be **indefinite** if its identity is unclear and/or unknown to the speaker and the listener
Indicative *l'indicatif*	This is the **mood** of the **verb** which is used to indicate fact
Indirect object *le complément* *d'objet indirect*	This is a **noun** or noun **phrase** preceded by *à*, or a **pronoun** containing the idea of 'to'
Indirect question *la question* *indirecte*	A **question** which is reported. The original words of the speaker are not used
Infinitive *l'infinitif*	This is the form of the **verb** which ends in -*er*, -*ir*, -*re* or -*oir*. It may be regarded as the name of the verb, e.g. 'aller', 'avoir', 'faire'. It is also the form from which **tenses** are generally considered to be formed
Interrogative **adjective** *l'adjectif* *interrogatif*	The **interrogative adjective** in French corresponds to the English 'which?'
Intransitive verb *le verbe intransitif*	A **verb** which has no **direct object**
Inversion *l'inversion*	When the **subject** of a **verb** and the verb itself change places with each other, this is called inversion
Masculine *masculin*	One of two types of **noun** in French

Main clause *la proposition principale*	A **clause** which makes complete sense on its own
Mood *le mode*	A set of forms of the **verb**. The three moods of the verb are the **indicative**, the **subjunctive** and the **imperative**
Negation *la négation*	The process of making a **verb** negative
Negatives *les négatifs*	Elements which may be attached to a **verb** to give it a **negative** sense
Noun *le nom*	A **noun** is a word which names a person, place, thing, quality or idea, e.g. *Jacques Chirac, Paris, diskette, beauté, communisme*
Noun phrase *le groupe nominal*	A group of words which together refer to something or someone, and of which the **noun** is the most important element
Number *le nombre*	The **referents** of all **nouns** and **pronouns** are either **singular** (one) or **plural** (more than one)
Number – cardinal *l'adjectif numéral cardinal*	Members of the series *un, deux, trois*, etc. up to infinity
Number – ordinal *l'adjectif numéral ordinal*	Members of the series *premier, deuxième/second, troisième*, etc.
Participle *le participe*	A part of the **verb** indicating **tense** (**present** or **past**) which does not itself have a **subject**
Partitive article *l'article partitif*	A type of **article** which shows that only a part of a noun is being discussed
Passive *le passif*	A form of the **verb** in which the **subject** undergoes the action of the verb, often committed by an agent or inflicted by an instrument
Past *passé*	A group of **tenses** which refer to previous events as seen from the speaker's viewpoint
Past historic *le passé simple*	A **tense** used only in writing to narrate events
Past participle *le participe passé*	A part of the **verb** which is used to form **compound tenses**. It may be recognised by the endings *-é, -i, -is, -u*
Perfect tense *le passé composé*	A **tense** of the verb consisting of the **present** tense of *avoir* or *être*, plus a **past participle**
Personal pronoun *le pronom personnel*	See **Pronoun**

Pronoun *le pronom*	A word which stands for a **noun**
Phrase *le groupe,* *l'expression,* *la locution*	A group of words which lacks a **verb** and which is smaller than a **clause** but is still a complete unit of meaning
Pluperfect *le plus-que-* *parfait*	A **past tense** which shows that one action or event preceded another, both events having taken place before the time that the speaker mentions them
Possessive *possessif*	**Possessive adjectives** show ownership and are attached to a **noun**. **Possessive pronouns** refer to a noun elsewhere in the text
Predicative *prédicatif*	An **adjective** is said to be predicative if it follows *être* or *devenir*
Preposition *la préposition*	**Prepositions** are invariable words which are attached to **nouns** and certain other words to show position or relationship
Present **participle** *le participe* *présent*	A part of the **verb** which has the ending *-ant*, which corresponds to the English ending *-ing*
Present tense *le présent*	A **tense** of the **verb** which indicates that what the speaker is talking about is happening **now**, or else that it **usually** happens
Qualificative **adjective** *l'adjectif* *qualificatif*	An **adjective** which adds descriptive elements to the meaning of the **noun**, rather than specifying it or defining it
Question *la question*	A **sentence** which requires information in the form of an answer
Reciprocal *réciproque*	A type of **reflexive verb** whose use indicates that the **subjects** of the verb do the action to each other
Referent *le référent*	The person, thing or concept to which a **noun** refers
Reflexive verb *le verbe de sens* *refléchi*	A type of **verb** which has a **direct object** pronoun or **indirect object** pronoun which refers back to the **subject** (i.e. they are same person or thing)
Relative clause *la subordonnée* *relative*	A **clause** which modifies the sense of a **noun**, **noun phrase** or **pronoun**. Relative clauses usually begin with *qui, que (qu'), dont, où* or involve a variant of *lequel*
Sentence *la phrase*	A unit of speech or writing which contains a **verb** and which makes complete sense
Subject *le sujet*	The **noun, noun phrase** or **pronoun** in a **clause** or **sentence** which commits the action of the **verb**, or about which the verb says something

Subjunctive *le subjonctif*	A **mood** of the **verb** which is used not so much to report facts as to reveal the speaker's attitude to those facts, or to suggest that what is reported is not real or is only potentially real
Subordinate clause *la (proposition) subordonnée*	A **clause** which adds extra detail to the sense of a **noun**, **noun phrase** or **verb**. Its meaning is secondary (subordinate) to that of the **main clause**. Thus a subordinate clause will not make sense on its own, but must be attached to a **main clause** or to another subordinate clause
Superlative *le superlatif*	The form of the **adjective** which shows that this is the **biggest**, **best**, **loudest**, etc.
Tense *le temps*	**Verbs** are marked for **tense**, that is, the form of the verb shows when an action took place in relation to the speaker's talking about it
Transitive verb *le verbe transitif*	A **verb** which has a **direct object**. If a **verb** has both a **direct object** and an **indirect object** it is known as a **di-transitive verb**
Verb *le verbe*	A type of word which forms the nucleus of a **sentence** or **clause**, and which refers to actions, processes, states, etc.

1

Nouns

A **noun** is the name of a person, place, thing, quality or idea.

GENDER

French nouns fall into two groups, **masculine** and **feminine**. Many beings which are male are grammatically masculine, and many females are grammatically feminine. This is not a hard and fast rule, and of course takes no account of inanimate objects, which also have a grammatical gender.

The following tables give guidance as to how to determine whether a noun is masculine or feminine.

1.1 *Masculine noun endings*

Most nouns which end in a consonant are masculine.

Consonantal endings	Examples	Exceptions
-b	le plomb	
-c	le sac	
-d	le pied, le nid	
-f	le chef	la clef, la soif, la nef
-g	le poing	
-k	le kayak	
-l	un animal, le détail	
-m	le tam-tam	la faim
-n	le nain, le vin	la fin (*see feminines for* -(i)on)
-p	le cap	
-q	le coq	

Consonantal endings	Examples	Exceptions
-r	le four	la chair, la tour (*tower*), la cuiller, la cour, la mer
-eur (*masculine agents*)	un travailleur	*most abstract nouns in* -eur
-t, -ment	le haricot, le commencement	la dent, la dot (*dowry*)

1.2 *Masculine nouns ending in* -e

The vast majority of nouns ending in *-e* are feminine, but the following endings on nouns are **masculine**.

Ending	Examples	Exceptions
-age	le fromage	la cage, une image, la nage, la page (*of a book*), la rage
-acle	le miracle	
-aire	le vocabulaire	une affaire, la grammaire, la paire
-amme	le programme	
-asme	le phantasme	
-aume	le royaume	
-ède	le remède	
-ège	le collège	
-ème	le problème	la crème
-ice	un exercice, le service	la justice, la police, la malice
-isme	le fascisme	
-iste	le fasciste	
-logue	le sociologue	
-oire	le territoire	une armoire, une histoire, la victoire

1.3 *The case of* -é

Where the *-é* indicates the past participle of a verb, the noun is masculine: *un employé, un attaché*. When the ending is *-té* or *tié*, the noun is feminine, with the exceptions of: *le comté, le comité, le côté, un été, le pâté, le traité*.

1.4   *Nouns ending in* -i, -o, -u

Nouns ending in *-i*, *-o*, and *-u* are usually masculine.

Ending	Examples	Exceptions
-eau	un chameau	l'eau, la peau
-i, -oi	le cri, le parti, un emploi	la fourmi, la foi, la loi, la paroi
-o	le zéro	la dynamo, la photo (*abbrev.*)
-ou	le genou	

1.5   *Masculine by category*

The following are **masculine** by category.

Category	Examples	Exceptions
Males	le garçon, le soldat, le bouc	la personne, la dupe, la recrue, la sentinelle, la vedette, la victime
Days	le dimanche, samedi dernier	*Festivals*: la Saint-Sylvestre, la Toussaint
Months	janvier, septembre	
Seasons	le printemps, l'automne	l'automne *is sometimes feminine in literature*
Minerals and metals	le fer, le cuivre	l'argile, la craie, la chaux, la houille (*coal*)
Trees and shrubs	le chêne, le pommier	une aubépine (*hawthorn*), la ronce (*bramble*), la vigne (*vine*)
Languages	le français, l'allemand	

1.6   *Feminine noun endings*

The majority of nouns ending in *-e* are feminine. The following are the most common *-e* endings.

Ending	Examples	Exceptions
-ace	la glace	
-ade	la limonade	le grade
-aie	la haie	
-aille	la paille	
-aine, -eine	la haine, la reine	

Ending	Examples	Exceptions
-ance	la redevance	
-ée	une araignée	le lycée, le musée, le trophée
-ence, -ense	la prudence, la défense	le silence
-èche	une flèche	
-èque	la bibliothèque	le chèque **NB** discothèque *is found as both M and F*
-euse	une vendeuse	
-ffe	la griffe	le greffe (*registry*)
-ie	la partie	le génie, un incendie, le parapluie
-ière	la bière	le cimetière
-ine	la cantine	
-ise	la cerise	
-lle	la balle, la fille	un intervalle, un mille, le porte-feuille
-mme	la pomme	un homme, le dilemme, le programme, le gramme (*and its compounds* – le kilogramme, *etc.*)
-nne	la canne	
-ppe	la grippe	
-rre	la terre	le beurre, le lierre, le parterre, le tonnerre, le verre
-sse	la princesse	le carosse
-tte	la cigarette	le squelette
-ude	la certitude	
-ure	la reliure	le mercure, le murmure

1.7 *Feminine nouns ending in consonants*

Some nouns ending in consonants are **feminine**. The following are the most common.

Ending	Examples	Exceptions
-eur (*abstract nouns*)	la chaleur	l'honneur, le déshonneur, le labeur, le bonheur, le malheur (*also*: le cœur, le chœur, l'équateur)

Ending	Examples	Exceptions
-aison	la saison	
-ion	la contagion	le million, le champion, le lion, le scorpion
-sion	la version	
-son, -çon	la poisson, la leçon	le bison, le poison, le garçon
-tion	la nation	

Un **courant** rapide nous emporta. Plus tard, je vis approcher les arbres de la rive. IIs s'avançaient vers nous confusément et notre **vitess**e se ralentit. On s'engagea alors dans un **chenal** entre deux **murailles** noires de **plantes.**

Henri Bosco, L'Enfant et la rivière

Internet: la **France** traîne pour se connecter – Dans son **rapport** parlementaire sur **Internet**, le **Sénateur** RPR Alez Türk dénonce le **retard** colossal qu'a déjà pris la France en la **matière**.

Le Point

EXERCICES

A Choisissez dans le tableau **1.1 un nom masculin** qui se termine par une consonne, pour compléter les phrases suivantes.

1 Le _____ ne s'utilise que rarement pour les conduites d'eau.
2 S'il y a un problème dans le bureau, il faut s'adresser au _____ de section.
3 Quelle bagarre! Coups de poing, coups de _____! Oh, l'affaire!
4 Quand je fais la cuisine, ma spécialité, c'est le _____ au vin.
5 Au supermarché, il faut présenter son _____ à la caisse.
6 Mettez le plat au _____.
7 Dans un contrat, le problème c'est toujours dans le _____.
8 Le _____ bordelais jouit d'une renommée mondiale.
9 Moi, je joue de la batterie. Je viens de m'acheter un _____.
10 Ma voiture a subi des dégâts en heurtant un _____ de poule (= *pothole*).

B Complétez **les noms féminins** de ces phrases avec la terminaison qui s'impose. Utilisez un dictionnaire s'il le faut.

1 La prince___ Diana a fait connaître au grand public la question des mines anti-personnel.
2 Une bav___ de police a entraîné la mort d'un jeune Algérien.

    3   Le moteur est en panne. Je pense qu'il manque une boug____.

    4   Mon père était furieux. Il a eu une algar____ avec mon frère.

    5   La Citroën DS – un calembour célèbre sur le mot 'dée___'.

    6   Il y a en ce moment une grave car____ en médecins.

    7   Le puzzle consiste en une gri___ de mots fléchés.

    8   La seconde gue___ mondiale s'est terminée après le lancement de la deuxième bombe atomique.

C   Complétez les phrases suivantes en ajoutant **le** ou **la**, selon la terminaison marquée.

    1   Mon ordinateur est en panne. ____ progr**amme** contenait un virus.

    2   ____ Roy**aume** du Danemark connaît aujourd'hui une véritable crise constitutionnelle.

    3   ____ redev**ance** est renouvelable.

    4   En ce qui concerne les embouteillages, les Parisiens paient cher ___ privil**ège** d'habiter la capitale.

    5   D'ici un siècle ___ Te**rre** risque de mourir en raison de la pollution.

    6   Le Front National est ___ part**i** qui pourrait bouleverser la France.

1.8   *Formation of the feminine*

The feminine form of certain nouns may be obtained by applying the following rules.

Rule	Masculine	Feminine
Nouns in -e do not usually change	*un communiste*	*une communiste*
Double the -l and add -e to -el	*un colonel*	*une colonelle*
Double the -n and add -e to: -en, -on	*un gardien, un espion*	*une gardienne, une espionne*
Double the -t, and add -e to: -et	*un cadet*	*une cadette*
Otherwise, add -e to consonantal endings: -d, -l, -s, -n, -t	*un truand* *un Lillois* *un voisin* *un Américain* *un commerçant* *un idiot*	*une truande* *une Lilloise* *une voisine* *une Américaine* *une commerçante* *une idiote* Exception: *le chat – la chatte*

Rule	Masculine	Feminine
The feminine form includes -s- (Rule 1): -eur → -euse Here, the noun is derived from a verb	un vendeur	une vendeuse Exception: enchanteur – enchanteresse; vengeur – vengeresse; mineur – mineure
The feminine form includes -s- (Rule 2): -oux → -ouse, -eux → -euse	un époux, un ambitieux	une épouse, une ambitieuse
The feminine form includes -s- (Rule 3): -e → -esse	le comte, un hôte, le maître, le prince, le traître	la comtesse, une hôtesse, la maîtresse, la princesse, la traîtresse **NB** le duc – la duchesse
Change -eau to -elle	un jumeau	une jumelle
Change -er to -ère	un épicier	une épicière
Change -f to -ve	un sportif	une sportive
Change -teur to -trice	un inspecteur	une inspectrice

1.9   *Irregular feminine forms*

Note the following irregular feminine forms:

Masculine	Feminine
ambassadeur *ambassador*	ambassadrice *ambassador*
copain *friend, boy-friend*	copine *friend, girl-friend*
compagnon *companion*	compagne *companion*
dieu *god*	déesse *goddess*
empereur *emperor*	impératrice *empress*
fils *son*	fille *daughter*
héros *hero*	héroïne *heroine*
homme *man*	femme *woman*
gendre *son-in-law*	bru *daughter-in-law*
mari *husband*	femme *wife*
neveu *nephew*	nièce *niece*
oncle *uncle*	tante *aunt*
parrain *godfather*	marraine *godmother*
père *father*	mère *mother*
roi *king*	reine *queen*
Suisse *Swiss (man)*	Suissesse *Swiss (woman)*

1.10 *Exceptions to the rules*

There are some peculiarities to note.

Rule	Examples
The following have the same form for the feminine as for the masculine	*bébé, camarade, concierge, élève, enfant*
The following, not surprisingly, have no masculine form!	*Amazone* (Amazon, female warrior), *nonne* (nun), *nourrice* (wet-nurse)

Accroupie devant le feu, se tenait la vieille **sorcière**. La fillette tisonnait. La **vieille**, une louche à la main remuait lentement dans le chaudron je ne sais quelle infernale nourriture.

Henri Bosco, *L'Enfant et la rivière*

J'ai 15 ans et je cherche des **correspondant(e)s** de 15 à 18 ans.

Science et Vie Junior

EXERCICES

A Écrivez le féminin des noms suivants.

ami – Juif – boulanger – paysan – veuf – neveu – fasciste – roi – chameau – héros – acteur – gendre – mari – mineur – Allemand – hôte – chien – étranger

B Écrivez le masculin des noms suivants.

copine – directrice – Parisienne – cousine – pâtissière – comtesse – Espagnole – impératrice – idiote – chatte – marchande – lionne – Suissesse – ambassadrice

EXERCICES DE CONSOLIDATION

A Complétez l'article suivant en remplissant les blancs.

L__ **Parlement** européen des jeunes regroupe des jeunes de quatorze à dix-huit ans, u__ **semaine** par **an**. Chacun des douze pays de l__ **Communauté** envoie u___ **délégation** de treize élèves de l'enseignement secondaire. L'objectif d__ **Parlement** européen des jeunes est de mettre au point u__ **outil** efficace, permettant des échanges d'idées entre les jeunes d'Europe. L__ **programme** comporte deux parties: l__ première **partie** – deux jours en forêt de Fontainebleau vise, au travers d'activités physiques et sportives, à créer des liens entre participants. L__ seconde partie dure cinq jours. Il s'agit d'u___ **simulation** d_ **Parlement** qui a pour **objectif** de débattre de sujets d'intérêt commun: éducation, environnement, affaires sociales.

B Relevez tous les noms dans le texte suivant. Classez-les selon leur genre.

COMMERCE & GESTION

ÉCOLE SUPÉRIEURE DE
MANAGEMENT & GESTION
ESDES

L'école de l'entreprise.

TITRE HOMOLOGUÉ par l'État

5 années d'études après le BAC (toutes séries)

- Une large ouverture aux sciences humaines et sociales.
- Admissions parallèles en 3ᵉᵐᵉ année après BTS, DUT, DEUG...
- Options :
  Finances Contrôle de Gestion, Marketing Vente, Gestion des Ressources humaines, Affaires internationales, Entrepreneur PME / PMI.

- 16 mois de stage au cours de la scolarité - 5ᵉᵐᵉ année professionnalisante en alternance.

Et aussi :

3ᵉᵐᵉ cycle Gestion des Ressources Humaines
3ᵉᵐᵉ cycle Management stratégique "création, reprise d'entreprise"
Préparation au D.E.S.C.F.

Université Catholique de Lyon

29, rue du Plat 69002 LYON

04 72 32 50 48

Etablissement d'Enseignement Supérieur Technique Privé

Service Lecteur : cerclez 170 en dernière page

1.11 *Nouns with both genders*

Some nouns have both genders. The meaning differs according to the gender.

Word	Masculine meaning	Feminine meaning
aide	*assistant*	*assistance*
critique	*critic*	*criticism*
crème	*white coffee*	*cream*
garde	*keeper*	*guardianship; corps*
livre	*book*	*pound (weight & money)*
manche	*long handle*	*sleeve; English Channel*
mémoire	*memoir, dissertation*	*memory*
mode	*way, manner*	*fashion*
mort	*dead man*	*death*
moule	*mould*	*mussel*
page	*page-boy*	*page (of book)*
pendule	*pendulum*	*clock*
physique	*physical appearance*	*physics*
poêle	*stove*	*frying-pan*
politique	*politician*	*politics, policy; computer type-face*
poste	*job*	*post-office*
solde	*balance (in account)*	*sale; soldier's pay*
somme	*nap, sleep*	*sum*
souris	*smile (literary usage)*	*mouse*
tour	*tour, turn, trick, stroll*	*tower*
trompette	*trumpeter*	*trumpet*
vapeur	*steamer*	*steam*
vase	*vase*	*mud*
voile	*veil*	*sail, sailing*

Presque tous les **postes** sont pris. Le principal, par surprise, à une heure et demie. Là, nous avons saisi huit cent fusils.

André Malraux, *La Condition humaine*

Qui voudrait racheter aujourd'hui la société concessionnaire du tunnel sous **la Manche**?

Libération

EXERCICES

A Choisissez dans le tableau **1.11** un nom pour compléter le sens des phrases suivantes.

1 J'espérais pouvoir envoyer cette lettre aujourd'hui, mais je n'ai pas de timbres et l_ _____ est fermée

2 On a trouvé u__ _____. Il paraît qu'il s'agit du cadavre d'un clochard.

3 Il faut que je parle au directeur de ma banque. L _ _____ de mon compte n'est pas très sain!

4 On a fait u__ _____ de tous les monuments de Paris, y compris l__ _____ Eiffel.

5 Pour traverser l_ _____, nous avons pris u_ _____ de Calais à Douvres.

6 L__ _____ est la science qui nous révèle que la réalité est tout autre qu'on ne le croyait.

7 Elle m'a reproché de toutes sortes de choses, mais c'était u__ _____ peu méritée.

8 Il y a u__ _____ dans le placard? Je viens de cueillir des fleurs dans le jardin.

9 Zut! J'avais complètement oublié. Je ne retiens plus rien. M__ _____ est une vraie passoire!

10 U__ _____ sterling vaut combien de francs en ce moment?

B Employez dans deux phrases chacun des mots suivants, d'abord **au masculin**, puis **au féminin**.

1 crème   2 critique   3 livre   4 mode   5 page   6 physique   7 voile

COMPOUND NOUNS

Compound nouns generally take the gender of the more important of the two parts. The presence or absence of hyphens in spelling should be noted.

Masculine	Feminine
Noun + noun	
un **camion** citerne	une auto-**école**
un **chou**-fleur	une **pause**-café
un **timbre**-poste	une **idée**-force
Noun + adjective	
un beau-**frère**	une belle-**sœur**
un **arc**-boutant	une basse-**cour**
Verb + noun (*most are masculine*)	
un abat-**jour**	une garde-**robe**
un gratte-**ciel**	une perce-**neige** (*also found*: **un** perce-neige)

Masculine	Feminine
Invariable word + noun	
un sous-**verre**	une arrière-**pensée**
un contre-**ordre**	une contre-**offensive**
Noun + prepositional phrase	
un **arc**-en-ciel	une **pomme** de terre
un **coup** de poing	une **tasse** à thé
	Exception: **un** tête-à-tête
Compound verbal phrases (all masculine)	
le ouï-**dire**	
le **savoir**-faire	

Le soleil n'avait pas paru ce matin-là, non plus que la veille, non plus que **l'avant-veille**…

Paul Arène

Douze millions de téléspectateurs ont regardé 'Driving School' («A **l'auto-école**», en français) sur la BBC.

Le Monde

EXERCICES

A Classez ces noms composés selon leur genre.

passeport	Monseigneur	chef d'œuvre	basse-cour	cure-dents
portemanteau	porte-avions	ver à soie	demi-bouteille	ouvre-boîtes
pot-de-vin	belle-mère	beau-père	voiture-restaurant	cache-nez

B Mariez les éléments de la colonne de gauche à ceux de la colonne de droite pour avoir des noms composés.

Exemple: un **abat**-jour

abat-	mère
casse-	président
chef-	heure
contre-	fils
demi-	lieu
grand'	jour
petit-	noisettes
vice-	ordre

1.12 *Geography*

COUNTRIES

The names of countries ending in *-e* are generally **feminine**. Note these examples and exceptions. The list is not exhaustive.

Masculine		Feminine	
le Canada	Canada	l'Allemagne	Germany
le Danemark	Denmark	l'Angleterre	England
les États-Unis	United States	la Belgique	Belgium
le Gabon	Gabon	la Corse	Corsica
le Grœnland	Greenland	l'Écosse	Scotland
le Japon	Japan	la France	France
le Kenya	Kenya	Israël (*no article*)	Israel
le Mali	Mali	la Libye	Libya
le Maroc	Morocco	la Malaisie	Malaysia
le Mexique	Mexico	l'île Maurice	Mauritius
le Portugal	Portugal	la Nouvelle-Zélande	New Zealand
les Pays-Bas	Netherlands	la Tunisie	Tunisia
le Pays de Galles	Wales	la Zambie	Zambia

CITIES AND TOWNS

The names of towns ending in *-e* are generally **feminine**, but some towns ending in *-e* are **masculine**. Similarly, towns ending in a **consonant** are **masculine**. Note these examples and exceptions. The list is not exhaustive.

Masculine		Feminine	
Londres	London	Nice	Nice
Mexico	Mexico City	Toulouse	Toulouse
Paris	Paris	Marseille	Marseilles
Le Touquet	Le Touquet	Rome	Rome
le Caire	Cairo	Athènes	Athens
Le Havre	Le Havre	Metz	Metz

> Les croix de mon pays… Elles jalonnent les chemins **en Bretagne** comme les fêtes sacrées et les rites religieux de la vie.
>
> Yves de Boisboissel, *Bretagne, ma mère bien-aimée*
>
> Où vont les Anglais? Jusqu'à une époque récente, dans leurs préférences, **la Grèce** concurrençait **Ibiza** ou **la Costa Brava**.
>
> *L'Événement*

EXERCICE

Quels sont les pays et les villes indiqués sur la carte?

1.13 *Number*

Nouns are marked to show whether they are **singular** or **plural**.

1.14 *The plural*

Nouns usually add *-s* in the written form of the plural. This *-s* is not usually pronounced. The following are **exceptional** ways of forming the plural:

Change	Singular	Plural
No change: nouns in *-s*	*le fils* (*-s* pronounced) *un os* (*-s* pronounced)	*les fils* (*-s* pronounced) *des os* (*-s* not pronounced)
No change: nouns in *-x*	*la voix*	*les voix*
No change: nouns in *-z*	*le nez* *le gaz* (*-z* pronounced)	*les nez* *les gaz* (*-z* pronounced)
Change *-ail* to *-aux*	*le travail*	*les travaux* Exception: *détails, éventails, gouvernails, portails* **NB** ail → *aulx*
Change *-al* to *-aux*	*le cheval*	*les chevaux* Exception: *bals, carnavals, chacals, cérémonials, festivals*
Change *-au* to *-aux*	*un étau* (vice)	*des étaux*
Change *-eau* to *-eaux*	*le gâteau*	*les gâteaux*
Change *-eu* to *-eux*	*le cheveu*	*les cheveux* Exception: *le pneu – les pneus*
Change *-ou* -to *-oux*	**Only** for: *bijou, caillou, chou, genou, hibou, joujou, pou.* All others add *-s*	*bijoux, cailloux, choux, genoux, hiboux, joujoux, poux*

1.15 *The plurals of compound nouns*

These are formed in various ways, according to the structure of the noun. Compound nouns using adjectives, prepositions and other nouns are formed as follows:

Rule	Plural pattern	Singular	Plural
Singular noun written as one word pluralises normally	des _____s	*le gendarme* *le pourboire*	*les gendarmes* *les pourboires*

Rule	Plural pattern	Singular	Plural
Possessive adjective + noun: both pluralise	des ____s____s	monsieur madame mademoiselle *Also*: un bonhomme	**mes**sieur**s** **mes**dame**s** **mes**demoiselle**s** des **bon**shomme**s**
Noun + noun: both pluralise	des ____s -____s	un mot-clé une idée-force une foire-exposition	des mot**s**-clé**s** des idée**s**-force**s** des foire**s**-exposition**s**
Noun + adjective/ adjective + noun: both pluralise	des ____s - ____s	un arc-boutant un grand-parent un beau-frère un chef-lieu	des arc**s**-boutant**s** des grand**s**-parent**s** des beau**x**-frère**s** des chef**s**-lieu**x**
Noun + preposition + noun: first noun is pluralised	des ____s __ ____	une tasse à café un arc-en-ciel un chef-d'œuvre *Exception:* un pot-au-feu un tête-à-tête	des tasse**s** à café des arc**s**-en-ciel des chef**s**-d'œuvre des pot-au-feu des tête-à-tête
Noun + (preposition understood) + noun: first noun pluralised	des ____s (-) ____	un timbre-poste une allocation-chômage	des timbre**s**-poste des allocation**s**-chômage
Invariable word + noun: noun pluralised	des _____-_____s	une contre-offensive un hors-bord	des contre-offensive**s** des hors-bord**s**

> Qui n'a souvent réfléchi à toute l'importance que l'on retire de ce modeste animal [le poulet], ornement de nos **basses-cours**?
>
> Gustave Flaubert, *Madame Bovary*

> Cinq producteurs de **choux-fleurs** du Finistère ont été condamnés mardi par le tribunal de Brest à des peines de prison avec sursis comprises entre trois et 18 mois et des amendes de 3 000 à 30 000 F.
>
> *Libération*

1.16 *Compound nouns using verbs*

Verbs used in compound nouns **never** show the plural marker.

Rule	Plural pattern	Singular	Plural
Verb + noun: in cases in which the noun never has a plural meaning, neither part pluralises	des ____-____	un abat-jour (chose qui abat le jour) un porte-monnaie (chose qui porte de la monnaie) un pare-brise (chose qui pare la brise)	des abat-jour des porte-monnaie des pare-brise
Invariable expressions: neither part pluralises	des ____-____	un ouï-dire un on-dit	des ouï-dire des on-dit
Verb + invariable word: neither part pluralises	des ____-____	un passe-partout	des passe-partout
With a compound of two verbs, neither shows the plural marker	des ____- ____	le garde-manger le laissez-passer le savoir-faire	les garde-manger les laissez-passer les savoir-faire
Verb + noun: when the noun is already plural, the form is as in the singular	des ____-____s	un porte-avion**s** un porte-clé**s** un essuie-main**s**	des porte-avion**s** des porte-clé**s** des essuie-main**s**
Verb + noun: the noun needs to be pluralised if it logically refers to more than one object	des ____- ____s	un tire-bouchon un soutien-gorge	des tire-bouchon**s** des soutien-gorge**s** **NB** soutiens-gorges *is also found*

En projet: un nouveau port de déchargement des **porte-conteneurs** qui rivaliserait avec Algésiras, saturé.

L'Étudiant

EXERCICES

A Donnez le pluriel des noms suivants.

un camion-citerne	un arrière-plan	un cache-nez
une mini-jupe	une pause-café	un qu'en dira-t-on?
un faire-part	un coup d'œil	un wagon-lit
un cerf-volant	un grand-père	une tasse à thé

B Donnez le singulier des noms suivants.

des brosses à dents	des choux-fleurs
des porte-parapluies	des timbres-poste
des contre-attaques	des non-lieux
des belles-filles	des pare-brise

2

Articles

An article is a word which determines whether a noun under discussion is **definite** (known to the listener), **indefinite** (unknown to the listener) or **partitive** (only part of the noun is under discussion).

THE DEFINITE ARTICLE

The form of the definite article depends in part on the first letter (or sound) of the noun to which it is attached. Nouns can begin with (1) a consonant (*b, g, n,* etc.), (2) a vowel (*a, e, i, o, u*) or (3) the letter *h.*

Now there are two types of *h* in French:

h mute (*h muet*) as in *homme* and *histoire*

h aspirate (*h aspiré*) as in *hibou* and *haie*

There is no difference in the pronunciation of the *h* (it is silent in **all** cases), but before nouns beginning with vowels and *h muet*, the definite article (*le, la*) becomes *l'*. Before nouns beginnng with consonants or with *h aspiré*, the full definite article is used - *le hibou, la haie.*

The plural is *les* in all cases. Before vowels and *h* mute, the *s* of *les* will be pronounced (as *z*) – *les_oranges.*

Other changes take place when the article is combined with *à* or *de* (see **2.1**).

2.1 *With nouns beginning with consonants and* h *aspirate*

	Masculine	**Feminine**	**Plural** (both genders)
'The'	le garçon le hibou	la fille la haie	les garçons, les filles les hiboux, les haies
With possessive *de*	du garçon du hibou	de la fille de la haie	des garçons, des filles des hiboux, des haies

	Masculine	**Feminine**	**Plural** (both genders)
With *à*	au garçon	à la fille	aux garçons, aux filles
	au hibou	à la haie	aux hiboux, aux haies

2.2 With nouns beginning with vowels and h mute

	Masculine	**Feminine**	**Plural** (both genders)
'The'	l'animal	l'alliance	les animaux, les alliances
	l'homme	l'histoire	les hommes, les histoires
With possessive *de*	de l'animal	de l'alliance	des animaux, des alliances
	de l'homme	de l'histoire	des hommes, des histoires
With *à*	à l'animal	à l'alliance	aux animaux, aux alliances
	à l'homme	à l'histoire	aux hommes, aux histoires

EXERCICE

Écrivez **le, la, l'** ou **les**, selon le cas. Consultez un dictionnaire si besoin est.

enfant – riverains – siècle – inquiétudes – bout – alternance – astronomes – phénomène – atmosphère – consommateur – couche – profondeurs – parachute – soleil – lune – planètes

2.3 The use of the definite article

Use	Examples
An item being discussed is known to both speakers	*Passe-moi **le** beurre* – Pass me **the** butter
To refer to a class of things	*L'homme est en danger de disparition, comme **les** éléphants* – Mankind is in danger of extinction, like the elephants
The names of countries, regions and *départements*	*la France, le Japon, les États-Unis; la Normandie* (region); *l'Oise* (*département*) – France, Japan, the USA, Normandy, Oise
The names of languages. **NB** With the verb *parler*, the article is dropped unless an adverb is present	*J'ai appris l'anglais et le japonais* – I've learnt English and Japanese **NB** *Parlez-vous français/allemand?* etc. – Do you speak French/German? etc. *André parle couramment le suédois* – André speaks Swedish fluently *Je ne parle que le français* – I speak only French
The names of the seasons	*Le printemps est toujours doux ici* – Spring is always mild here

Use	Examples
With periods of the day	*le matin* – **in** the morning; *l'après-midi* – **in** the afternoon; *le soir* – **in** the evening; *la nuit* – **at** night
With certain expressions of time (*semaine, mois, année*) when these are qualified by an adjective	*la semaine dernière* – last week *le mois prochain* – next month *l'année prochaine* – next year
When referring to certain places. English omits the article	*à la maison* – at home; *à l'école* – to/at school; *à l'église* – to/at church
When referring to parts of the body	*Elle a **les** cheveux blonds* – She has fair hair *Il a secoué **la** tête* – He shook **his** head *Je me suis cassé **le** bras* – I've broken **my** arm
People's titles, particularly when used on formal occasions	*Le roi Louis XIV* – King Louis XIV *Monsieur **le** maire* – Mr Mayor *Madame la Directrice* – (the) Headmistress *L'oncle Jules* – Uncle Jules
In greetings and farewells	*Salut, **les** jeunes!* – Hi, kids! *Au revoir, **les** enfants* (film title) – Goodbye, children
When a name is qualified by an adjective	*Le petit Alain* – Little Alan *Le Grand Meaulnes* (book by Alain-Fournier) – Big Meaulnes (the title is usually translated as *The Lost Domain* or *The Wanderer*)
When people in a group each have one item	*Tous les garçons avaient **la** tête rasée* – All the boys had **their** heads shaved
With prices (corresponding to 'per')	*50 francs **la** pièce* – 50 francs each *25 francs **le** kilo* – 25 francs per kilo *8 francs **la** livre* (500g) – 8 francs a pound *300 francs **la** bouteille* – 300 francs a bottle *125 francs **le** mètre* – 125 francs a metre *100 kilomètres à **l'**heure* – 100 kilometres **per** hour
With the names of festivals	*La Saint-Jean* (*la (fête de) Saint Jean*) - Saint John's Day
With the names of days to indicate repetition	*Le samedi, on va toujours regarder le foot* – **On** Saturdays we always go to watch the football
With *la majorité de* and *la plupart de*	*La majorité **des** filles* – Most girls...
With the superlative of adjectives – the article agrees with the noun	*C'est la chose **la** plus curieuse que j'aie jamais vue* – It was the strangest thing I've ever seen
With the superlatives of adverbs – the article is always *le*	*Il faut le faire **le** plus rapidement possible* – It must be done as quickly as possible

Tchen tenterait-il de lever **la** moustiquaire? Frapperait-il au travers? **L'**angoisse lui tordait **l'**estomac… **La** seule lumière venait **du** building voisin…

André Malraux, La Condition humaine

1 Chauffez **l'**huile dans une sauteuse à feu doux. Faites-y revenir 2–3 min **les** échalotes hachées. Ajoutez **la** carotte, **le** céléri et **le** poivron; cuisez 10 mn à feu doux en remuant souvent.

2 Ajoutez **les** lentilles et **l'**orge; cuisez 2 mn à feu doux en remuant souvent.

Avantages

EXERCICE

Complétez les phrases suivantes en traduisant en français les sections marquées en italique.

1 Passez-moi *the milk and the sugar* s'il vous plaît.

2 Tu as vu *the newspapers*?

3 *Dolphins and whales* deviennent de plus en plus rares.

4 Vous avez visité *Mexico or Argentina*? – Non, mais j'ai visité *the United States and Canada*.

5 Vous ne parlez pas *Spanish*? – Non, je ne parle que *French and English*.

6 Moi, je trouve que *summer* est intolérable dans les pays humides.

7 *Little Philippe* est le garçon qui a *brown hair* et les *green eyes*. Il a eu un accident *last week*. Il s'est cassé *his arm*.

8 *Mr Mayor, members of the municipal council*, c'est avec grand plaisir que je prends la parole devant cette réunion importante.

9 C'était la liquidation. On vendait tout à des prix fous – Château-neuf-du-pape, 20 francs *a bottle*, du fromage à dix francs *a pound,* des fruits à 50 centimes *each*!

10 *On Sundays* on va voir mes parents d'habitude, mais *last Sunday* c'était *St. Andrew's Day,* la fête de mon fils, donc *in the morning* on est allés *to church*, et *in the afternoon* on est restés *at home*.

THE INDEFINITE ARTICLE

The indefinite article cannot be abbreviated, unlike the definite article.

If the noun begins with a vowel or *h* mute, there will be liaison between the masculine indefinite article (*un*) and the noun: *un͜ arbre*

The distinction between *h muet* and *h aspiré* can be heard in the lack of liaison with *h aspiré* between the article and the noun. Compare: *un͜ homme* and *un hibou*. Similarly, *des͜ hommes* versus *des hiboux*.

Pronunciation	Masculine	Feminine	Plural (both genders)
No liaison in masculine singular	un garçon	une fille	des garçons, des filles
Liaison in masculine singular	un‿animal, un‿homme	une‿histoire	des‿animaux, des‿hommes, des‿histoires
No liaison in masculine singular or in plural of both genders	un hibou	une‿haie	des hiboux, des haies

EXERCICES

A Mettez devant les noms suivants soit **un** soit **une**. Consultez un dictionnaire si besoin est.
âge – calme – cage – choix – cour – dialecte – doctrine – énigme – insecte – intervalle – manque – nuage – ordre – ombre – principe – sphère – ustensile – victime

B Marquez la liaison là où il le faut, e.g. un‿arbre
un aide – un hall – un héros – un homard – un homme – un hoquet – un horaire – un hôtel – un hublot – un igloo – un oiseau – un uniforme

2.4 *Use of the indefinite article*

Use	Examples
The speaker mentions a previously unused item in the conversation	*Tu as **un** bic?* – Have you got a biro? *Il y a **une** grande différence entre les deux* – There's **a** big difference between the two
An abstract noun is accompanied by an adjective	*Il est d'**une** intelligence incroyable* – He's incredibly intelligent
Emphasis is laid on singularity – *seul* is added for emphasis	*J'ai pris **un seul** gâteau* – I took **only one** cake
The plural *des* often corresponds to 'some'. It cannot usually be omitted, even where it is dropped in English	*J'ai **des** achats à faire* – I have **some** shopping to do *Dans la cour il y avait **des** pions et **des** élèves* – There were supervisors and pupils in the yard
If an expression using *de* would be followed by a partitive article (see **2.7**) the partitive article is dropped	*J'ai besoin **de** vis et **de** boulons* – I need nuts and bolts *Il a travaillé pour le fermier en échange **de** lait et **d'**œufs* – He worked for the farmer in exchange for milk and eggs

> Dans la plaine rase, sous la nuit sans étoiles, d'**une** obscurité et d'**une** épaisseur d'encre, **un** homme suivait seul la grande route de Marchiennes à Montsou… Depuis **une** heure il avançait ainsi, lorsque sur la gauche, à deux kilomètres de Montsou, il aperçut **des** feux rouges, trois brasiers brûlant au plein air et comme suspendus. D'abord il hésita, pris de crainte; puis il ne put résister au besoin douloureux de se chauffer **un** instant les mains.
>
> Zola, *Germinal*
>
> Il est au moins **un** cas où la recherche d'**une** solution à **un** problème écologique planétaire a **des** conséquences économiques directes: celui de l'ozone.
>
> Hervé Kempf, *L'Économie à l'épreuve de l'écologie*

EXERCICE

Insérez dans les phrases suivantes **un**, **une**, **des**, **de** ou **d'**.

1 Qu'est-ce que c'est qu'___ vélodrome?
2 La vague a heurté la plage avec ___ puissance inattendue.
3 Pour les maçons, il y a ___ sandwichs et ___ thermos de café.
4 Je n'ai pas vu ___ seul épisode de ce feuilleton.
5 Il me faudra ___ litre ___ lait et ___ douzaine ___œufs.

2.5 *Omission of the article*

Note: this section is numbered for the purposes of the exercise which follows.

Explanation	Examples
1. When the noun is the complement of *avoir* or *être*, no article used	*Mon père est **infirmier*** – My father is **a** nurse *Edith Cresson est devenue **Premier Ministre*** – Edith Cresson became **Prime Minister** *Moi, j'ai **faim*** – I'm hungry
2. If the noun is qualified, however, the article is used	*Sa mère est **une chirurgienne** mondialement connue* – Her mother is **a** world-famous **surgeon**
3. A noun in apposition requires no article	*Louis XIV, **roi** de France* – Louis XIV, **king** of France
4. Titles of books	***Réflexions générales*** – General Thoughts ***Grammaire française*** – French Grammar
5. The noun is preceded by a preposition, and the sense is vague or general	*Alain est en **ville*** – Alain is in **town** *Elle portait un bonnet en **laine*** – She was wearing a **woolly** hat

Explanation	Examples
6. Common expressions, see above (5)	*à/en* **vélo** – on a bike; *à* **cheval** – on horseback; *à* **pied** – on foot; *avec* **plaisir** – with pleasure; *en* **bateau** – by boat; *en* **voiture** – by car; *par* **an** – per year; *par* **jour** – per day; *par* **exemple** – for example; *sans* **crainte** – without fear, *de* **jour** *en* **jour** – from day to day, etc.
7. Nouns closely linked to a verb and forming a single unit of meaning	*avoir* **besoin** *de* – to need; *avoir* **chaud** – to be hot; *faire* **attention** *à* – to pay attention to; *faire* **fortune** – to make a fortune; *mettre* **fin** *à* – to put an end to; *reprendre* **courage** – to regain one's courage; *rendre* **service** *à* – to do someone a favour; *trouver* **moyen** *de* – to find a way to
8. After *avec, par, ni* and *sans*	*avec* **élan** – with verve; *par* **erreur** – by mistake; *sans* **pitié** – without pity; *sans* **attaches** *ni* **perspectives** – without commitments or prospects
9. With *ni... ni..., soit... soit...* and *jamais*	*Les refugiés n'ont ni* **vêtements** *ni* **nourriture** – The refugees have neither **food** nor **clothing** *Soit* **fatigue**, *soit* **peur**, *il se mit à grelotter* – Either from **tiredness** or from **fear**, he started to shiver *Jamais* **chose** *pareille ne s'était passée* – Such **a thing** had never happened before
10. After *quel* in exclamations	*Quel* **dommage!** – What **a pity!** *Quelle* **horreur!** – How **awful!**
11. After *tout/toute* followed by a singular noun	*Tout* **homme politique** *le sait* – Every **politician** knows it
12. In enumerations	**Papiers, stylos, crayons, bloc-notes, trombones** – *tout était jonché par terre* – **Paper, pens, note-pads, paper clips** – everything was strewn on the floor
13. In proverbs, where the sense is general	**Pauvreté** *n'est pas* **vice** – It's no **sin** to be poor

En ce temps là, deux autorités reconnues régnaient dans toute préfecture qui se respecte, abritées chacune par un palais administratif, et c'étaient l'évêque et le préfet. **Pouvoir civil** et **pouvoir ecclésiastique**, **Église** et **État**; **pôles** entre lesquels oscillait ce qu'on est convenu d'appeler la société.

Édouard Estaunié, *Monseigneur*

En 1992, date d'entrée dans l'étude, les habitants consommaient globalement trop de graisses saturées (**beurre**, **chips**, **frites**, **viandes**, **charcuteries**, **fromages**, **gâteaux**, etc.) au détriment des graisses instaurées, cardioprotectrices (**huiles végétales type Isio 4**, **huile d'olive**, **de colza**…)

Maxi

EXERCICES

A Expliquez la raison de l'omission de l'article en donnant à chacune des phrases suivantes un numéro qui correspond aux sections de la grammaire ci-dessus.

Exemple: Pierre qui roule n'amasse pas mousse = 13

1 Toute **femme** qui connaît bien son mari pourra vous dire ses défauts = ?
2 Philippe IV, dit le Bel, **roi** de France entre 1286 et 1314 a exterminé les Templiers = ?
3 *Manuel* de français = ?
4 J'ai **chaud** = ?
5 Ma grand'mère était **directrice** d'une institution pour les handicapés = ?
6 Il faisait si chaud que je portais une chemise en **coton** = ?
7 John Wayne était une **vedette** de cinéma qui s'identifiait au peuple américain = ?
8 Il a complété l'exercice sans **erreur** = ?
9 Quelle **honte**! = ?
10 Jamais désastre écologique à une telle échelle ne s'était vu = ?

B Insérez l'article là où il le faut. Attention – parfois il faut omettre l'article.

1 Mon père est _____ scientifique.
2 Mon arrière grand-père était _____ amiral célèbre.
3 Lui est _____ Français, sa femme est _____ Belge.
4 Quel _____ beau château!
5 Alain Lecronon, _____ député pour le Finistère, a pris la parole.

THE PARTITIVE ARTICLE

2.6   Forms

	Masculine	Feminine
Before consonant or h *aspirate*	du	de la
Before vowel or h *mute*	de l'	de l'
Before a plural noun	des	des

Note: these forms are also used when *de* + article = of the, from the.

*Le vent **du** nord* – The north wind (i.e. the wind **from the** north)

*Les côtes **de l'**Australie* – The coast **of** Australia

2.7   Use of the partitive article

Rule	Examples
The partitive article indicates an indefinite number or amount. It agrees in number and gender with the noun to which it is attached	*Il faudra **du** temps et **des** efforts pour que ce problème puisse se résoudre* – It will take time and effort for this problem to resolve itself
The partitive article is often equivalent to 'some' or 'any'	*Tu as **des** bonbons? – Non, mais j'ai **du** chewing gum* – Do you have **any** sweets? – No, but I've got **some** chewing gum
The partitive article may not be omitted in French, even if it does not appear in English	*Pour cette recette, il faut **des** œufs, **de la** farine, **du** lait et **du** sucre* – For this recipe, you'll need flour, eggs, milk and sugar
The partitive article is reduced to *de* after expressions indicating quantity or containers	*Un kilo **de** farine et une livre **de** sucre* – A kilo of flour and a pound of sugar *Tu vas prendre un verre **de** vin?* – Will you have a glass **of** wine?
The partitive is reduced to **de** after negative verbs and other negative expressions	*Il **n'**y a jamais **de** flics quand on en a besoin* – There are never any cops around when you need one ***Pas de** problème!* – **No** problem!
The partitive article disappears after expressions involving *de*, e.g. *beaucoup de, assez de, tant de, moins de, en échange de*	***Beaucoup de** jeunes quittent le foyer familial à cause de mésententes* – **Many** young people leave home because of a lack of understanding *Je n'avais jamais vu **tant de** monde* – I'd never seen **so many** people

Rule	Examples
When a partitive article precedes a plural adjective it is reduced to *de*. This rule is less observed in speech	*Il y a **de** bonnes raisons d'écouter tes parents* – There are good reasons to listen to your parents
When the adjective and the noun form a single unit of meaning, *des* is the correct form	*Il y a **des** jeunes gens devant la maison* – There are **some** *youngsters* outside the house

Bientôt tout le compartiment se mit en mouvement. On déplaça **de** lourdes valises, **des** cartons, **des** paniers, et surgirent **des** serviettes de table, **des** torchons rayés ou à carreaux, qu'on étala sur les genoux, **des** bouteilles **de** vin bouché, **d'**eau de Vichy qu'on décapsulerait contre la portière, **des** monceaux **de** victuailles: charcuterie, poulet rôti, œufs durs et cornets de papier contenant le sel, fromages, pots de beurre…

Robert Sabatier, Les Noisettes sauvages

L'administration américaine a émis la possibilité de mener **de** nouvelles attaques contre **des** cibles terroristes, au lendemain **de** tirs de missiles de croisière qui ont détruit une usine accusée de fabriquer **des** composantes **d'**armes chimiques…

Le Monde

EXERCICES

A Complétez les phrases suivantes avec la forme du partitif qui convient.

1 Pour le pique-nique, il faudra _____ jambon, _____ tomates et _____ chips.
2 Il ne faut pas qu'on se fasse _____ soucis à ce sujet.
3 Y a-t-il suffisamment ___ place?
4 Elle n'a vraiment pas ___ patience.
5 Dans cette rue-là, il y a _____ grandes maisons qui appartiennent au Ministre de l'Intérieur.
6 Y a-t-il ___ autres possibilités?
7 Moi, je n'ai plus _____ papier. Tu peux m'en prêter?
8 Il y a _____ tasses ici, mais je ne pense pas qu'il reste beaucoup ___ café.

B Vous vous lancez dans une nouvelle affaire commerciale et il faut équiper vos locaux qui consistent en un bureau, un petit entrepôt et une petite salle pour les employés avec toilette. Dressez la liste de ce qu'il faudra en termes généraux.
«Bon, il nous faudra **du** papier, **des** diskettes, **des** trombones…»
Attention! Votre budget n'est pas illimité!

C   Répondez aux questions suivantes avec une phrase à l'affirmatif.

Exemple: Tu n'as pas **de** fric, alors? – Si, j'ai **du** fric.

1   Il n'y a pas **de** pain ou **de** beurre, alors?

2   Tu n'as pas **de** cousins, alors?

3   Il ne restait pas **de** places, alors?

4   Ton frère n'avait pas **d'**argent, alors?

5   On ne t'a pas rendu **de** monnaie, alors?

EXERCICES DE CONSOLIDATION

A   L'article partitif et le genre des noms. Selon la terminaison d'un nom, il est possible de prédire la forme de l'article partitif qu'il vous faudra. En vous référant aux paragraphes **1.1–1.10**, complétez le tableau suivant, selon l'exemple.

Forme de l'article partitif	Terminaison du nom
de la	pat**ience**
	limon**ade**
	plom**b**
	ser**vice**
	from**age**
	chapel**ure**
	pa**in**
	far**ine**

B   Complétez les phrases suivantes avec l'article défini, indéfini ou partitif.

1   ____ France connaît des difficultés économiques en ce moment.

2   Pendant la guerre du Golfe, les pilotes britanniques ont agi avec ____ courage incroyable.

3   ____ éléphants sont en voie de disparition.

4   ____ samedi je reste toujours planté devant la télé à regarder le foot.

5   Vous avez ____ papier? Je veux écrire une lettre.

Adjectives

There are two types of adjective. The first type give us information about:

- number (how many?),
- possession (who owns the noun?),
- position (this noun **here**, or that one **there**?),
- definition (**which** noun?),
- indefiniteness (**some** nouns? **certain** nouns?).

These are known as **determinative** adjectives, and in general (though with some exceptions) are placed **before** the noun in the sentence.

The second type signal features such as:

- size (a **big** noun or a **small** noun?),
- colour (a **red** noun or a **green** noun?),
- quality (a **loveable** noun or a **hateful** noun?).

This latter type are known as **qualificative** adjectives and, in general, **follow** the noun, though there are many notable exceptions.

DETERMINATIVE ADJECTIVES

3.1 *Numeral adjectives (cardinal numbers)*

Many of the cardinal numbers are simple in form: *un, deux, trois, vingt,* etc. Others are formed by juxtaposition or co-ordination with others, e.g. *dix-sept, vingt et un,* etc., or by multiplication: *quatre-vingts.* In *quatre-vingt-dix-sept* there is both multiplication and addition. (Historically, this method of counting derives from the Gauls who were the Celtic inhabitants of Gaul (France) at the time of the Roman invasion.)

Rule	Examples	Comment/Exception	Explanation
Up to 1600, use *cents*, not *mille* + figure	1100 = *onze* **cents** 1600 = *seize* **cents**		
Over 1600, the use of *mille* is possible	1700 = *dix-sept* **cents** OR **mille** *sept cents*	*En* **mil** *sept cent quatre-vingt-neuf, ce fut la Révolution* – In 1789, the Revolution started	The spelling *mil* is used for dates
un million	1 000 000	*quelques* **millions**	*million* is a noun and may be pluralised
un milliard	1 000 000 000	**billion** in the financial sense	
A space is used in figures to separate hundreds and thousands	3 567 = *trois mille cinq cent soixante-sept*		
A comma corresponds to the English decimal point	3,9%	The comma is **said** as *'virgule'*	
No *-s* is added to *mille* in the plural	2000 = *deux* **mille**	*Londres est à quelques* **milles** – London is a few **miles** away	*milles* in plural = miles
millier = about a thousand	*plusieurs* **milliers** – several thousand	This is imprecise in sense	
No *-s* on *cent* and *quatre-vingts* if another number follows	*deux* **cents** but *deux* **cent** *un; quatre-vingts* but *quatre-***vingt-***un*		
Hyphens join compound numbers	*vingt-deux*	*vingt et un*	**No hyphens** in numbers with *et*
No *et* is necessary in numbers following *cent* and *mille*	101 = *cent un;* 1012 = *mille douze*	*Les Mille* **et** *Une Nuits*	This is a set literary phrase
The number follows when defining **books**, **chapters**, **pages**, **acts** in a play	*livre* **cinq**		
In years, the number follows	*l'an* **deux mille**		
In apposition, the number follows	*le chiffre* **trois**		

Rule	Examples	Comment/Exception	Explanation
After *plus/moins*, *de* is inserted. This is an amount	*plus de sept cents; moins de trois pour cent*	*Il est **plus** grand **que** moi* – He's taller than me	This is a **comparison**, not an amount
quelque (= about) + number is invariable	*les **quelque** 3 000 chômeurs* – about 3000 unemployed	***quelques** chômeurs* – some unemployed people	Here *quelques* is an adjective and agrees

EXERCICES

A Lisez à haute voix les chiffres suivants
1 300 – 1 900 – 3 000 000 – 2 000 000 000 – 5 675 – 14,7% – 6 000 – 203 – 1 013
Voir la clé (page 228) pour vérifier vos réponses.

B Écrivez en mots les chiffres contenus dans les phrases suivantes.
1   Une force de 21 navires de guerre attend au large de la république rebelle.
2   J'ai payé 80 francs le nouveau bouquin de Roger Peyrfitte.
3   Il y a 1 070 élèves dans ce lycée.
4   Le maire a reçu plus de 5 000 voix aux élections municipales.
5   Plus de 1 500 personnes ont participé à ce concours.

C Calculez. Lisez les résultats à haute voix. Voir la clé (page 228) pour vérifier vos réponses.

1	209 + 368 = ?	5	999 – 332 = ?	9	3 001 x 5 = ?
2	817 + 777 = ?	6	797 – 102 = ?	10	560 ÷ 4 = ?
3	685 + 954 = ?	7	167 x 3 = ?	11	999 ÷ 3 = ?
4	1 200 – 678 = ?	8	1 070 x 8 = ?	12	48^2 = ?

3.2 *Numeral adjectives (ordinal numbers)*

These are the adjectives used to place or locate nouns in a sequence.

Rule	Examples	Exceptions
For most numbers, add -*ième* to the cardinal number	*trois* → *troisième* *six* → *sixième*	Numbers ending in -*e* drop the -*e*: *quatrième, onzième* *Cinq* adds a -*u* before the ending: *cinquième*
'First' is *premier*	Henri **premier** – Henri **the First**; *le* **premier** *janvier* – the **first** of January	*le vingt et* **unième,** *le quarante et* **unième,** etc.
'*Deuxième*' means second in a longer series	*Le* **deuxième** *des trois livres est le plus intéressant* – The **second** of the three books is the most interesting	*la* **seconde** *guerre mondiale* – (there have only been two) BUT *la* **deuxième** *guerre mondiae* is also found
With more than one ordinal, only the last has -*ième*	*A la* **cinq** *ou* **sixième** *interview, il a tout avoué* – At the **fifth** or **sixth** interrogation, he confessed everything	
Ordinals agree in number and gender with their noun	*Les trois* **premiers** *ministres se sont réunis à Versailles* – The three **prime** ministers met at Versailles	
Fractions are usually expressed by ordinals	*Neuf* **dixièmes** *d'un iceberg ne sont pas visibles* – Nine-**tenths** of an iceberg are invisible	*la moitié* = half; *le quart* = quarter; *le tiers* = third

Ce n'est pas le **premier** hiver que la neige nous bloque, mais je ne me souviens pas d'avoir jamais vu son empêchement si épais.

André Gide, *La Symphonie pastorale*

Marianne atteint son **sixième** mois. Notre hebdomadaire a renforcé ses positions… Vente France: fin juillet notre plafond était (hors des **premiers** numéros) de 216 000 et notre plancher de 150 000.

Marianne

EXERCICES

A Examinez le tableau ci-dessous. Expliquez la position des pays suivants en ce qui concerne les hommes ayant plus de 65 ans – **la Belgique**, **la Grèce**, **l'Italie**, **le Danemark**, **le Royaume-Uni**, **l'Allemagne**.

Exemple: Le Danemark arrive en **première** place.

L'Europe du troisième âge Part des hommes de 65 et plus dans la population totale de l'UE (en %)	
Belgique	6,8
Danemark	7,7
Espagne	6,5
France	6,4
Grèce	7,0
Irlande	5,9
Italie	6,7
Luxembourg	5,9
Pays-Bas	6,3
Portugal	6,2
Allemagne	6,1
Royaume-Uni	7,2

B Donnez les noms des monarques suivants.

François I – Philippe II – Louis XIII – Louis XVIII – Élisabeth I – Georges VI – Édouard VIII

C Réécrivez les phrases suivantes en utilisant une fraction.

Exemple: 20 sur 60 cmployés ont voté une grève perlée.

   Le tiers des employés ont voté une grève perlée.

1 **50 sur 100** des élèves souhaitent avoir des professeurs plus qualifiés.

2 **250 sur 1 000** directeurs d'entreprises ne sont pas satisfaits de la politique gouvernementale.

3 **30 sur 90** des commerçants interrogés souhaiteraient avoir deux jours de congé par semaine.

4 **3 voitures sur 7** ont des défauts cachés.

5 **7 jeunes sur 10** croient avoir de bons rapports avec leurs parents.

3.3   *Numeral adjectives (further notes)*

Rule	Examples
The following numbers, and these *only*, are used to indicate a collective or approximate number: *une huit**aine**, dix**aine**, douz**aine**, quinz**aine**, vingt**aine**, trent**aine**, quarant**aine**, cinquant**aine**, soixant**aine**, cent**aine***	*un homme d'une **quarantaine** d'années* – a man of **about** forty *On attend une **vingtaine** de personnes* – We're expecting **about twenty** people *Quelques **centaines** de chômeurs sont descendus dans les rues* – A **few hundred** unemployed people demonstrated
The suffix *-aire* indicates approximate age: *quadragén**aire*** (40), *quinquagén**aire*** (50), *sexagén**aire*** (60), *septuagén**aire*** (70), *octogén**aire*** (80), *nonagén**aire*** (90), *centen**aire*** (100), *millén**aire*** (1000). These adjectives may be used as nouns	*une femme **quadragénaire** – a woman **in her** forties un **septuagénaire** – a man **in his seventies** Des menhirs **millénaires** se dressent partout dans le paysage breton* – Megaliths **thousands of years** old are to be found standing everywhere in the Breton landscape
With expressions such as *le prix* and *le taux*, *de* precedes the numeral	*Le prix est **de** quarante francs* – The price is **forty** francs *Le taux de change de la livre est **de** 8,9 francs* – The rate of exchange is **8.9** francs to the pound

3.4   *Possessive adjectives: forms*

The forms of the possessive adjectives (my, your, his, her, etc.) are as follows. Note the similarity between the initial letters of certain strong pronouns (**Owner** column) and the possessive adjectives.

Owner	One possession, masculine	One possession, feminine	Several possessions
moi	mon	ma	mes
toi	ton	ta	tes
lui/elle	son	sa	ses
nous	notre	notre	nos
vous	votre	votre	vos
eux/elles	leur	leur	leurs

3.5 *Possessive adjectives: uses*

Rule	Examples
The person or thing possessed, not the possessor, determines the choice of possessive adjective. Hence the use of *son* in the following example	*Hélène a deux frères.* **Son** *frère aîné est handicapé* – Hélène has two brothers. **Her** elder brother is handicapped
Each noun in a sequence requires the possessive adjective	*J'ai ramassé **mon** manteau et **mes** papiers et je suis sorti à la hâte* – I picked up **my** coat and (**my**) papers and hurried out
Plural subjects demand the singular possessive adjective if each owner has only one possession	*Les garçons avaient tous laissé **leur** anorak dans la hutte* – The boys had all left **their** anoraks in the cabin

Rule	Examples
Tout le monde, on and *chacun* use *son/sa/ses* as the possessive adjective	*Tout le monde a **sa** propre opinion là-dessus* – Everybody has **their** own opinion about that
The strong pronoun is added when emphasis is required, as possessive adjectives are weak form	*C'était **sa** faute **à elle*** – It was **her** fault
The masculine forms *mon, ton* and *son* are used before a feminine noun beginning with a vowel or *h* mute	*Je suis sortie avec **mon** amie* – I went out with out with **my** girl-friend *Cécile n'a rien dit. **Son** hésitation a tout révélé* – Cécile said nothing. **Her** hesitation revealed everything
'Of mine', 'of hers', etc. is rendered by the possessive adjective	***Une de ses copines** est arrivée* – **A friend of hers** arrived

Ma femme est un jardin de vertus; et même dans les moments difficiles qu'il nous est arrivé parfois de traverser, je n'ai pu douter un instant de la qualité de **son** cœur; mais **sa** charité naturelle n'aime pas à être surprise.

André Gide, *La symphonie pastorale*

Le Monde: Quotidien du soir fondée en 1944 par Hubert Beuve-Méry, dirigé depuis 1991 par l'économiste Jacques Lesourne. «Journal de référence» caractérisé par **son** exhaustivité, **sa** rigueur dans le traitement de l'information. Reconnu notamment pour la richesse de **ses** articles en politique étrangère.

Label France

EXERCICE

Voici des notes biographiques sur un personnage fictif, André Rolin. Écrivez des phrases sous forme de notes sur sa vie. Voir la clé (page 229) pour une version modèle.

Exemple: Son père, Hubert Rolin, est décédé en 1987.

André Rolin – né 2 février 1950 – père: Hubert Rolin, mort 1987 – mère Alice Rolin (née Laval), née 1931 – 1 frère, Grégoire, avocat – 2 sœurs: Huguette (née 1948), peintre; Cécile (née 1952), professeur d'art dramatique – ambition enfantine: d'être acteur – livres les plus connus: *Voyage autour de mon cœur* (1987), *Un fidèle rapport* (1989), *Va, je ne te hais point* (1994); ambition actuelle: Prix Goncourt

3.6   *Interrogative adjectives: forms*

	Masculine	Feminine
Singular	quel	quelle
Plural	quels	quelles

3.7   *Interrogative adjectives: uses*

Rule	Examples
The interrogative adjective agrees in number and gender with its noun	*Quelles émissions préférez-vous?* – **Which** programmes do you prefer?
The interrogative adjective may be separated from its noun by *être*	*Quels sont les avantages d'un tel système?* – **What** are the **advantages** of such a system?
The interrogative adjective is used in indirect questions	*Est-ce que vous savez quels ont été les résultats de l'élection?* – Do you know **what** the results of the election were?
The various forms of *quel* are used to express 'What...!', 'What a...!' or 'How...!'	*Quel toupet!* = **What** cheek! *Quelle horreur!* = **How** horrible!

Une heure après, j'étais au bord de la rivière. **Quelle** splendeur! L'onde était devenue limpide et le bleu d'un ciel vif, lavé, où le vent poussait en riant deux petits nuages, se reflétait sur ces eaux claires.

Henri Bosco, *L'Enfant et la rivière*

Label France: **Quelles** sont les perspectives du marché pour le TGV dans les années à venir? ... Sur **quels** réseaux français vous appuyez-vous pour votre politique internationale?

Label France

EXERCICE

Vous comprenez mal ce dont votre ami vous parle et vous lui demandez de clarifier ce qu'il veut dire.

Exemple: Vous: Les **perspectives** sont excellentes.

Lui: De_____ est-ce que tu parles?

= De **quelles perspectives** est-ce que tu parles?

1   Ce **livre** est vraiment bien.

2   Les **calculs** que j'ai faits sont assez décevants.

3   Tu as vu les **résultats**?

4   Il y a donc plusieurs **possibilités**.

5   C'est un **logiciel** superbe!

3.8   *Demonstrative adjectives: forms*

	Masculine	Feminine
Singular	ce cet (*before vowels and* h *mute*)	cette
Plural	ces	ces

3.9   *Demonstrative adjectives: uses*

Demonstrative adjectives are often used in answer to questions involving some form of *quel* (above). Demonstrative adjectives can mean 'this', 'that', 'these' or 'those', according to context.

Rule	Examples
Ce is used before masculine nouns beginning with a consonant or h aspirate	*Il avait vraiment honte de ce crime* – He was really ashamed of this crime
Cet is used before masculine nouns beginning with vowels and *h* mute	***Cet** arbre date de la Révolution* – **This** tree dates from the time of the Revolution *Les actions de **cet** homme ont choqué tout le monde* – **That man**'s actions shocked everybody
If emphasis is required, add *-ci* or *-là* to indicate 'this' or 'that'	***ce** mur-**ci** –* **this** wall; *ce mur-**là** –* **that** wall; ***ces** murs-**ci** –* **these** walls; ***ces** murs-**là** –* **those** walls

Il eût été difficile de rencontrer plus grand contraste, plus ironique dissemblance, qu'entre **ces** deux personnages, dont l'un faisait songer à un vieux furet sorti de son terrier, et l'autre à un héron traversant hautement les marais.

Maurice Druon, *La Loi des mâles*

Les nombreuses lettres émanant de jeunes mais aussi de responsables des structures d'accueil... témoignent en faveur de **ce** programme (le service volontaire européen).

Tribune pour l'Europe

EXERCICES

A Donnez la forme correcte de l'adjectif démonstratif pour chacun des noms suivants.
architecture – casques – ciseaux – église – hamster – journal – lampe – livre – possibilité

B Traduisez en français.
1 *This dictator's actions have horrified the world.*
2 *Have you seen this item of news* in the paper? (*item of news = nouvelle)*
3 *Pass me that shirt, please – no, no, **that** shirt!*
4 *This airport holds the record for delays.*
5 *Which (= Lesquelles) do you prefer – **these** socks or **those** socks?*

3.10 *Indefinite adjectives*

Indefinite adjectives give a vague idea of quality or quantity connected with the noun
to which they are linked. They agree in number and gender with the noun and usually
precede it. Those marked with an asterisk in the table below may also be used alone as
pronouns (see 4.31).

Adjective	Rule	Examples
aucun*	aucun (fem. aucune) is negative (= no, not a single, not any) and requires ne	Je ne vais utiliser **aucun** produit de cette société-là – I'm not going to use **any** product made by that company
autre*	autre = other, else. With chose, it often appears without an article	Le travail doit servir à **autre** chose que de payer les factures! Il doit y avoir une **autre** raison que celle-là. – Work must be for something **other** than paying the bills. There must be a reason **other** than that
autres*	des is reduced to d' before the plural adjective autres	Il y a d'**autres** patients qui attendent, Docteur – There are **other** patients waiting, Doctor
certains*	certains (fem. certaines) = certain, some (unspecified)	**Certains** sociologues croient que l'effondrement de la civilisation est inévitable – **Some** sociologists believe that the collapse of society is inevitable
chaque	chaque means 'each', 'every'. It is always followed by a singular noun	**Chaque** homme choisit son propre destin – **Each** man chooses his own destiny
même	même (= same) precedes the noun, and agrees in number. Used after the noun, it means 'self', 'very'. **NB** the adverb même = even	Le ministre a démissionné pour les **mêmes** raisons que son prédécesseur – The minister resigned for the **same** reasons as his predecessor Voilà les documents **mêmes** qu'on cherchait – Those are the **very** documents that we were looking for

Adjective	Rule	Examples
n'importe quel(le)	*n'importe quel* = any. The *quel* must agree with the following noun	*Je veux lire quelque chose.* **N'importe quel** *livre fera l'affaire* – I want something to read. **Any** book will do
nul, nulle	*Nul* is negative (= no, not a single) and agrees with its noun. It requires *ne* with the verb	**Nulle** *empreinte digitale* **ne** *restait sur les meubles que les cambrioleurs avait saccagés* – There was**n't a single** finger-print on the furniture which the burglars had wrecked
*plusieurs**	*plusieurs* = several. Always plural. The feminine form is the same as the masculine	*Il avait décidé de faire cela pour* **plusieurs** *raisons* – He had decided to do that for **several** reasons
quel (quelle, quels, quelles) que	Whatever... *Quel* must agree with its noun. Noun and verb are inverted in relation to English	**Quels que** *soient* **les résultats** *de cette élection, la politique gouvernementale devra changer* – **Whatever the results** of this election are, government policy will have to change
quelque(s)	Some... Usually plural. Used with the subjunctive (see **5.57** *quelque... que...*) it means 'whatever'	**Quelques** *heures plus tard il est revenu bredouille* – **Some** hours later, he returned empty-handed *Il faut que le public veille sur l'autorité gouvernementale, à* **quelque** *niveau* **qu'***elle s'exerce* – The public must keep a watchful eye on government power, at **whatever** level it is exercised
quelconque	This corresponds to 'some… or other'. The noun usually precedes the adjective	*On lui racontait une histoire* **quelconque** – They were telling him **some** story **or other**
*tel (telle, tels, telles)**	1. Used to mean 'such' 2. Used to give examples (= like)	1. *Je n'avais jamais eu une* **telle** *surprise* – I had never had **such** a surprise 2. *On en voit de plus en plus d'exemples,* **tel** *cet enfant qui a volé deux mille francs* – You see more and more examples of this, **like** the child who stole two thousand francs
*tout**	*Tout*, used as an adjective, means 'all', 'the whole'. In the plural it can mean 'every'. It agrees in number and gender with its noun	**tout** *le genre humain* = the **whole** human race **Tous** *les visiteurs doivent se présenter à la réception* – **All** visitors must report to reception *On y va* **tous** *les jours* – We go there **every** day *Il faut obéir à* **toutes** *les règles* – You have to obey all the rules

Il se trouve dans **certaines** villes de province des maisons dont la vue inspire une mélancolie égale à celle que provoque les cloîtres les plus sombres, les landes les plus ternes ou les ruines les plus tristes.

Honoré de Balzac, *Eugénie Grandet*

Un million de francs **chaque** année. Un chiffre d'affaires de quatre milliards de francs.

Ouest France

EXERCICE

Choisissez dans le tableau ci-dessus un adjectif indéfini pour compléter le sens des phrases suivantes.

1 Battez les cartes et distribuez-les. _____ joueur en reçoit sept.

2 _____ enfants attendaient devant le magasin – cinq ou six, peut-être.

3 Jusque-là, on n'avait reçu _____ nouvelle de Jules.

4 _____ femmes pensent que le féminisme a déjà atteint ses buts, mais _____ femmes croient qu'on en est loin de là.

5 _____ _____ Français vous dira que la langue anglaise l'emporte sur le français en matière de publicité.

6 _____ _____ soient vos idées là-dessus, vous feriez mieux de vous taire à ce sujet.

7 Une _____ idée ne m'était jamais passée par la tête.

8 Ma fille a été horrifiée. Elle portait la _____ robe que sa mère!

QUALIFICATIVE ADJECTIVES

3.11 *Agreement*

The basic form of the adjective is the masculine singular. Other forms are based on this. The basic scheme of agreement is as follows:

	Masculine	Feminine
Singular	-	-e
Plural	-s	-es

3.12 *General rules*

Explanation	Examples
Adjectives agree in number (singular/plural) and gender (masculine/feminine)	*pour la* **première** *fois* – for the **first** time *les deux* **premiers** *exemples* – the **first** two examples
A plural adjective is used with two singular nouns if it qualifies both	*un chat et un chien* **maltraités** – a dog and a cat that had been **mistreated**
A singular adjective goes with a plural noun if it qualifies each referent individually	*Les forces* **serbe** *et* **kosovar** – The **Serbian** and **Kosovar** forces
The masculine form of the adjective is used with nouns of mixed gender	*un frère et une sœur* **intelligents** – an **intelligent** brother and sister
Two adjectives, *demi* and *nu*, are invariable before a noun, but agree when placed after one	*ma* **demi**-*sœur* – my **half**-sister *On est sorti* **nu**-*pieds* – We went out **bare**-foot BUT *une heure et* **demie** – an hour and a **half** *Les victimes restaient là,* **nues**, *affamées et grelottantes* – The victims stood there, **naked**, starving and shivering
Compound colour adjectives are invariable, as are colours which are really nouns	*Il avait les yeux* **bleu foncé** – He had **dark-blue** eyes *Elle a les cheveux* **paille** – She has **straw-coloured** hair

3.13 *Specific rules of agreement*

Explanation	Examples
Adjectives ending in -*e* do not change in the feminine	*une jeune fille* – a **young** girl *une femme riche* – a **rich** woman
Silent final consonants in the masculine are heard in the feminine, being no longer final	*un pullover gris* BUT *une chemise grise* a **grey** pullover – a **grey** shirt
Seven types of adjective double the final consonant in the feminine. In the case of adjectives ending in -*n*, the nasal vowel becomes an oral vowel in the feminine: *bon – bonne* Exception: *ras – rase* – shaven; *gris – grise* – grey; *dévot – dévote* – devout ; *idiot – idiote* – idiotic	*cruel – cruelle* – cruel; *pareil – pareille* – equal; *ancien – ancienne* – old, former; *bon – bonne* – good; *sujet – sujette* – subject; *gras – grasse* – fat *Dans les pièces comiques traditionnelles il y a souvent une* **cruelle** *marâtre* – In traditional comedies there is often a **cruel** stepmother

Explanation	Examples
Six adjectives ending in -et do not double the consonant in the feminine but add a *grave* accent	*complet – complète* – complete, full; *concret – concrète* – concrete; *discret – discrète* – discreet; *inquiet – inquiète* – worried; *replet – replète* – full; *secret – secrète* – secret *Malheureusement **la pension** était **complète*** – Unfortunately the **hotel** was **full** ***Elle** est **discrète*** – **She** is **discreet**
Adjectives ending in -f (e.g. *sportif*) change to -ve in the feminine (i.e. become voiced)	*C'est **une fille** très **sportive*** – She is a very **sporty girl** *La **lettre** que j'ai reçue était très **brève*** – The **letter** that I received was very **short**
Adjectives ending in -x (e.g. *heureux*) change to -se in the feminine Exception: *doux – douce* – sweet; *faux – fausse* – false; *roux – rousse* – red-haired	***Elle** était très **heureuse*** – **She** was very **happy** *Ma femme est **rousse*** – My wife is **a red-head**
Adjectives ending in -er (e.g. *premier*) change to -ère in the feminine	***Elle** a été la **première** à arriver* – **She** was the **first** to arrive *Cette **étoffe-ci** est plus **légère** que celle-là* – **This material** is **lighter** than that one
Adjectives such as *flatteur* which are based on the present participle (*flattant*) have the feminine in -euse Exception: *défendeur – défenderesse* – defending *demandeur – demanderesse* – requesting *gouverneur – gouvernante* – governing *vengeur – vengeresse* – avenging	***Cette remarque flatteuse** me fit un effet extraordinaire* – **This flattering remark** had an extraordinary effect on me *Les **étudiantes voyageuses** courent d'énormes risques aujourd'hui* – **Travelling girl-students** run enormous risks these days
Adjectives such as *conservateur*, which are not based on the present participle (*conservant*) have their feminine in -trice	*Les **institutions** académiques en France sont très **conservatrices*** – **Academic instutions** in France are very **conservative** cf. *accusateur* – accusing, *créateur* – creative, *observateur* – observational
Majeur, mineur and *meilleur* and those ending in -*érieur* form their feminine regularly	*Cela ne s'est pas produit dans les **meilleures** conditions* – That didn't take place in the **best** conditions *La Commission **Supérieure** du Nucléaire a ouvert une enquête* – The Nuclear **Upper** Council has opened an enquiry
Adjectives ending in -gu change to -guë	*Les deux surfaces sont **contiguës*** – The two surfaces are **adjacent**

Du thé **bouillant**, des paroles **aimables** accueillent l'institutrice… N'est-il pas comique de partir vers une maison de campagne **isolée**, d'imaginer par avance un paysage **agreste**, des prairies, des forêts et puis, en ouvrant pour la **première** fois la croisée de sa chambre, d'apercevoir une cheminée d'usine, **haute**, **agressive** et qui, bouchant et salissant le ciel, crache un panache **opaque** de fumée **noire**.

Eve Curie, *Madame Curie*

Les 142 marches de Brelevenez: «Le **gros** village est devenu une ville.» **Forte** de 18 000 habitants. Trois fois plus qu'en 1960. Sur la souche **lannionnaise***ont poussé bien des rameaux. Des **petits** cousins **venus** de Paris, de la Normandie ou du pays d'Oc. … Devant l'objectif des photographes, aux **beaux** jours, «les **vieux** pignons rigolent de leur succès.»

Ouest France

* lannionnais – de Lannion (ville bretonne)

EXERCICES

A *Une voiture **originaire de France** est une voiture **française**.* Remaniez les expressions suivantes en faisant attention à l'accord de l'adjectif.

1 un camion originaire de Hollande
2 des citoyens originaires de Belgique
3 la langue originaire d'Allemagne
4 des refugiés originaires de Bosnie
5 du café originaire d'Amérique du Sud
6 des produits originaires de France

B Complétez ce texte avec la forme des adjectifs qui s'impose.

Jamais chose (pareil) ne s'était produite dans ce (petit) village (tranquille). Mme Lebec n'avait pas la réputation d'être très (discret) et elle avait été la (premier) à faire courir le bruit dans cette (petit) commune (breton). Ce bruit était certainement (faux). Danielle était tout à fait (heureux) et n'avait aucune intention de quitter son mari (ivrogne). Sa mère avait été la (dernier) à avoir des nouvelles de sa fille (roux), et en avait été très (inquiet).

3.14 *Irregular feminine adjectives*

The following adjectives have more or less irregular feminine forms.

Masculine	Meaning	Feminine
absous	*absolved*	absoute
bénin	*benign*	bénigne
bref	*brief*	brève
doux	*sweet*	douce
épais	*thick*	épaisse
exprès	*express*	expresse
faux	*false*	fausse
favori	*favourite*	favorite
frais	*fresh, cool*	fraîche
gentil	*kind*	gentille
coi	*quiet*	coite
dissous	*dissolved*	dissoute
long	*long*	longue
malin	*malign*	maligne
nul	*no*	nulle
oblong	*oblong*	oblongue
paysan	*peasant, country-style*	paysanne
roux	*red (hair)*	rousse
tiers	*third*	tierce

3.15 *Adjectives with special forms*

The following five adjectives have special forms:

Masculine form before consonant	Masculine form before vowel or *h* mute	Feminine form
beau – *beautiful*	bel	belle
fou – *mad*	fol	folle
mou – *soft*	mol	molle
nouveau – *new*	nouvel	nouvelle
vieux – *old*	vieil	vieille

Examples:

Il y avait devant la **vieille** maison un **bel** arbre séculaire – *Before the **old** house stood a **beautiful**, centuries-old tree*

Le **nouvel** hélicoptère a dû subir des épreuves au **vieil** aéroport – *The **new** helicopter had to undergo tests at the **old** airport*

De **folles** mèches de cheveux blonds sortaient de sous son chapeau de toile bleue – *Rebellious wisps of fair hair peeped out from beneath her blue canvas hat*

EXERCICE

Complétez le texte suivant, en changeant, là où il le faut, la forme des adjectifs. Attention! Il ne faut pas les changer tous!

IBM... France

L'insertion (professionnel) des personnes (handicapé) dans les conditions (ordinaire) de travail est sans doute une disposition (légal), mais aussi un enjeu (économique) et (social) pour les entreprises.

L'objectif est (clair). (Tout) personne dans l'entreprise doit pouvoir exercer un métier ou des responsabilités sur le (seul) critère de la compétence. Cela suppose d'acquérir les connaissances et d'apprendre à se servir des outils (exigé) par la fonction.

IBM, entreprise (citoyen), mène cette (double) action.

3.16 *Formation of the plural*

Rule	Examples
All feminines add -*s* to the singular	*Les femmes **travailleuses** n'ont pas toujours les mêmes droits que les hommes* – **Working** women do not always have the same rights as men
Masculine adjectives in -*s* and -*x* do not change	*De **gros** soupirs se firent entendre* – **Heavy** sighs were heard *Trois petits enfants **malheureux** ont survécu à l'accident* – Three **unfortunate** children survived the accident
Masculine adjectives in -*eau* add -*x*	*les **beaux** monuments de Paris* – Paris's beautiful monuments
Masculine adjectives in -*al* change to -*aux* Exception: *banal – banals* – banal; *fatal – fatals* – inevitable; *glacial – glacials* – glacial; *natal – natals* – native; *naval – navals* – naval	*les éléments **principaux** de ce plan* – the **main** constituents of this plan
With the above exceptions, masculine adjectives add -*s*	*Trois **grands** camions attendaient* – Three large lorries were waiting *Je trouve ses livres **intéressants*** – I find her books interesting

3.17 *Comparison*

There are three degrees of comparison – inferiority, equality and superiority. The English 'as' or 'than' is rendered by *que*.

– Inferiority	= Equality	+ Superiority
Ce film est **moins** intéressant **que** celui que j'ai vu hier – *This film is **less** interesting **than** the one I saw yesterday*	L'intrigue en est **aussi** compliquée **que** celle de l'autre – *The plot is **as** complicated **as that of** the other one*	Le dénouement en est **plus** improbable **que** celui de l'autre – *The outcome is **more** improbable **than** that of the other one*
Ce film n'est **pas aussi/si** intéressant **que** celui que j'ai vu hier – *This film is **not as/so** interesting as the one I saw yesterday*	L'intrigue n'en est **pas moins** compliquée **que** celle de l'autre – *The plot is **no less** complicated **than** that of the other one*	
Ce film est **encore moins** intéressant **que** 'Godzilla' – *This film is **even less** interesting **than** 'Godzilla'*		Le dénouement en est **encore plus** spectaculaire **que** celui de l'autre – *The outcome is **even more** spectacular **than** that of the other one*

3.18 *Irregular comparatives*

Adjective	Comparative	Notes
bon	*meilleur, meilleure*	Better, not to be confused with *mieux* (adverb). See **6.10**.
mauvais	*pire*	*Plus mauvais* is more common (= worse in quality). *Pire* is usually used to express emotion rather than fact (= morally worse). Not be confused with *pis*. See **6.10**
petit	*moindre*	*Plus petit* (smaller) is more common. *Moindre* suggests 'less important', and is used with abstract nouns

EXERCICES

A   Lisez les détails ci-dessous, puis complétez les phrases qui y font suite avec **plus** ou **moins**.

superficie de l'Asie = 44 493 000 km^2

superficie de l'Afrique = 30 293 000 km^2

superficie de l'Amérique du Nord = 24 454 000 km^2

superficie de l' l'Amérique du Sud = 17 838 000 km^2

superficie de l'Europe = 10 245 000 km^2

1   L'Amérique du Sud est _____ grande que l'Amérique du Nord.

2   L'Amérique du Nord est _____ grande que l'Europe.

3   L'Asie est _____ grande que l'Afrique.

4   L'Europe est _____ grande que l'Amérique du Sud.

5   L'Amérique du Nord est _____ grande que l'Afrique.

B   Lisez les détails suivants.

Marc fait 1 mètre 40.

Jeanne fait 1 mètre 38.

Céline fait 1 mètre 36.

Marc a un quotient intellectuel (QI) de 120.

Jeanne a un QI de 123.

Céline a un QI de 130.

Maintenant, comparez ces trois personnes.

Exemple: Marc est **plus grand que Jeanne**, mais il est **moins doué** qu'elle, et **encore moins doué** que Céline.

3.19 *Superlatives*

The superlative expresses the idea of 'the biggest', 'the highest', 'the best', etc. The appropriate definite article (*le*, *la*, *les*) is added to the comparative to form the superlative.

Masculine singular	Masculine plural	Feminine singular	Feminine plural
C'est le film **le plus intéressant** que j'aie jamais vu – *It's the most interesting film that I've ever seen*	Ce sont les films **les plus intéressants de** l'histoire du cinéma – *These are the most interesting films in the history of cinema* **NB de** *not* **dans**	C'est l'histoire **la plus banale** que j'aie jamais lue – *It's the most banal story that I have ever read*	C'étaient les expériences **les plus émouvantes de** ma vie – *These were the most moving experiences of my life* **NB de** *not* **dans**

Cet homme se nommait Barthélemy Piéchut, maire de la commune de Clochemerle, dont il était **le plus gros** propriétaire et possédait **les meilleures** pentes exposées au sud-est, celles qui produisent les vins **les plus fruités**.

Gabriel Chevalier, Clochemerle

Le peuple de l'été de l'automne 40, il faut le voir tel qu'il est: écrasé sous le poids de **la plus effroyable** défaite de son histoire…

Le Figaro Magazine

C'EST LE PLUS LONG MÈTRE PLIANT DU MONDE.

G. Mathieu

EXERCICES

A Appariez les noms de la colonne de gauche aux records à droite auxquels ils correspondent.

le stégosaure	la plus vieille femme du monde
la girafe	la boisson la plus connue du monde
le Pacifique	le jeu-vidéo le plus vendu du monde
Pluton	la voiture la plus rapide du monde
Thrust SSC	la planète la plus froide du système solaire
Lockheed SR-71A (Merle)	l'animal le plus grand du monde
Tomb Raider	l'océan le plus profond du monde
Coca-Cola	le dinosaure le plus stupide qui ait vécu
le Prince Abdul Aziz Bin Fahd	l'avion le plus rapide du monde
Jeanne Calment (morte 1999)	le teenager le plus riche du monde

B Écrivez une phrase pour exprimer votre opinion sur les choses suivantes. Vous trouverez des exemples dans la clé (page 232).

Exemple: *Autant en emporte le vent* – C'est le film le plus ennuyeux du monde!

1 *Titanic*
2 les Spice Girls
3 le Concours de l'Eurovision
4 le Mundial
5 une soirée sans télévision

3.20 *Adjectives which precede the noun*

The following qualificative adjectives are **always** placed before the noun, like articles and determinative adjectives.

Rule	Examples	Notes
Ordinal numbers (*premier, deuxième*, etc.) precede the noun	*Pour la* **première** *fois de ma vie, j'étais toute seule* – For the **first** time in my life, I was completely alone	The names of monarchs have the number *following*: François **Premier** – *François* **the First** Philippe **Quatre**, dit Le Bel – *Philippe* **the Fourth**, *known as the Fair*
Adjectives qualifying a proper noun precede	*Le* **Petit** *Paul m'écouta lire à haute voix* Le Dernier des Mohicans – **Little** Paul listened to me reading *The Last of the Mohicans*	

The following adjectives **usually** precede the noun but some may occur after it for stylistic effect:

autre, beau, bon, cher (= *beloved*), double, excellent, gentil, grand, gros, jeune, joli, long, mauvais, meilleur, moindre, nouveau, petit, pire, saint, seul, vaste, vieux, vilain, vrai.

> Tors-Col haussa sa **grosse** épaule, ferma les yeux et eut une moue lassée.
> Maurice Druon, Le Lis et le lion
>
> Après quelques **petits** boulots, il s'est lancé dans la bande dessinée et a déjà sorti cinq albums.
> Les Clés de l'actualité

3.21 *Preceding adjectives modified by adverbs*

Rule	Examples
Preceding adjectives modified by the adverbs *aussi, bien, fort, plus, moins, si,* and *très* normally remain before the noun	*On habitait une **si petite** maison que l'on y tenait à peine* – We lived in **such a tiny** house that we could hardly all fit in
Adjectives which normally precede will follow the noun if they have a long adverb attached to them	*C'était une femme **extraordinairement belle*** – She was an **extraordinarily beautiful** woman
Adjectives which normally precede will follow the noun if they have a long complement after them	*Il s'agissait d'un garçon **haut comme deux pommes*** – It was a boy **who was knee-high to a grasshopper**

NB The latter two examples follow the end-weight principle. See **9.4**.

3.22 *Adjectives with* quel *and* que

Rule	Examples
In exclamations using *quelle*, adjectives from the list in paragraph **3.20** precede the noun	***Quelle belle** maison!* – **What a beautiful** house!
In exclamations using *que*, the adjective follows *être*	***Que** cette maison est **belle!*** – **How beautiful** that house is!

3.23 *Adjectives which always follow the noun*

The following types of adjective are **always** placed after the noun.

Rule	Examples
Nouns used adjectivally	*une robe **Coco Chanel*** – a **Coco Chanel** dress
Adjectives of nationality and region	*les institutions **françaises*** – **French** institutions; *les villes **bourguignonnes*** – **Burgundy** towns
Adjectives joined by *et* and *ou*	*Les sapins **noirs et raides** frappent de stupeur l'enfant de la plaine* – The child from the lowlands was stupefied by the **rigid black** pines
Adjectives which have a complement dependent on them	*Ce sont des problèmes **communs à tous*** – These are problems **common to all**

3.24 *Adjectives which usually follow the noun*

The following types of adjectives are **usually** placed after the noun.

Rule	Examples
Adjectives expressing physical characteristics	*Il avait le visage **glabre*** – His face was **clean-shaven**
Adjectives of colour Exception: *une **verte** semonce* – a good talking to (metaphorical use); *faire **grise** mine* – to look grumpy	*un vieillard vêtu d'un tricot de laine **violette*** – an old man dressed in a **purple** cardigan
A long (polysyllabic) adjective follows a short noun	*Il menait une **vie irresponsable*** – He led an **irresponsible life**
Past and present participles used adjectivally. **NB** *prétendu* (alleged) and *soi-disant* (self-styled) always precede: *Le **soi-disant** roi de ce pays africain* – The **self-styled** king of this African country	*C'était vraiment un enfant **gâté*** – He was a **spoiled** child *Les vagues **étincelantes** venaient déferler sur les sables* – The **sparkling** waves broke on the sands

Une longue maison **rouge**, avec cinq portes **vitrées**, sous des vignes vierges, à l'extrémité du bourg; une cour **immense** avec préaux et buanderie, qui ouvrait en avant sur le village par un grand portail

Alain-Fournier, Le Grand Meaulnes

Si la mode des femmes **maigres** nous vient des États-Unis, c'est aussi de là-bas que la protestation contre cette tendance arrive en Europe. De nombreuses femmes **américaines** rappellent qu'avec la mode des femmes **rondes**, elles trouvaient plus facilement à s'habiller.

Les Clés de l'actualité

3.25 *Two adjectives qualifying a noun*

Rule	Examples
Two adjectives which normally precede may combine	*une **jolie petite** fille* – a **pretty little** girl
Two adjectives used to qualify a noun retain their normal positions	*un **petit** livre **intéressant*** – an **interesting little** book
Adjectives linked by *et* or *ou* follow the noun, whatever their normal position	*Ils entrèrent dans un bâtiment **vaste et vide*** – They entered a **vast, empty** building

Le kulig… Est-ce assez dire que c'est un bal? Non, naturellement! C'est dans l'excitation du carnaval, un voyage tournoyant et féerique. Ce sont deux traîneaux qui partent le soir, dans la neige, emportant, blotties, sous les couvertures, Mania Sklodowska et ses trois cousines, **masquées et vêtues** en paysannes carcoviennes. Des garçons, qui arborent des habits **pittoresques et rustiques**, les escortent à cheval, en brandissant des torches… Le traîneau des musiciens approche… Ils joueront ces **petits** juifs **frénétiques** jusqu'à ce que dix autres traîneaux les retrouvent dans la nuit. Malgré les cahots et les descentes vertigineuses sur les pentes glacées, ils ne manqueront pas un seul coup d'archet et ils conduiront triomphalement jusqu'à la première étape, la **fantastique** farandole **nocturne**.

Eve Curie, *Madame Curie*

Il sont vingt. Solides gaillards de première F d'un lycée technique du 20e, on les destine aux métiers de gestion. Age moyen: 18 ans. Bien plus que les élèves **instruits et concernés** du Lycée Jean-Baptiste-Say, ils représentent le lycéen ordinaire. Quand ils voudront savoir, les derniers témoins de la **Seconde** Guerre **mondiale** auront disparu.

L'Événement du jeudi

EXERCICE

Mettez les adjectifs à la bonne place.

1 un homme (petit, chauve)
2 la raison (légitime, seule)
3 des mouvements (frénétiques, saccadées)
4 une plaine (nue, vaste)
5 le port (nouveau, breton)
6 une église (élégante, grande)
7 une vie (irresponsable, dissipée)
8 des résultats (inattendus, effrayants)
9 les forces (orientales, militaires)
10 les prix (premiers, deux)

3.26 *Adjective position and meaning*

Some adjectives change their meaning according to their position in relation to the noun. These include the following.

The adjective precedes	The adjective follows
un **ancien** soldat – *a former soldier*	un bâtiment **ancien** – *an old building*
un **brave** homme – *an honest man*	un homme **brave** – *a courageous man*
certaines gens – *some people*	une victoire **certaine** – *certain victory*
Mon cher Robert – *Dear Robert*	un achat **cher** – *an expensive purchase*
un **curieux** type – *an odd bloke*	une vieille **curieuse** – *an inquisitive old woman*
mon **dernier** sou – *my last penny*	la semaine **dernière** – *last week*
un **grand** homme – *a great man*	une femme **grande** – *a tall woman*
un **gros** problème – *a serious problem*	un enfant **gros** – *a fat child*
la **haute** mer – *the open sea*	la mer **haute** – *high tide*
la **même** lettre – *the same letter*	la lettre **même** – *the letter itself*
une **nouvelle** robe – *a new (another) dress*	une robe **nouvelle** – *a new-style dress*
la **pauvre** petite! – *poor (pitiable) little girl!*	des gens **pauvres** – *poverty-stricken people*
mon **propre** appartement – *my own flat*	une chemise **propre** – *a clean shirt*
une **pure** perte de temps – *a complete waste of time*	un ciel **pur** – *a cloudless sky*
les **rares** lanternes – *the few, scattered lanterns*	les animaux rares – *rare animals*
le **seul** problème – *the only problem*	une femme **seule** – *a single/lonely woman*

Le sénéchal de Joinville, qu'on n'avait fait lever qu'à la **dernière** minute afin de ménager ses forces, se tenait à la porte du roi, en compagnie de Bouville... La lumière qui tombait d'une embrasure lui montra le visage de l'**ancien** chambellan...

Maurice Druon, *La Loi des mâles*

C'est un demi-succès qu'a enregistré ce week-end la Nasda, l'agence spatiale japonaise qui œuvre à la mise au point d'une **nouvelle** navette spatiale... le tir de lundi constitue bel et bien une première étape de l'entrée du Japon dans le cercle très fermé possédant une telle navette, alors que l'Europe a gelé son **propre** projet de navette «Hermès».

Le Soir (journal belge)

EXERCICE

Traduisez en français.

1 *last month*

2 *a former judge*

3 *the evidence itself*

4 *the only solution*

5 *an inquisitive child*

6 *a clean room*

7 *the few hamlets*

8 *some men*

9 *a complete lie*

10 *an expensive car*

3.27 *Adjective position and style*

While the above rules give generalities, it is almost impossible to give hard and fast rules on the position of adjectives. Writers of all types vary the positions of adjectives in order to achieve stylistic effects. The more unusual the place that the adjective occupies, the more striking it is to the reader. The End-weight Principle (see **9.4**) often plays an important role in determining the position of the adjective.

Examples:

Victor émit un **fort** ronflement – Robert Sabatier, *Les noisettes sauvages*

Ces **violents** contrastes climatiques provoquent érosion et désertification – *Ça m'intéresse*

Premier effet de ce **brutal** accroissement de la population – *Profession Parents*

The more factual and down-to-earth a piece of writing is, the more the adjectives will remain in their usual place. The more emotional or evocative a piece is, the more likely it is that the adjectives will occupy unusual positions.

EXERCICE DE CONSOLIDATION

Insérez les adjectifs dans le texte suivant et faites-les accorder avec les noms qu'ils qualifient.

La porte des îles anglo-normandes

Le port de Saint Quay a trouvé sa compagnie. Émeraude Lines exploite une liaison avec Jersey (**quotidien**). Dix mille passagers en deux mois. Émeraude Lines vient de faire une percée à Saint-Quay-Portrieux (**beau**). La compagnie a l'habitude du trafic avec les îles (**anglo-normand, malouin***).

Le né des ports exprime ainsi sa vocation (**dernier, breton, plein**). Ses promoteurs n'ont pas lésiné sur les moyens: 800 000 mètres de roches pour protéger un bassin de 17 hectares (**cube**); 10 pontons pour l'accueil de 950 voitures (**quelque**); 700 places de parking pour les automobiles sur 5 hectares de terre-plein et un centre (**commercial**).

Émeraude Lines a pris un départ (**bon**).

* malouin = de St. Malo

Pronouns

Pronouns stand in place of a noun, an adjective or a prepositional phrase that has already been mentioned, or is about to be mentioned. Pronouns replacing nouns are marked for number and gender.

4.1 *Subject pronouns*

The subject pronouns are:

je	*I*	nous	*we*
tu	*you (sing.)*	vous	*you (plural/polite)*
il	*he, it*	ils	*they*
elle	*she, it*	elles	*they*
on	*one, you, people*		

4.2 *Use of the subject pronouns*

Rule	Examples
Subject pronouns agree in number and gender with the noun to which they refer	*Mon père* était un original. *Il* portait toujours un tricot, été comme hiver – **My father** was eccentric. **He** always wore a cardigan, summer and winter *La voiture* n'était pas là. *Elle* était en retard – **The car** wasn't there. **It** was late
Tu is used when speaking to **one** person with whom one is on familiar terms. It is also used when speaking to an animal	*Tu* vas rester ici, Alain? – Are you going to stay here, Alain? *Médor, où es-**tu**?* – Médor, where are **you**? (Médor is a dog's name)

Rule	Examples
Vous is used (a) to address one or more people politely, (b) to address more than one person with whom one is familiar	***Vous*** *désirez, monsieur?* – What would **you** like, sir? *Qu'est-ce que **vous** faites, les gars?* – What are **you** doing, lads?
On is used in situations similar to those in which English uses 'one'	***On*** *doit obéir à la loi* – **One** must obey the law
On may be used to mean 'we'	*Qu'est-ce qu'**on** fait, alors?* – What shall **we** do then?

Phil plia les fauteuils de bois, retourna la table en rotin. **Il** ne souriait pas, en la passant, à sa petite amie

Colette, *Le Blé en herbe*

Ne gardez pas **les champignons** frais plus de deux jours au refrigérateur: au delà, **ils** sèchent ou **ils** moisissent.

Avantages

4.3 *Disjunctive pronouns*

The disjunctive pronouns are:

moi	*I, me*	**nous**	*we*
toi	*you (sing.)*	**vous**	*you (plural/polite)*
lui	*he, him, it*	**eux**	*they, them*
elle	*she, her, it*	**elles**	*they, them*
soi	*one, you, people*		

4.4 *Use of the disjunctive pronouns*

'Disjunctive' means 'not joined'. Disjunctive pronouns can thus stand alone, unlike subject pronouns. Various other uses are explained below.

Rule	Examples
Disjunctive pronouns may stand alone	*Qui a fait cela?* – **Moi** – Who did that? – **Me**
Disjunctive pronouns follow prepositions such as *avec*, *chez*, *pour* and *sans*	*Où est Jean?* – *Il est **chez lui*** – Where's Jean? He's **at home** *Chacun pour **soi*** – Every man for **himself**

Rule	Examples
If the subject is emphasised, the disjunctive form may be used alone	*Lui* veut y aller, *moi* non – **He** wants to go there, **I** don't
Disjunctive forms emphasise the subject pronoun	*Moi, je* veux y aller. *Toi, tu* as envie de m'accompagner? – **I** want to go there. Do **you** feel like coming with me?
This emphasis may also be added at the end	*Je* veux y aller, *moi*. *Tu* as envie de m'accompagner, *toi*? – **I** want to go there. Do **you** feel like coming with me?

4.5 *Direct object (DO) and indirect object (IDO) pronouns*

Direct object pronouns replace nouns functioning as the **direct object** of the sentence (see table of grammatical definitions) and **indirect object pronouns** replace nouns functioning as the **indirect object** of the sentence (see table of grammatical definitions). The pronouns are as follows:

Direct object pronouns	Meaning	Indirect object pronouns	Meaning
me	*me*	me	*to me*
te	*you*	te	*to you*
le	*him, it*	lui	*to him*
la	*her, it*	lui	*to her*
nous	*us*	nous	*to us*
vous	*you*	vous	*to you*
les	*them*	leur	*to them*

Note: Direct object pronouns will cause agreement to be put on past participles in compound tenses (see **5.16**). Indirect objects **never** cause any agreement on past participles.

4.6   *Pronoun function*

In choosing pronouns to replace nouns, it is important to be sure what function the original noun plays in the sentence. If it is a direct object, choose the appropriate pronoun from the **direct object pronoun** table (example 1). If the noun is an indirect object, choose from the **indirect object pronoun** table (example 2).

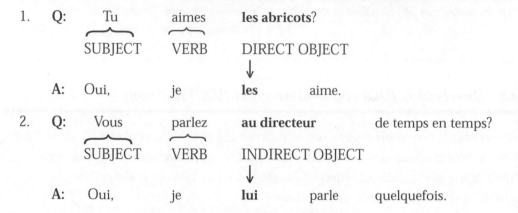

1. Q: Tu   aimes   **les abricots**?

            SUBJECT   VERB   DIRECT OBJECT
                                         ↓

    A: Oui,   je   **les**   aime.

2. Q: Vous   parlez   **au directeur**   de temps en temps?

            SUBJECT   VERB   INDIRECT OBJECT
                                         ↓

    A: Oui,   je   **lui**   parle   quelquefois.

4.7   *Use of direct and indirect object pronouns*

Rule	Examples
Direct object pronouns agree in number and gender with the noun to which they refer	*Françoise Sagan avait été témoin de **ces événements**, et elle **les** a notés dans son journal –* Françoise Sagan had witnessed **these events** and she noted **them** in her diary
Indirect object pronouns agree in number and gender with the noun to which they refer	*J'ai téléphoné **à mes copains**, et je **leur** ai parlé de ce qui s'était passé –* I phoned **my friends** and told **them** what had happened
DO and IDO pronouns precede the verb in negative commands	*Ne **t'**inquiète pas! –* Don't worry! *Ne **vous en** faites pas! –* Don't worry!
Le and *en* may be used to complete the sense of a sentence	*Lui, il est fatigué, moi je ne **le** suis pas (i.e. fatigué) –* He's tired, but I'm not *Il y a moins d'éléphants qu'il n'y **en** avait en 1980 (i.e. d'éléphants) –* There are fewer elephants now than there were in 1980

Dès que le dîner fut fini, Chantal **me** prit par le bras.

Guy de Maupassant, Mademoiselle Perle

Des agents bilingues aideront les visiteurs de la capitale. Divers produits **leur** seront également proposés.

Le Figaro

EXERCICES

A Complément d'objet direct ou indirect? Complétez les phrases avec **le**, **la**, **les**, **lui** ou **leur**.

1 J'ai vu André et Marianne en ville et je _____ ai demandé de venir à la boum.

2 Je comprends bien l'anglais, mais je ne ___ parle pas très bien.

3 J'ai une nouvelle voisine. Je ___ connais de vue, mais je ne ___ ai pas encore parlé.

4 Il y a de très beaux rideaux dans le nouveau catalogue, mais je ne vais pas ___ acheter parce qu'ils sont trop chers.

5 J'ai un manuel pour mon ordinateur, mais je ne _____ comprends pas.

B Répondez aux questions suivantes en utilisant un pronom au lieu du nom ou de l'expression en gras.

Exemple: Vous connaissez **le monsieur qui habite à côté**?

Oui, je **le** connais.

1 Vous aimez **ce disque**?

2 Vous avez acheté **cet ordinateur dont on parlait**?

3 Vous connaissez **la jeune fille qui attend au comptoir**?

4 Vous **m'**avez téléphoné?

5 Vous **nous** avez écrit?

4.8 *Reflexive and reciprocal pronouns*

Pronouns are used with certain verbs when (a) a person does the action to himself/herself and (b) when two people do the action to each other. The first type are known as **reflexive** pronouns, the second type as **reciprocal** pronouns. Some verbs use reflexive pronouns even though they are not reflexive or reciprocal in sense (e.g. *il s'agit de* – it's a question of).

4.9 *Reflexive pronouns: forms*

The reflexive pronouns are as follows:

me	*myself*	nous	*ourselves*
te	*yourself*	vous	*yourself, yourselves*
se	*himself, herself, oneself*	se	*themselves*

4.10 *Reflexive pronouns: uses*

There is no difference in the form of DO reflexive forms and the IDO reflexive forms. Whether a pronoun is being used as a DO or an IDO, may however, influence the form of a past participle in the written form (but rarely the spoken form). See **5.16**.

IDO forms will be used with verbs which take *à* after them, e.g. *demander, dire, poser,* etc. and the construction *se faire* + infinitive (i.e. to get something done to oneself). If one injures onself, verbs such as *casser, couper* and *brûler* will require an IDO reflexive pronoun. IDO pronouns cause no agreement with the past participle.

Direct object use	Indirect object use
Je **me** suis levé à sept heures – *I got up at seven o'clock*	Je **me** demande ce qui se passe – *I wonder what's happening*
Tu **te** promènes tous les jours? – *Do you go for a walk every day?*	Tu **t'**es fait couper les cheveux? – *Have you had your hair cut?*
Il **se** plaint de ce qui s'est passé – *He's complaining about what's happened*	Il **se** disait que ce ne pouvait pas être vrai – *He said to himself that this couldn't be true*
Elle **se** dépêche vers la sortie – *She hurries towards the exit*	L'accident se produit ainsi – elle glisse, elle tombe et elle **se** casse le bras* – *This is how the accident happened – she slipped, she fell and she broke her arm*

* The present tense is used in this example to render the action more vivid.

Direct object use	Indirect object use
On **s'**interroge toujours sur ce point-là – *We always wonder about that*	On **se** demande que faire – *We're wondering what to do*
Nous **nous** couchons toujours très tard – *We always go to bed very late*	Nous **nous** posons la même question – *We ask ourselves the same question*
Si vous **vous** blessez, ne venez pas à moi pour vous en plaindre – *If you hurt yourselves, don't come complaining to me*	Vous **vous** faites couper les cheveux régulièrement? – *Do you have your hair cut regularly?*
Ils/Elles **se** heurtent à des obstacles – *They come up against obstacles*	Ils/Elles **se** sont fracturé la jambe – *They have broken their legs*

Mais moi, si je **me** tais, c'est pour le plaisir de **me** taire.

Henri Bosco, L'Enfant et la rivière

Pour attirer les jeunes hors des frontières, ils ne **se** contentent plus d'inscrire à leur programme une langue étrangère.

Le Figaro

EXERCICES

A Décidez s'il s'agit de l'emploi d'un pronom complément d'objet **direct** ou **indirect** dans les phrases suivantes.
1 Mes parents **se** levaient toujours à six heures, hiver comme été.
2 Mon copain n'a pas pu venir à la boum, parce qu'il **s'**était cassé la cheville.
3 Nous **nous** demandons ce qu'il faut faire.
4 Hélène **s'**est fait maquiller par une maquilleuse professionnelle.
5 Je **me** suis fait percer l'oreille la semaine dernière.

B Traduisez en français.
1 *The fire broke out in the hall.*
2 *Everybody rushed toward the exit.*
3 *I wondered what to do.*
4 *My girl-friend complained about what was happening.*
5 *She broke her ankle.*

4.11 *Reciprocal uses*

Reciprocal use of IDO forms occurs with verbs which are followed by *à* (e.g. *écrire à, téléphoner à*).

Direct object form	Indirect object form
Ils **se** sont insultés – *They insulted **each other***	Ils **se** téléphonent tous les jours – *They phone **each other** every day*
Elles **se** détestent l'une l'autre – *They hate **each other***	Elles **s'**écrivent au moins une fois par semaine – *They write **to each other** once a week*

4.12 *y*

The little word *y* functions sometimes as a pronoun and sometimes as an adverb, but it generally replaces a longer phrase involving *à* (or some other preposition) and a noun, and precedes the verb (except in commands).

Noun reference	Use of *y*
Tu as jamais été **à Rome**? – *Have you ever been **to Rome**?*	Oui, j'**y** ai été l'année dernière – *Yes, I was **there** last year*
Les boîtes étaient donc **dans le placard**? – *So the tins were **in the cupboard**!*	Oui, elles **y** étaient – *Yes, they were (**there**)*
Madeleine est parvenue **à contacter ses parents?** – *Did Madeleine manage **to contact her parents?***	Oui, elle **y** est parvenue – *Yes, she managed it*

4.13 *en*

The pronoun *en* replaces a noun phrase which contains *de* (or some form of it such as *du* or *des*), and precedes the verb (except in commands).

Noun reference	Use of *en*
Tu as **des ciseaux**? – *Have you got **any scissors**?*	Oui, j'**en** ai ici – *Yes I've got **some** here*
Vous avez **des frères**? – *Do you have **any brothers**?*	Oui j'**en** ai deux – *I've got two (**of them**)*
Papa a besoin **de cette revue**? – *Does Dad need **this magazine**?*	Oui, il **en** a besoin – *Yes, he does need **it***

4.14 *Multiple pronouns*

If a sentence requires more than one pronoun before the verb, they occur in a fixed order, as follows. If negatives or past participles are used, they occur at the points noted.

	me							
	te	le						
(ne)	se	la	lui	y	en	**VERB**	(neg.)	(past participle)
	nous	les	leur					
	vous							

4.15 *Nouns to pronouns*

In choosing pronouns, it is important to establish the function of the pronoun in the sentence (see above, **4.6**).

Once the function of the pronouns has been decided, their order follows the pattern set out in **4.14**.

Noun reference	Order with pronouns
J'ai décidé de mentionner **ce problème à Louis** – *I decided to mention* **this problem to Louis**	Je **le** *lui* ai mentionné le lendemain – *I mentioned* **it** *to him* the following day
On a donné **de l'argent** *aux jeunes*? – *Did they give* **the youngsters** **any money**?	Non, on ne **leur en** a guère offert – *No, they hardly offered* **them** **any**

Note, too, this use with *il y a:*

Il **y** a **de la peinture**? – *Is there* **any paint**?	Non, il n'**y en** a pas – *No, there isn't any*

Je ne **te** l'avais jamais dit, mais j'ai des obligations de chemin de fer; j'en ai pour sept cent quatre vingts francs.

Marcel Pagnol, Le château de ma mère

Plus surprenant, mais qui **s'en** plaindra, le jazz, le rock, les musiques venues de toutes les cultures du monde auront droit de cité.

Les Clés de l'actualité

EXERCICES

A Décidez si l'ordre des pronoms dans les phrases suivantes est correct ou non. Si l'ordre est incorrect, corrigez-le.

1 Il y avait des sucres d'orge dans cette petite confiserie, et j'**en y** ai acheté pour ma sœur.

2 Le ministre a demandé le dossier, et le fonctionnaire confus **le lui** a remis.

3 Le directeur m'a interrogé sur ce projet et j'**en lui** ai donné des détails.

4 Mon frère m'a demandé les photos qui étaient dans le bureau, et je **les lui** ai envoyées.

5 Suzanne m'avait demandé de remettre le livre dans la bibliothèque, donc j'**y l'**ai remis.

B Substituez des pronoms aux expressions marquées.

Exemple: J'ai retrouvé **mon copain** *au coin de la rue*.

Je **l'y** ai retrouvé.

1 J'ai remis **les papiers** *à mon chef*.

2 Marguerite a vu **son fils** *dans le cinéma*.

3 Les deux garçons ont trouvé **de l'argent** *dans la vieille maison*.

4 Le gouvernement a accordé **de nouveaux droits** *aux automobilistes*.

5 Le fonctionnaire qui s'occupait **de cette affaire** a parlé *aux délégués* dans la grande salle.

4.16 *Positive commands*

It is in **positive** commands that the usual rule about pronouns preceding the verb fails to apply. Here the pronouns follow the verb, and, in the written form, are linked to it by hyphens.

Note: the strong forms of *me* (*moi*) and *te* (*toi*) are used in positive commands, except before *en*, where they shorten to *m'* and *t'*. The order of pronouns is as follows:

	moi		
le	toi		
la	lui	y	en
les	nous		
	vous		
	leur		

4.17 *Nouns to pronouns in commands*

The typface in the following examples shows the connection between noun and pronoun.

Noun reference	Order with pronouns in command
Voulez-vous que je donne **ces informations** *au directeur*? – *Do you want me to give* **these details** *to the manager*?	Oui, donnez-**les**-*lui*, s'il vous plaît – *Yes, give* **them** *to him* please
Tu veux que je **te** prête **mes disques**? – *Do you want me to lend* **you my records**?	Oui, prête-**les**-*moi*, s'il te plaît – *Yes, please lend* **them** *to me*
Est-ce que je dois donner **du papier** *à tous les élèves*? – *Do I have to give* **paper** *to all the pupils*?	Oui, donnez-*leur*-**en** à tous, s'il vous plaît – *Yes, give* **them** all **some**, *please*
Tu veux que je **te** parle **de la soirée**? – *Shall I tell* **you about the party**?	Mais oui, parle-*m'***en**! Ça me ferait grand plaisir – *Yes, do tell* **me about it**!, *I'd like that very much*

Changez les demandes suivantes en ordres.
Exemple: Voulez-vous **me les** donner?

Donnez-**les-moi**!

1 Voulez-vous me le prêter?
2 Voulez-vous le lui passer?
3 Voulez-vous nous en donner?
4 Veux-tu lui en prêter?
5 Veux-tu le leur dire?
6 Veux-tu m'en donner?

4.18 *Pronouns used with two verbs*

With verbs which are followed by an infinitive, the pronouns may occupy one of two places.

Type 1   With *faire* + infinitive, all pronouns precede *faire*:

Vous avez *fait communiquer* **ces informations** à *tous les managers*?
Oui, je **les** *leur* ai *fait communiquer*.

This order also applies to: *écouter, emmener, entendre, envoyer, laisser, regarder, sentir, voir.*

The typeface in the following examples shows the connection between noun and pronoun.

Noun reference	Order with pronouns and auxiliary
Vous avez laissé partir **vos enfants** en vacances? – *Have you let **your children** go away on holiday?*	Oui, je **les** ai laissés partir – *Yes, I've let **them** go* (See **4.19** for the agreement of the past participle)
Tu avais entendu arriver **les derniers invités**? – *Had you heard **the last guests** arriving?*	Non, je ne **les** avais pas entendus arriver – *No, I hadn't heard **them** arrive*

Type 2   This includes all other verbs which may be used as an auxiliary with an infinitive, e.g. *aller, venir, devoir, pouvoir, vouloir, savoir.* The pronouns are placed **between** the auxiliary and the infinitive.

Noun reference	Order with pronouns and auxiliary
Tu peux prêter **tes crayons de couleur à Anne**? – *Can you lend **your coloured pencils to Anne**?*	Je peux **les** *lui* prêter, mais je ne veux pas! – *I can lend **them** **to her**, but I won't!*
Vous devez aller **chez le médecin**? – *Do you have to go **to the surgery**?*	Oui, je dois **y** aller – *Yes, I have to go (**there**)*

L'oncle Jules, en bras de chemise, les manches retroussées, finissait le déchargement de ses meubles, c'est-à-dire qu'il **les** faisait basculer du bord de la voiture sur le vaste dos d'un déménageur.

Marcel Pagnol, *La Gloire de mon père*

Un certain pourcentage de sièges pourrait **y** être réparti selon le scrutin proportionnel…

Tribune pour l'Europe

EXERCICE

Réécrivez les phrases suivantes en substituant un pronom à l'expression en italique.

Exemple: J'ai entendu *le groupe* partir.

Je **l'**ai entendu partir.

1   On a envoyé chercher *le médecin*.
2   On ne peut pas permettre *la liberté totale*.
3   Ma tante est venue voir *ses neveux*.
4   Les élèves doivent finir *leur travail* avant de rentrer à la maison.
5   Le chef sent *les légumes* brûler dans la casserole.

6 Ma mère écoute *les enfants* jouer dans le jardin.

7 Nous allons visiter tous *les monuments de Venise*.

8 On a regardé le *Titanic* partir de Queenstown pour la première et la dernière fois.

9 Mon grand-père ne laissait jamais *ses enfants* écouter la radio le dimanche.

10 Je veux apprendre *le russe* depuis longtemps.

4.19 *Preceding direct objects*

In the written form of the language, if a pronoun object occurring before *avoir* (or *être* with reflexives) in any compound tense is feminine or plural, then the past participle agrees in number and gender with the pronoun. The agreements follow the pattern of adjectives. See **3.11**.

The object follows (no agreement)	The object precedes (with agreement)
Vous avez **vu** cette émission hier soir? – *Did you see that programme last night?*	Oui, je l'ai **vue** – *Yes, I saw it*
Tu as **lu** ces BD? – *Have you read these cartoon books?*	Non, je ne les ai pas **lues** – *No, I haven't read them*
C'est vous qui avez **écrit** ces articles? – *Did you write these articles?*	Non, ce n'est pas moi qui les ai **écrits** – *No, I didn't write them*
Alain a **blessé** Philippe? – *Did Alain hurt Philippe?*	Non, ils *se* sont **blessés** tous les deux – *No, they both hurt each other*

> J'ai vu mon type qui discutait avec un copain. Celui-ci a désigné du doigt un bouton juste au-dessus de l'échancrure du pardessus. Puis l'autobus m'a emmené et je ne **les** ai plus **vus**.
>
> Raymond Queneau, *Exercices de style*
>
> [Jacqueline Boyer] C'est sa mère qui **l'**a **poussée** à chanter contre l'avis de son père.
>
> *France-Soir*

EXERCICES

A Ajoutez la terminaison qu'il faut.

Exemple: Sandrine? Je l'ai vu__ dans le jardin.

Sandrine? Je l'ai vu**e** dans le jardin.

1 Les documents? Je les ai laissé__ sur la table.

2 Catherine? Je l'ai entendu___ dans sa chambre.

3 Les enfants? Je les ai vu___ sortir il y a quelques minutes.

4 Les données? Je les ai déjà enregistré___.

5 Mes clés? je les ai oublié___ malheureusement.

B Décidez s'il faut faire l'accord ou non. Rappel – seul le pronom personnel objet **direct** exige l'accord.

Exemples: La lettre? Oui, je l'ai écri**te** (= Pronom personnel objet direct)

Françoise? Oui, je lui ai téléphoné (= Pronom personnel objet indirect)

1 Marie? Oui, je lui ai écrit___ il y a quelques jours.

2 Les ministres? Oui, on les a interviewé___ à la radio.

3 Le téléphone? Oui, je l'ai entendu___ sonner il y a quelques minutes.

4 Les détails? Je regrette, mais je ne les ai pas encore reçu___.

5 Les participants? Oui, on leur avait écrit___ le mois dernier.

4.20 *Emphatic pronouns*

The emphatic pronouns are:

moi-même	*myself*	**nous-mêmes**	*ourselves*
toi-même	*yourself (sing.)*	**vous-même(s)**	*yourself/yourselves*
lui-même	*himself, itself*	**eux-mêmes**	*themselves*
elle-même	*herself, itself*	**elles-mêmes**	*themselves*
soi-même	*oneself*		

These are generally used in a similar way to the corresponding English pronouns:

Qui a fait ça? – Je l'ai fait **moi-même** = *I did it **myself***

Note: Adjectives such as *sûr* (sure), *confiant* (confident) and *fier* (proud) are followed by *de* and require only the disjunctive form of the pronoun:

Il faut être très sûr de **soi** (*not* **soi-même**) = *You need to be very sure of **yourself***

4.21 *Possessive pronouns: forms*

Possessive pronouns correspond to **mine**, **yours**, **his**, etc. in English. They should not be confused with possessive adjectives (*mon, ma, mes,* etc.). They refer to a noun but are not attached to one. The forms of both the article (*le, la, les*) and the pronoun depend on the noun or nouns to which they refer.

Meaning	One possession masculine	Several possessions masculine	One possession feminine	Several possessions feminine
mine	le mien	les miens	la mienne	les miennes
yours	le tien	les tiens	la tienne	les tiennes
his, hers	le sien	les siens	la sienne	les siennes
ours	le nôtre	les nôtres	la nôtre	les nôtres
yours	le vôtre	les vôtres	la vôtre	les vôtres
theirs	le leur	les leurs	la leur	les leurs

4.22 *Possessive pronouns: uses*

Noun reference	Possessive pronoun reference
Tu peux lire ton **livre**,... – *You can read your* **book**...	...moi, je vais lire **le mien** – *me, I'm going to read* **mine**
Alain va prendre sa **voiture**,... – *Alain will take his car*...	...moi, je vais prendre **la mienne** – *I'll take* **mine**
Sandrine n'aime pas aller voir ses **parents**,... – *Sandrine doesn't like going to see her* **parents**...	...mais moi, je suis toujours content de voir **les miens** – *but I'm always happy to see* **mine**
Moi, j'avais perdu mes **clés**,... – *I'd lost my* **keys**	...mais heureusement que Louis avait **les siennes** – *but fortunately Louis had* **his**
Honorine a perdu toutes ses **possessions** lors du cyclone,... – *Honorine lost all her* **possessions** *in the hurricane*...	...mais **les nôtres** étaient en toute sécurité – *but* **ours** *were quite safe*
Catherine avait oublié ses **disques**,... – *Catherine had forgotten her* **records**...	...mais les garçons avait **les leurs** – *but the boys had* **theirs**

Sganarelle:	Je veux la battre si je le veux; et je ne veux pas la battre si je ne le veux pas.
M. Robert:	Fort bien.
Sganarelle:	C'est ma femme, et non pas **la vôtre**.
M. Robert:	Sans doute.

Molière, *Le Médecin malgré lui*

EXERCICE

Complétez les phrases avec la forme de l'article et du pronom possessif qui s'imposent:

Exemple: Tu n'as pas **tes livres**, mais heureusement, moi, j'ai l___ m_____.

Tu n'as pas **tes livres**, mais heureusement, moi, j'ai **les miens**.

1 Henri avait apporté **son pique-nique**, mais malheureusement, j'avais oublié l___ m____.

2 **Ma mère** avait immédiatement accepté de venir, mais Karine n'avait pas pu persuader l__ s_____.

3 J'avais **mes documents** sur moi, mais Conrad s'est rappelé qu'il avait vu l___ s_____ sur la table.

4 Voici **mes résultats**. Où sont l____ t_____?

5 Votre chambre est vraiment trop petite. On va faire la boum dans l___ m_____.

4.23 *Demonstrative pronouns: forms*

These are as follows:

	Masculine	Feminine
Singular	celui	celle
Plural	ceux	celles

They are followed by:

- *de*, to indicate possession,
- *-ci* or *-là* to indicate position,
- a relative clause beginning with *qui*, *que* (*qu'*) or *dont*. See also **4.27**.

4.24 *Demonstrative pronouns: uses*

Rule	Examples
The pronoun used agrees in number and gender with the noun to which it refers	*Si on prenait **ma moto**? – Non, je préférerais prendre **celle de** Jacques* – Shall we take my motorbike? – No, I'd prefer to take **Jacques**' (*celle de* = the one belonging to)
-ci or *-là* are added to indicate proximity or distance	*Il y a trois **couteaux** sur la table. Passe-moi **celui-là**!* – There are three knives on the table. Pass me **that one**!
A relative pronoun (*qui, que*) may follow the demonstrative pronoun. (**NB** *que* shortens to *qu'*, but *qui* cannot be abbreviated)	*Des deux disques, lequel préfères-tu – **celui qui** passe en ce moment ou **celui qu'**on vient d'écouter?* – Of the two records, which one do you prefer – **the one that**'s playing at the moment or **the one that** we've just heard?
The relative pronoun *dont* may also follow the demonstrative pronoun. Note the word order in constructions of this type	*A vrai dire, je préfère **celui dont** j'oublie le nom!* – To tell the truth, I prefer **the one whose** name I've forgotten (**of which** I have forgotten the name)

EXERCICES

A Complétez les phrases suivantes avec le pronom démonstratif qui s'impose.
   Exemple: J'ai besoin d'un nouveau bic. _____-ci ne marche plus.
        J'ai besoin d'un nouveau bic. **Celui**-ci ne marche plus.

1 Mon grand-père doit avoir une nouvelle canne. _____ dont il se servait s'est cassée.
2 Je viens d'acheter des crayons pour mon fils. _____ qu'il avait étaient tout usés.
3 J'ai perdu mes clés. Je ne trouve que _____ de Céline.
4 Tu peux m'apporter un tourne-vis, chérie? _____ que j'utilisais a disparu.
5 Il faut que nous nous achetions un nouvel ordinateur. _____ que nous avons actuellement est tout à fait démodé.

B Insérez dans les phrases suivantes **de**, **dont**, **qui** ou **que**.
1 Nous avons deux téléviseurs – celui _____ est au coin du salon et celui _____ vous avez vu dans la salle à manger.
2 Les chambres de nos fils sont en haut. Celle _____ Pierre est à gauche et celle _____ Grégoire est à côté de la nôtre.
3 Il y a trois sœurs. Celle _____ je vous parlais habite juste à côté.

   4   Il faut que nous changions tous les fils électriques de la maison. Ceux ____ y sont actuellement sont gainés de plomb!

   5   Tu te trompes. Il y a des jumelles dans la famille. Celle _____ tu te souviens s'appelle Marie. Celle ___ habite toujours chez ses parents s'appelle Angéline.

4.25 *The pronoun* ce

Rule	Examples
Ce is used to introduce a definition (or to ask for one)	*Qu'est-ce que **c**'est qu'un mirloton? – **C**'est un instrument de musique* – What's a *mirloton*? – **It**'s a type of musical instrument
If *être* has a plural complement, *sont* follows *ce*, not *est* (though *c'est* is often used in speech)	***Ce** ne **sont** pas de raisons valides pour ce refus (written definition)* – **These are** not adequate reasons for a refusal ***Ce** n'**est** pas là de bonnes raisons! (spoken)* – **Those aren't** good reasons!

Rule	Examples
With emphatic pronouns, *est* follows *ce*, except with *eux/elles*	***C****'est* **toi** *qui as fait ça* – **You**'re the one who did that *Ah,* **c***'est* **vous**! – Oh, **it**'s you ***Ce*** *sont* ***elles*** *qui viennent* – **They** are **the ones** who are coming
Ce is used to introduce a relative clause, when the sense is 'what', 'the thing which'	***Ce qui*** *est important, c'est d'être là* – What's important is to be there *Je ne sais pas* **ce que** *Robert a dit* – I don't know what Robert said
Ce is also the subject pronoun in a relative clause that begins with *dont*	*Je ne me rappelle plus* **ce dont** *j'avais besoin* – I can't remember **what** I needed
Ce is used when *être* is followed by (1) a verb, (2) an adverb, (3) a preposition or (4) a conjunction	(1) *Vouloir* **c'est pouvoir** – You can do something if you really want to (2) **C'est beaucoup** *dire* – **That's** saying **a lot** (3) **C'est pour** *moi* – **It's for** me (4) *C'est* **parce que** *Louise ne peut pas venir* – **It's because** Louise can't come
Ce is used before *devoir* and *pouvoir* when these are followed by *être*	**Ce doit** *être elle* – **It must be** her **Ce** *ne* **peut** *pas être le cas* – **That can**'t be the case
C'est… que is used for emphasis to highlight particular elements. **NB** The present is often used in French where another tense is used in English	**C'est** *à Rouen* **que** *Flaubert est né, pas à Croisset* – **It was** at Rouen **that** Flaubert was born, not at Croisset **C'est** *à Paris* **que** *l'exposition aura lieu* – **It will be** in Paris **that** the exhibition takes place

CE QUI ME PLAÎT DANS L'ARMÉE, C'EST LE CÔTÉ "VIE AU GRAND AIR"

EXERCICE

Complétez les phrases suivantes en utilisant **ce** (x2), **c'est** (x5), **ce sont** (x1), **ce qui** (x1), **ce que** (x2), **ce dont** (x1).

1 _____ à la FNAC qu'il faut chercher les livres dont vous avez besoin.

2 _____ doit être Philippe qui a fait cela.

3 _____ les Français qui ont gagné le Mundial de 1998.

4 _____ est essentiel, _____ d'avoir égard aux besoins d'autrui.

5 _____ parce que son père est malade qu'Aline ne peut pas assister au concert.

6 _____ vous avez besoin, _____ d'une perceuse électrique.

7 _____ peut certainement être le cas.

8 _____ Madeleine cherche, _____ un homme qui soit prêt à lui acheter tout _____ elle désire.

4.26 *The pronouns* ceci *and* cela

These pronouns express the generalised notions of ***this*** and ***that***.

Rule	Examples
Ceci refers forward	*Je te dis* **ceci** *– il faut faire attention –* I tell you **this** – you need to pay attention
Cela (or *ça* in spoken French) refers back to something already mentioned	*Il y a toujours le problème de l'exclusion, mais on ne ressent pas beaucoup* **cela** *dans le XVIe arrondissement de Paris –* There remains the problem of social exclusion, but **that** is little felt in the XVIth *arrondissement* of Paris
Cela + verb of emotion + *de* refers forward	**Cela** *m'etonne* **d'***apprendre que Pierre est mort –* I'm astonished to learn (lit. It astonishes me to learn) that Pierre has died
Before an adjective, *ceci* requires *de*	*Il y a* **ceci de** *curieux – la fenêtre était ouverte –* **This** is the curious thing – the window was open

EXERCICE

Remettez dans le bon ordre les phrases suivantes.

Exemple: ceci intéressant y d' a Il – ne sait personne il où habite

→ Il y a **ceci** d'intéressant – personne ne sait où il habite

1 dit il On qu' borgne est – n'ai **cela** remarqué Je jamais

2 bon de payer se luxe petit un fait **Cela** un

3 noter faut **ceci** Il – difficile examen cet sera

4.27 *Relative pronouns*

Relative pronouns stand at the head of a clause referring to a noun, i.e. a clause which tells us more about that noun. The relative pronouns are *qui, que, dont, où, quoi* and *lequel* – in its various forms (see **4.29**).

Rule	Examples
When the relative pronoun is the **subject** of its clause, *qui* is used	*Marcel Proust – un auteur* **qui** *était obsédé par le temps* **qui** *passe* – Marcel Proust, an author **who** was obsessed by the passing of time
Qui may follow a preposition (e.g. *à, avec*) if reference is being made to a **person**	*Le petit garçon* **à qui** *je parlais avait complètement disparu* – The little boy **to whom** I was speaking had completely vanished
When the relative pronoun is the object of its clause, *que* is used	*Les mesures* **que** *le Sénat a recommandées sont tout à fait inadéquates* – The measures **which** the Senate has recommended are hopelessly inadequate
If a verb is followed by *de*, the relative pronoun used must be *dont*	*C'était le type* **dont** *j'avais entendu parler* – *(entendre parler* **de***)* – This the guy **that** I'd heard **about**
Dont may be used to mean 'whose'	*Le monsieur* **dont** *la maison est à vendre est mort il y a longtemps* – The man **whose** house is for sale died a long time ago
Où is used to mean 'where', 'in which', or with expressions of time (*au moment, à l'époque,* etc.), 'when'	*La ville* **où** *j'habitais était très petite* – The town **in which** I lived was very small *Juste au moment* **où** *je sortais, maman est arrivée* – Just **as** I was going out, Mum arrived
Quoi has no specific reference to a noun. It means 'what', and follows prepositions such as *de* and *à*	*Dites moi de* **quoi** *vous parliez* – Tell me what you were talking **about** *Voilà à* **quoi** *tu pensais* – That's **what** you were thinking about
The various forms of *lequel* (see **4.29**) are used after prepositions and have specific reference	*Dans le musée on peut voir les stylos* **avec lesquels** *Colette a fait les premières esquisses de ses romans* – In the museum you can see the pens **with which** Colette first sketched out her novels
If a relative clause has a preposition at its head (*à, de*) and a possessive construction with *de* within it, then an appropriate form of *lequel* is used. See **4.29**	*Le général* **aux mémoires duquel** *j'ai fait allusion est mort l'année dernière* – The general **to whose memoirs** I referred died last year

It is necessary to place the **relative pronoun** as close as possible to the **noun** to which it refers (its antecedents). Thus *le temps* **qui**…; *les mesures* **que**….; *le type* **dont**…

Le stil est un bipède au cou très long **qui** hante les autobus de la ligne S vers midi. Il affectionne particulièrement la plate-forme arrière **où** il se tient, morveux…

Raymond Queneau, *Exercices de style*

Sous le mouvement historique, on voit se dessiner la redéfinition de la théorie économique dominante **qui** ignore la question environnementale… elle conduit à la redéfinition d'une société moderne **dont** la dimension planétaire est toujours plus évidente…

Hervé Kempf, *L'Économie à l'épreuve de l'écologie*

EXERCICE

Choisissez parmi les formes données celle qui convient le mieux au sens des phrases suivantes.

1   Le premier chapitre _____ j'ai lu m'a vraiment choqué (**que, dont**).

2   Je ne comprenais pas ce _____ il parlait (**dont, qu'**).

3   On peut voir dans le musée le couteau avec _____ il a commis ces terribles meurtres (**quoi, lequel**).

4   Ça, c'est le monsieur _____ la maison a été incendiée la semaine dernière (**dont, qui**).

5   A l'époque _____ vivait Louis XIV, les aristocrates considéraient la pauvreté comme normale (**que, où**).

6   Il faut avoir un passeport, faute de _____ vous ne pourrez pas franchir la frontière (**lequel, quoi**).

7   Les mesures _____ a proposées le Sénat doivent être approuvées (**qui, qu'**).

8   L'agent avec _____ j'ai parlé m'a dit qu'il faudrait me présenter au commissariat de police (**quoi, qui**).

4.28 *Interrogative pronouns*

These are pronouns which are used for asking questions.

Rule	Examples
Qui? (who?) is used to refer to one or more persons	*Qui vient à la boum ce soir?* – **Who**'s coming to the party tonight? *Qui as-tu vu?* – Who(m) did you see?
Que? corresponds to 'what?'	*Que vont-ils faire?* – **What** are they going to do?
Following a preposition, *quoi*, not *que* is used	*En quoi je peux vous être utile?* – **In what way** can help you?

4.29 *Lequel*

The forms of this interrogative pronoun are:

	Masculine	Feminine
Singular	lequel	laquelle
Plural	lesquels	lesquelles

4.30 *Interrogative pronouns: uses*

Noun reference	Form of *lequel*
Ici il y a trois **disques** (m.)	**Lequel** prends-tu ? – *Which one* are you having?
Il y a deux **revues** (f.)	**Laquelle** vas-tu prendre? – *Which one* are you going to have?
Il y a plusieurs **garçons** (m.) ici	**Lesquels** cherchez-vous? – *Which ones* are you looking for?
Il y a pas mal de **chemises** (f.) ici	**Lesquelles** sont à toi? – *Which ones* are yours?

Note: These pronouns may also be used as **relative pronouns** after a preposition: *La maison **dans laquelle** j'habitais* – The house **in which** I lived; *Le marteau **avec lequel** il a cassé la vitrine* – The hammer **with which** he broke the window. See **4.27**.

EXERCICES

A Corrigez les phrases suivantes, dans lesquelles le pronom interrogatif est incorrect.
1   De **que** est-ce que vous parlez?
2   Il faut que tu prennes *trois* de ces disques. **Lequel** veux-tu?
3   **Que** va assister au concert – Éliane et Georges?
4   Il faut porter de bonnes chaussures pour faire cette promenade – **laquelle** vas-tu porter?
5   **Qui** est-ce qu'ils comptent faire? Du patinage?

B Reliez les phrases suivantes par *lequel, laquelle, lesquels* ou *lesquelles*, précédé d'une préposition.
Exemple: Roger Peyrefitte est un écrivain français. J'éprouve une certaine admiration pour lui.
Roger Peyrefitte est un écrivain français **pour lequel** j'éprouve une certaine admiration.
1   On est restés sur le pont. Des bateaux-mouches passaient sous le pont.
2   Mondeville est un grand centre commercial. J'aime bien faire des achats dans ce centre.

3 La banque centrale européenne pourra prendre des décisions. Nous n'aurons pas d'influence sur ces décisions.

4 Le monétarisme est une politique économique. Je n'attache pas beaucoup d'importance à cette politique.

5 Jacques Chirac et Tony Blair ont assisté à un congrès. Chacun a prononcé un discours important devant ce congrès.

4.31 *Indefinite pronouns*

Unlike personal pronouns, indefinite pronouns do not refer to a specific person or thing. In the following examples, indications are given for the form of the verb when the pronoun is the **subject**.

Explanation	Examples
Aucun(e) – none. The pronoun assumes the gender of the noun to which it refers	*J'ai posé la question à toutes les filles. **Aucune** n'a répondu* – I put the question to all the girls. **None** replied
Autrui – other people. *Autrui* always follows a preposition	*Il fait peu de cas des opinions **d'autrui*** – He pays little heed to **other people's** opinions
L'autre – the other. The third person singular of the verb is used	*Une des deux femmes est partie, **l'autre** est restée* – One of the two women left, **the other** stayed
Certain(e)s – some people. The 3rd person plural of the verb is used	***Certains** affirment qu'Elvis Presley est toujours en vie* – **Some people** say that Elvis Presley is still alive
Chacun(e) – each one. The pronoun has the gender of the noun to which it refers	***Chacune** des filles a pris son sac à dos et s'est mise en route* – **Each** of the girls took her rucksack and set off
Nul, nulle – none, not one. The pronoun requires the gender of the noun to which it refers, and, being negative, requires *ne*	*On cherche des traces des kidnappés. Jusqu'à maintenant, **nulle ne** s'est présentée* – They are searching for traces of the kidnap victims. So far, **none** has been found
On – you, people, one. The reference is unspecific	***On** peut avoir des prix avantageux sur les ordinateurs* – **You** can get good deals on computers
Plusieurs – several (of them). It has no feminine form. A third person plural verb is required	*La majorité des invités étaient déjà partis, mais **plusieurs** étaient toujours dans le salon* – Most of the guests had left, but **several** were still in the living room
Quelque chose – something. This pronoun is masculine	*Il y a **quelque chose** sous le canapé?* – Is there **something** under the sofa?

Explanation	Examples
Quelqu'un – somebody, someone. The third person singular of the verb is required	***Quelqu'un** attendait dans l'obscurité du vestibule* – Someone was waiting in the darkness of the hall
Quiconque – anybody who. The pronoun requires a third person singular verb	***Quiconque** a lu toute l'œuvre de Proust a vécu une expérience extraordinaire* – Anybody who has read all of Proust's work has experienced something extraordinary
Quelques-un(e)s – some. If used as a subject, the pronoun requires the gender of the noun to which it refers	*J'ai presque tous les disques d'Alan Stivell, mais il m'en manque **quelques-uns*** – I have nearly all Alan Stivell's records, but I'm still missing **some**
Qui que ce soit/N'importe qui – anybody. Both require the third person singular of the verb if used as a subject	***Qui que ce soit/N'importe qui** peut faire ce travail – il ne faut pas posséder de connaissances spéciales* – **Anybody** can do this work – you don't need any special knowledge
Quoi que ce soit/N'importe quoi – anything (at all). Both require the third person singular of the verb if used as a subject	***Quoi que ce soit/N'importe quoi** me conviendra – je ne suis pas difficile* – **Anything** will do – I'm not fussy
Les un(e)s... les autres – some... (the) others. If used as a subject, the pronoun requires the gender of the noun to which it refers	*Les refugiés fourmillaient dans le grand hall. **Les uns** avaient quelques possessions, **les autres**, rien* – The refugees were milling around in the great hall. **Some** had a few possessions, **others**, nothing

Knock: Savent-ils même ce que c'est qu'un microbe?

Bernard: J'en doute fort! **Quelques-uns** connaissent le mot, mais ils doivent se
figurer qu'il s'agit d'une espèce de mouche.

Jules Romains, Knock

EXERCICE

Traduisez en français.

1 *Anybody can learn to play a musical instrument.*
2 *Some people think that the year 2001 is the real beginning of the new millennium.*
3 *You must pay attention to other people's feelings.*
4 *Two men stood beside the door. Each was armed.*
5 *Simenon wrote more than 100 books. I have some of them.*
6 *One of the policemen went out. The other stayed sitting facing me.*
7 *Quick! Pass me a cloth or something! Anything will do!*
8 *After the air-crash several survivors were found. Several were very emaciated. None had eaten for several days.*

Verbs

'Verb' means 'word' and the verb is *the* word in a sentence. It is like the nucleus of an atom around which the other atomic particles move. The verb is the heart of the sentence, telling us what happens or what the state of affairs is.

A handbook for French school students, Larousse *Conjugaison*, recognises 115 different types of verbs! This is clearly too great a number for foreign learners, and we must reduce the verb system to a smaller number of regularities and exceptions.

SIMPLE (SINGLE WORD) TENSES: INDICATIVE MOOD

5.1 *The present tense*

There are three major groups of regular verbs (whose infinitives end in *-er, -ir, -re*). Some smaller groups have minor but predictable irregularities and there are a number of verbs which are completely irregular, and therefore unpredictable. These latter have to be learnt individually. In the majority of cases, endings for the present are added to a stem which is formed from the infinitive. The principal irregular verbs are listed in the Irregular verb tables (**p. 262-279**). The three major groups of regular verbs are as follows:

Subject	-er type regarder	-ir type (1) finir	-re type vendre
je	regarde	finis	vends
tu	regardes	finis	vends
il, elle, on	regarde	finit	vend
nous	regardons	finissons	vendons
vous	regardez	finissez	vendez
ils, elles	regardent	finissent	vendent

NB *cueillir, accueillir, ouvrir, couvrir, découvrir, recouvrir* and *offrir* are only *-ir* verbs in the infinitive form. In their present tense forms they follow the *-er* pattern. Thus: *couvrir: je couvre, tu couvres*, etc.

Type 2 *-ir* verbs follow the pattern below. Note: *servir – nous servons*, etc.

Subject	*partir*	Subject	*partir*
je	par**s**	nous	par**tons**
tu	par**s**	vous	par**tez**
il, elle, on	par**t**	ils, elles	par**tent**

This group includes *mentir, partir, ressentir, (se) sentir, servir* and *sortir.*

A number of verbs have alterations within the present tense. In these verbs, the forms of the **singular** and and those of the **third person plural** (*ils/elles*) share a feature in common, while the **first** and **second person plural** forms resemble each other in a different way. This latter form is generally similar to that of the infinitive.

Type	Infinitive	*je, tu, il/elle, ils/elles* forms	*nous* and *vous* forms
1	je**t**er	je je**tt**e, tu je**tt**es, il je**tt**e, ils je**tt**ent	nous je**t**ons, vous je**t**ez
2	ach**e**ter	j'ach**è**te, tu ach**è**tes, il ach**è**te, ils ach**è**tent	nous ach**e**tons, vous ach**e**tez
3	esp**é**rer	j'esp**è**re, tu esp**è**res, il esp**è**re, ils esp**è**rent	nous esp**é**rons, vous esp**é**rez
4	p**ay**er	je p**ai**e, tu p**ai**es, il p**ai**e, ils p**ai**ent	nous p**ay**ons, vous p**ay**ez
	env**oy**er	j'env**oi**e, tu env**oi**es, il env**oi**e, ils env**oi**ent	nous env**oy**ons, vous env**oy**ez
	ess**uy**er	j'ess**ui**e, tu ess**ui**es, il ess**ui**e, ils ess**ui**ent	nous ess**uy**ons, vous ess**uy**ez

Verbs of these types are as follows:

Type	Infinitive
1	(s') appeler, (se) rappeler, épeler, étinceler, feuilleter, jeter, rejeter, renouveler
2	acheter, achever, crever, geler, peser, mener, amener, emmener, (se) promener, ramener
3	céder, compléter, délibérer, espérer, exagérer, excéder, (s') inquiéter, libérer, refléter, répéter, sécher, suggérer, tolérer
4	bégayer, débrayer, embrayer, essayer, étayer, rayer (**NB** *In this group* je paye, j'essaye *and related forms are found*); coudoyer, employer, fourvoyer, nettoyer, (se) noyer, (se) tutoyer, (se) vouvoyer, (s') ennuyer, désennuyer

Spelling: In order to show that *-c-* and *-g-* are pronounced as soft consonants (*-s-* and *-j-*), a number of verbs have a modified *nous* form. These are as follows:

Infinitive	*nous* form	Other verbs of this type
manger	nous mang**e**ons	bouger, partager, protéger, voyager
commencer	nous commen**ç**ons	avancer, forcer, lancer

EXERCICE

Donnez la forme de la première personne du singulier (**je**) et de la première personne du pluriel (**nous**) des verbes suivants.

   épeler – rappeler – achever – mener – espérer – partager – essayer – employer – nettoyer

5.2   *Use of the present tense*

Note: for the purposes of Exercise A, the sections below are numbered.

Rule	Examples
1. For universal truths, such as sayings and proverbs	*Pierre qui* **roule** *n'***amasse** *pas mousse* – A rolling stone gathers no moss
2. To describe events happening at the present moment	*La population de la Chine* **augmente** *d'année en année* – The population of China **is increasing** annually
3. To narrate an action which is repeated regularly or is habitual	*A l'Arc de Triomphe on* **rallume** *chaque soir la flamme éternelle* – At the Arc de Triomphe, the eternal flame **is re-lit** every evening
4. To render a past event more vivid	*En 1820, Napoléon* **meurt** – In 1820, Napoleon **died**
5. To show that an action which began in the past continues into the present. Note the use of *depuis*	*J'***apprends** *l'anglais depuis trois ans* – **I've been learning** English for three years
6. To show that an action is continuing, *être en train de* + infinitive may be used	*Je* **suis en train de ranger** *mes papiers – j'en ai pour une heure!* – **I'm tidying up** my papers – it'll take me an hour!
7. 'I have come to' is rendered by the present tense in French	*Je* **viens** *vous dire quelque chose* – **I've come** to tell you something
8. The present of *venir* + *de* expresses a recently completed action: **have just, has just**, etc.	*Je* **viens de recevoir** *une lettre de ma belle-sœur* – **I've just received** a letter from my sister-in-law

> Mon âme **est** joyeuse et légère aujourd'hui comme un oiseau qui aurait fait
> son nid dans le ciel. C'**est** aujourd'hui qu'il **doit** venir; je le **sens**, je le **sais**; je
> voudrais le crier à tous; j'**ai** besoin de l'écrire. Je ne **peux** plus cacher ma joie.
>
> André Gide, La Porte étroite
>
> Il **convient** d'abord d'examiner où se **situe** l'hélice 'gauche' sur la molécule
> d'AND et comment elle se **forme**.
>
> Science et Vie

EXERCICES

A Selon le numérotage du tableau (page 95), décidez de quel emploi du présent il s'agit.

Exemple: Depuis des années, l'économie est en pleine expansion. = 5

1 Le gouvernement vient d'annoncer sa nouvelle politique sur la toxicomanie.
2 En 1940, c'est l'invasion de la France.
3 Le magasin ferme tous les soirs à 20 heures.
4 Pauvreté n'est pas vice.
5 Je viens vous annoncer quelque chose d'important.
6 Les sauveteurs sont en train de fouiller les décombres.

B Complétez les phrases suivantes avec la forme du verbe qui convient.

1 De gros embouteillages se (**former**) au niveau de Bourges.
2 Les disques se (**vendre**) à des prix plus bas chez Leclerc.
3 Le samedi, les cours (**finir**) à midi.
4 J'(**acheter**) rarement des bouquins de ce genre-là.
5 En général, c'est moi qui (**nettoyer**) ma chambre.
6 Les politiciens européens s'(**inquiéter**) de la situation en Albanie.
7 J'(**essayer**) de persuader mes copains de m'accompagner en vacances.
8 Nos enfants s'(**ennuyer**) à Noël.

5.3 *Imperatives: forms*

NB Imperatives are really a separate mood.

In commands, the *tu* and *vous* are dropped from the second person singular and plural of the verb. In the written form, the *-s* is dropped from the *tu* form of regular verbs ending in *-es* and *-as*. *Avoir* and *être* have irregular forms.

To make a suggestion (Let's…), the *nous* is dropped from the first person singular of the verb.

	regarder	acheter	finir	vendre	aller	avoir	être
tu	regarde!	achète!	finis!	vends!	va!	aie!	sois!
vous	regardez!	achetez!	finissez!	vendez!	allez!	ayez!	soyez!
nous	regardons	achetons	finissons	vendons	allons	ayons	soyons

5.4 *Imperatives: uses*

Rule	Examples
The imperative form of the verb is the form that is used for giving commands (*tu* and *vous*) and for making suggestions (*nous*)	***Arrête!*** – Stop! ***Arrêtez!*** – Stop! ***Allons*** *au restaurant* – Let's go to the restaurant
Reflexive verbs require the object pronoun after the imperative. **NB** *toi* is used for the *tu* form	***Lève****-toi!* – Get up! ***Réveillez****-vous!* – Wake up! ***Allons****-nous-en!* – Let's go!
The imperative form may be used to issue an invitation	***Venez*** *me voir quand vous serez à Paris* – Come and see me when you are in Paris
The imperative may be used to express a wish	***Amuse****-toi bien!* – Have a good time!
The imperative may express a condition	***Continuez*** *à faire ça et vous aurez affaire à moi!* – **Keep** doing that and you'll have me to deal with!
The *-s* is retained on *vas* before *y*	***Vas-y**, mon petit!* – **Go on**, kid!

Bien droit sur ses deux jambes, le personnage inconnu suivait avec intérêt, mais très calme, la bataille, répétant de temps à autre d'une voix nette: «**Allez**… Courage… **Revenez**-y… *Go on, my boys*…»

Alain-Fournier, Le Grand Meaulnes

FRANCE TELECOM vous aide à découvrir les meilleures solutions de Bureautique Communicante. Pour en savoir plus, **consultez** dès maintenant votre Agence Commerciale FRANCE TELECOM. Et n'**oubliez** pas l'annuaire électronique de la Bureautique Communicante 3616 SCRIP.

Science et Vie

EXERCICES

A Complétez le tableau suivant avec la forme de l'impératif qui convient.

Infinitif	tu	vous	nous
donner	donne		
offrir		offrez	
aller			allons
faire		faites	
avoir	aie		
être			soyons
boire	bois		
manger		mangez	

B Utilisez dix des formes données pour écrire des phrases. Ces impératifs peuvent être au négatif si vous voulez.

5.5 *The future tense*

The future tense of the majority of verbs is based on the infinitive. For those verbs whose infinitive end in *-re*, the *-e* is dropped to provide a stem to which endings are added. The stem of **all** verbs in the future, both regular and irregular, ends in *-r*. All verbs in the future tense have the same set of endings which is, essentially, the present tense of *avoir*.

REGULAR VERBS

Subject	*regarder*	*finir*	*vendre*
je	regarder**ai**	finir**ai**	vendr**ai**
tu	regarder**as**	finir**as**	vendr**as**
il, elle, on	regarder**a**	finir**a**	vendr**a**
nous	regarder**ons**	finir**ons**	vendr**ons**
vous	regarder**ez**	finir**ez**	vendr**ez**
ils, elles	regarder**ont**	finir**ont**	vendr**ont**

IRREGULAR VERBS

Since all verbs in the future share the same endings, it is necessary only to know the *je* form of any irregular verb. The following are irregular verbs whose future stem is not based directly on the infinitive. The future stem is marked in bold type.

Infinitive	Future tense	Infinitive	Future tense
acquérir	j'**acquerr**ai to acquire/ purchase	faire	je **fer**ai
aller	j'**ir**ai	mourir	je **mourr**ai
s'asseoir	je m'**assiér**ai	pouvoir	je **pourr**ai
avoir	j'**aur**ai	recevoir	je **recevr**ai
courir	je **courr**ai	savoir	je **saur**ai
cueillir	je **cueiller**ai to pick/ catch	tenir to hold/keep	je **tiendr**ai
devoir	je **devr**ai	venir	je **viendr**ai
envoyer	j'**enverr**ai	voir	je **verr**ai
être	je **ser**ai	vouloir	je **voudr**ai

EXERCICE

Donnez la forme de la première personne du singulier du futur des verbes suivants. Consultez le tableau des verbes irréguliers si besoin est.

  obtenir – consommer – comprendre – annoncer – revoir – servir – convaincre – enrichir

5.6   *Use of the future tense*

Rule	Examples
An action which will happen in the future may be expressed by the **future** tense	*D'ici deux ans, je **changerai** d'emploi* – In two years' time, **I'll change** job
In a hypothetical future, a **future tense** follows *quand* or *lorsque*; cf. 'When I go…' (the present is used in English)	*Quand/Lorsque j'**irai** à Paris, je **visiterai** la FNAC pour m'acheter des livres* – When **I go** to Paris, **I'll visit** FNAC to get myself some books
In a sentence whose main verb is in the future, a hypothesis (*si* = if) is expressed by the present tense	*Si je **vais** à Paris, je **visiterai** la FNAC pour m'acheter des livres* – If **I go** to Paris, **I'll visit** FNAC to get myself some books
In a command attached to a *quand* clause, it is suggested that the action will happen in the **future**, and the future tense is used in the *quand* clause	*Dites-le-lui quand vous lui **téléphonerez*** – Tell her when you **phone** her *Dites-leur bonjour de ma part quand vous les **verrez*** – Say hello to them from me when you see them

J'aime tant à l'entendre prononcer mon nom… Il **sera** là! Je **mettrai** ma main dans sa main. Je **laisserai** mon front s'appuyer contre son épaule. Je **respirerai** près de lui.

André Gide, *La Porte étroite*

Taureau: Cœur – Tout entier livré au cœur, semble-t-il. Personne ne vous en **voudra**, surtout pas votre partenaire, pour autant que vous ne le partagiez avec lui.

Scorpion: Santé – Beaucoup d'activités, vous ne **saurez** plus où donner de la tête et des jambes, et cela risque de vous affecter quelque peu.

Avantages

EXERCICES °

A Transformez les phrases suivantes en utilisant le futur, selon l'exemple.

Exemple: Je **vais visiter** Rome. → Je **visiterai** Rome.

1   Nous **allons assister** au concert de Phil Collins au Stade National.

2   Les élections cantonales **vont avoir** lieu le mois prochain.

3   S'il neige, mes parents ne **vont** pas **pouvoir** venir passer Noël chez nous.

4   Si je suis recalé à mon examen, je **vais devoir** me représenter l'année prochaine.

5   Si les sans-abri ne reçoivent pas de secours, plusieurs centaines **vont mourir** cet hiver.

B Complétez les prévisions météorologiques en utilisant le futur.

Bretagne, Pays-de-Loire, Basse Normandie. – Le ciel gris et pluvieux de l'Ouest breton (s'étendre) aux Pays-de-Loire l'après-midi. Il ne (faire) pas plus de 11 degrés.

Limousin, Auvergne, Rhône-Alpes. – La grisaille humide présente du Masif Central au Lyonnais le matin (laisser) passer des embellies ensoleillées l'après-midi.

Languedoc-Roussillon, Provence-Alpes Côte d'Azur, Corse. – Le soleil (parvenir) à s'imposer une bonne partie de la journée, alors qu'il (être) davantage contesté l'après-midi en Languedoc-Roussillon. Il (faire) de 19 à 22 degrés.

5.7 *The conditional*

This tense expresses a hypothesis, indicating what would happen if certain conditions obtained. It closely resembles the future in form, with different endings. These endings are also used for the imperfect tense. See **5.9**.

REGULAR VERBS

Subject	*regarder*	Subject	*regarder*
je	regarder**ais**	nous	regarder**ions**
tu	regarder**ais**	vous	regarder**iez**
il, elle, on	regarder**ait**	ils, elles	regarder**aient**

IRREGULAR VERBS

All verbs in the conditional use the same set of endings. Those verbs whose stem is not based on the infinitive use the same stem as the future. Thus:

Infinitive	Conditional tense
acquérir	j'**acquerr**ais
aller	j'**ir**ais
avoir	j'**aur**ais
s'asseoir	je m'**assiér**ais
courir	je **courr**ais
etc.	etc.

See table for irregular verbs in the future tense, above, **5.5**.

5.8 *Use of the conditional*

Explanation	Examples
The conditional is used to report speech originally in the future	*Elle a dit qu'elle* **viendrait** *le lendemain* – She said that she **would come** the following day (*'Je viendrai demain'* – 'I'll come tomorrow')
In a sentence whose main verb is in the **conditional**, a hypothesis (*si*) is expressed by the imperfect tense	*Si j'***allais** *à Paris, je* **visiterais** *la FNAC pour m'acheter des livres* – If **I went** to Paris, **I'd go** to FNAC to get myself some books
A hypothetical clause in the pluperfect may require a conditional in the main clause	*Si j'***avais** *bien* **fait** *attention à ce qu'on me disait, je ne* **serais** *pas dans ce pétrin!* – If I had paid attention to what I was told, I wouldn't be in this mess

Explanation	Examples
'Even if' is expressed by *quand même* and is followed by the conditional. The main clause also requires the conditional	*Quand même tous les partis politiques **seraient** d'accord, on ne **trouverait** pas de solution à ce problème* – Even if all the political parties were in agreement, they wouldn't find a solution to this problem
The conditional is used, particularly in journalism, to indicate hearsay or uncertainty. The speaker/writer does not vouch for the truth of the sentence	*Selon des rapports qu'on vient de recevoir, les rebelles congolais **seraient** déjà à quelques kilomètres de Kinshassa* – According to reports that we've just received, the Congolese rebels are already only a few kilometres from Kinshassa
The conditional is used instead of the present in requests to add a nuance of politeness	*Je **voudrais** un kilo de tomates, s'il vous plaît* – **I'd like** a kilo of tomatoes please ***Pourriez**-vous m'envoyer un catalogue, s'il vous plaît?* – **Could you** send me a catalogue, please?
'If…' may be expressed by *au cas où* which is followed by the conditional. The main clause also uses the conditional	*Au cas où on n'**aurait** pas suffisament d'assiettes, il **faudrait** en demander au traiteur* – If we **didn't have** enough plates, **we'd have to** ask the caterer for some
The conditional of *devoir* is used to mean 'ought to'. There is a sense of moral obligation. The infinitive of the verb follows	*Tu **devrais** finir tes devoirs avant de regarder la télé* – You **ought to** finish your homework before watching telly *La classe politique **devrait** se mettre d'accord sur la question de l'exclusion sociale* – Politicians **ought to** come to an agreement on the question of social exclusion

– Quelle question venez-vous de lui poser? demanda Clapique à mi-voix.

– Ce qu'il **ferait** si le médecin condamnait sa femme.

– Le maître ne **croirait** pas le médecin.

André Malraux, La Condition humaine

… un changement de cap sur l'Éducation **serait** évidemment perçu par l'opinion comme un recul. Pour Lionel Jospin… ce **serait** un aveu d'immobilisme.

Libération

EXERCICES

A Rapportez les phrases suivantes en discours indirect.

Exemple: Josyane: «Je pourrai me payer un nouveau jean en fin de semaine.»

Josyane a dit qu'elle **pourrait** se payer un nouveau jean en fin de semaine.

1 Grégoire et Stéphane: «Nous pourrons louer une voiture à la gare.»

2 Le Président: «La France n'hésitera pas à exercer son droit de véto contre ces mesures.»

3 Le PDG: «La société Perma enregistrera de meilleurs bénéfices l'année prochaine.»

4 L'ambassadeur: «Les terroristes ne jouiront pas de la protection diplomatique.»

5 Le directeur: «Les élèves devront s'accoutumer aux nouveaux programmes scolaires.»

B Mariez les deux parties des phrases suivantes.

1 Si on abattait tous les arbres du Brésil,	A il pourrait payer des asiles pour les SDF.
2 Si l'État percevait plus d'impôts,	B peut-être qu'ils auraient plus de connaissances générales.
3 Si on brûlait moins de combustibles fossiles,	C le monde risquerait de mourir de manque d'oxygène.
4 Si les jeunes regardaient moins la télé,	D on aurait plus confiance en eux.
5 Si les politiciens étaient sincères,	E la pollution atmosphérique se réduirait.

C Un journaliste rapporte les faits suivants, mais sans en garantir la vérité. Changez la forme du verbe contre celle du **conditionnel**.

Exemple: Le Président **est** prêt à libérer les trois prisonniers politiques.

Le Président **serait** prêt à libérer les trois prisonniers politiques.

1 Les fonctionnaires responsables de cette bavure **sont** actuellement absents de Paris.

2 Les autorités **souhaitent** mettre fin à ces abus.

3 M. Normand **possède** plus de 2 millions de francs.

4 Les jeunes beurs **craignent** de sortir le soir dans les rues de la cité.

5 Les actions **risquent** de perdre 50% de leur valeur cette semaine.

5.9 *The imperfect tense*

The *nous* form of the present tense forms the basis of the imperfect tense (*l'imparfait*). The stem for the imperfect is derived by removing *-ons* and adding the same endings as those used for the conditional. The **only** exception to this rule is the verb *être*.

Subject	*regarder*	*finir*	*vendre*
je	regard**ais**	finiss**ais**	vend**ais**
tu	regard**ais**	finiss**ais**	vend**ais**
il, elle, on	regard**ait**	finiss**ait**	vend**ait**
nous	regard**ions**	finiss**ions**	vend**ions**
vous	regard**iez**	finiss**iez**	vend**iez**
ils, elles	regard**aient**	finiss**aient**	vend**aient**

NB *Être*	
j'ét**ais**	nous ét**ions**
tu ét**ais**	vous ét**iez**
il ét**ait** elle ét**ait** on ét**ait**	ils ét**aient** elles ét**aient**

Those verbs which use a *-ç-* or *-ge-* in the *nous* form of the written form of the present tense (see page 95) retain it for the *je*, *tu*, *il/elle/on* and *ils/elles* forms of the imperfect, because *-a-* follows, but use *-c-* and *-g-* in the *nous* and *vous* forms, as the following *-i-* softens them.

Infinitive	*je* and *nous* forms	Other verbs of this type
manger	je man**g**eais, nous man**g**ions	bouger, partager, protéger, voyager
commencer	je commen**ç**ais, nous commen**c**ions	avancer, forcer, lancer

5.10 *Use of the imperfect*

Rule	Examples
To describe a **state in the past**	*Ma mère **avait** les yeux bleus* – My mother **had** blue eyes *La guillotine se **dressait** Place de la Révolution* – The guillotine **stood** on the Place de la Révolution
To express an action which was **repeated**	*On **allait** tous les jours voir le vieillard* – We **used to go** every day to see the old man
To say what **was happening** at a given moment	*Papa **lisait** et les enfants **jouaient** devant la télévision* – Dad **was reading** and the children **were playing** in front of the television
To express an action which had begun further back in the past and which was still continuing. This use follows *depuis*	*Il la **regardait** depuis quelques minutes* – He **had been watching** her for several minutes *Les forces congolaises **attendaient** depuis quelques semaines le moment d'attaquer* – The Congolese forces **had been awaiting** the moment to attack for some weeks
In a hypothetical clause using *si*, the imperfect is used when the verb in the main clause is in the conditional	*Si je **gagnais** le Gros Lot, j'**irais** habiter aux Antilles* – If I **won** the jackpot, I'd go and live in the West Indies *Si le taux de chômage **baissait**, le taux d'inflation **augmenterait*** – If the unemployment rate **were to fall**, the rate of inflation **would go up**
In reported speech, the imperfect replaces the present tense	*«Je ne me **sens** pas bien»* → *Elle a dit qu'elle ne se **sentait** pas bien* – 'I **don't feel** well' → She said that she **didn't feel** well
The imperfect of *venir* + *de* expresses a recently completed action in the past: '**had just**'	*Je **venais d'ouvrir** la lettre de ma belle-sœur quand le téléphone a sonné* – I **had just opened** the letter from my sister-in-law when the phone rang

---

Quand j'**étais** tout enfant, nous **habitions** à la campagne. La maison qui nous **abritait** n'**était** qu'une petite métairie isolée au milieu des champs. Là nous **vivions** en paix. Mes parents **gardaient** avec eux une grand'tante paternelle, Tante Martine.

Henri Bosco, *L'Enfant et la rivière*

Jusqu'au milieu des années 60, la Fiat 500 n'**était** urbaine que par défaut. Petite car économique, un point c'est tout, elle ne **visait** pas a priori une clientèle particulière…

Le Monde

EXERCICES

A Complétez le texte suivant avec l'imparfait des verbes entre parenthèses.

A Kerveillant, on n'(**être**) pas loin de l'école. Même pas trois quarts d'heure à naviguer dans la boue des chemins creux, puis les nids de poule et on (**arriver**) au bourg tout de suite, malgré les vents et les pluies. L'hiver, on (**partir**) de nuit, on (**revenir**) de nuit. Nous (**être**), dit mon père, les enfants de la chandelle de résine. A midi, on (**manger**) un quignon ou une soupe dans une maison amie ou parente pour les plus chanceux, dans l'encoignure d'une porte pour les autres et c'(**être**) fait. Mon père étant l'aîné, ma grand'mère lui (**confier**) quelques sous avec lesquels il se (**charger**) de nourrir les autres.

Pierre Jakez Hélias, *Le Cheval d'orgueil*

B Exercice de consolidation. Réécrivez les phrases suivantes en utilisant l'imparfait et le conditionnel.

Exemple: Si les États-Unis *s'engagent* dans ce conflit, les conséquences en **seront** graves.

Si les États-Unis *s'engageaient* dans ce conflit, les conséquences en **seraient** graves.

1 Si le tribunal *libère* ce jeune voyou, il s'**agira** d'une vendetta entre les familles.

2 Si Florence ne *va* pas en Fac, qu'est-ce qu'elle **fera**?

3 Si on ne *trouve* pas les informations dans cette encyclopédie, il **faudra** chercher ailleurs.

4 Nous ne **pourrons** pas aller à Paris si la voiture n'*est* pas réparée à temps.

5 Bon nombre de gens **risqueront** de perdre de l'argent si les valeurs *continuent* à baisser.

5.11 *The past historic*

This tense (*le passé simple*) is restricted to the written language, and is thus to be found mainly in literature. For regular verbs, its stem is formed from the infinitive, less its ending, to which endings are added.

Subject	*regarder*	*finir*	*vendre*
je	regard**ai**	fin**is**	vend**is**
tu	regard**as**	fin**is**	vend**is**
il, elle, on	regard**a**	fin**it**	vend**it**
nous	regard**âmes**	fin**îmes**	vend**îmes**
vous	regard**âtes**	fin**îtes**	vend**îtes**
ils, elles	regard**èrent**	fin**irent**	vend**irent**

Many verbs in *-oir*, some in *-re* (and *être*) have the following pattern:

Subject	*devoir*
je	d**us**
tu	d**us**
il, elle, on	d**ut**
nous	d**ûmes**
vous	d**ûtes**
ils, elles	d**urent**

Verbs following this pattern include the following:

Infinitive	*je* form	Infinitive	*je* form
avoir	j'**eus**	pouvoir	je **pus**
croire	je **crus**	savoir	je **sus**
être	je **fus**	vouloir	je **voulus**
lire	je **lus**	vivre	je **vécus**

For other irregular verbs, see the irregular verb tables.

Venir and verbs which are related to it (*devenir, revenir, se souvenir, tenir, retenir, s'abstenir, soutenir*) have the following pattern:

Subject	*venir*	Subject	*venir*
je	vin**s**	nous	vîn**mes**
tu	vin**s**	vous	vîn**tes**
il, elle, on	vin**t**	ils, elles	vin**rent**

5.12 *Use of the past historic*

Rule	Examples
To express a single action at a single point in time	*Philippe **entra** dans la mairie* – Philippe **went into** the town hall
To express an action of long duration, but which is closely defined in time	*Pendant deux semaines il alla tous les jours chez le notaire, mais ne **reçut** pas de nouvelles* – Every day for two weeks he **went** to the notary's office, but **received** no news
The past historic of *savoir* is used to express the meaning of 'realise'	*Elle **sut** tout à coup que son mari l'avait quittée et qu'il ne reviendrait plus* – She suddenly **realised** that her husband had left her and that he wouldn't be coming back

Le car **eut** un sursaut qui **projeta** le prisonnier contre son maître. Celui-ci, se retournant, le **toisa** en silence. Le chauffeur venait d'éteindre le plafonnier et la nuit **tomba** sur son regard chargé de haine que le brusque contact de l'Allemand avait ranimé. Hans se **recula** et **retomba** dans sa rêverie.

Michel Boutron, *Hans*

Le 7 décembre dernier, Helder, international espoir et olympique portugais et milieu de terrain au club de Boavista Poro, **fut** accueilli par Charles Biétry comme le sauveur du PSG.

France-Soir

Complétez le texte suivant avec la forme qui convient du passé simple.

> Petit à petit les arbres se (**desserrer**) et un vent pur et frais (**venir**) à la rencontre du promeneur. Des fraisiers posaient dans l'herbe plus pâle leurs fines fleurs nacrées comme de minuscules anémones. Enfin les arbres (**lâcher**) prise et il ne (**rester**) plus qu'une prairie où s'inscrivaient, éclatantes et royales, les gentianes bleues... Hans s'(**asseoir**) quelques instants sur l'herbe courte, recevant avec bonheur la coulée tiède du soleil sur son visage. Une cloche (**sonner**), venue de très loin. Puis un ronronnement (**rompre**) la paix de ce haut lieu. Il (**croire**) apercevoir l'éclat métallique d'un avion, au même instant, des prairies (**monter**) le tintement de grelots de brebis prises de panique. Tout (**redevenir**) calme, aérien; invisibles, les oiseaux (**reprendre**) leurs chants.

Michel Boutron, *Hans*

COMPOUND TENSES: INDICATIVE MOOD

These tenses (perfect, pluperfect, future perfect and conditional perfect) consist of an **auxiliary verb** (*avoir* or *être*) and the **past participle**. The compound tenses of the subjunctive are also formed in this way (see **5.40**).

5.13 *The past participle*

The past participle (p.p.) (*participe passé*) of **regular verbs** is formed as follows:

-er	Past participle	*-ir*	Past participle	*-re*	Past participle
regard**er**	regard**é**	fin**ir**, serv**ir**	fin**i**, serv**i**	vend**re**	vend**u**

Irregular verbs generally have irregular past participles. Some common examples are as follows:

Infinitive	Past participle	Infinitive	Past participle
avoir	**eu**	mettre	**mis**
croire	**cru**	pouvoir	**pu**
devoir	**dû**	savoir	**su**
être	**été**	vouloir	**voulu**
lire	**lu**	vivre	**vécu**

It will be noted that in many cases the past participle is **similar** in form to the **past historic**.

5.14 *The perfect tense*

The perfect tense consists of the **present tense** of either *avoir* or *être* followed by the **past participle**.

5.15 *Verbs taking* avoir

Most of the verbs in the language are conjugated with *avoir* in their compound tenses. All reflexives and a small group of other verbs require *être*.

Rule	Examples
The perfect has the appropriate part of *avoir*, followed by the past participle	*J'ai acheté un nouvel ordinateur* – I have bought a new computer *Le premier ministre a démissionné* – The Prime Minister **resigned**
In the written form, the past participle does not agree with the subject	*Hélène a fait un petit tour en Bretagne* – Hélène went on a short tour of Brittany *Mme Chirac a accompagné son mari à l'Ambassade Britannique* – Mme Chirac accompanied her husband to the British Embassy
All unstressed pronouns precede the auxiliary	– *Tu as prêté ton vélo à Philippe?* – *Oui, je **le lui** ai prêté* (See **4.14**) – Have you lent your bike to Philippe? – Yes, I've lent **it to him**

*Moi aussi, **j'ai voyagé*** – Title of short story by Henri Queffélec

Reprenant le vieux principe du pollueur-payeur déjà en vigueur dans l'industrie, la ministre de l'Environnement **a proposé** un panel de mesures visant à pénaliser l'utilisation de produits toxiques.

Le Soir (journal belge)

EXERCICE

Complétez les phrases suivantes avec le participe passé d'un verbe irrégulier.

Exemple: Il a __ un litre d'eau, tant il avait soif.

Il a **bu** un litre d'eau, tant il avait soif.

1 André a ___ que Cécile allait le retrouver à la gare, mais quand il y est arrivé, elle n'était pas là.

2 Anne a été obligée de s'absenter. Elle a ___ retourner chez elle.

3 C'est dimanche et je m'ennuie. J'ai ___ tous les journaux et il n'y a rien à faire.

4 Martin va manquer le train. Il a ___ son passeport quelque part, et il ne le trouve plus.

5 J'ai ___ dans plusieurs grandes villes, mais c'est Paris qui me plaît le plus.

5.16 *Preceding direct objects*

In the written form of the compound tenses, the past participle will agree in number and gender with a preceding direct object (**PDO**). This happens when the direct object (**DO**) is a pronoun, a noun phrase introduced by *combien* or *quel* or a relative clause. The agreements are the same as adjective endings (see **3.11**).

Rule	Examples
In the question in the example, the **object** follows the past participle, so there is no agreeent. In the answer, it precedes, so there is agreement	– *Vous avez trouvé **les clés**?* – *Oui, je **les** ai trouvées* – Have you found **the keys**? – Yes, I've found **them**
In the case of a direct object and an indirect oject, the **PDO** causes agreement. The indirect object (**IDO**) does not. **NB** In this example, the agreement on the past participle will change the pronunciation of the participle (*transmis – transmises*)	– *Le ministère avait-il transmis **ces informations** au Premier Ministre?* – *Oui, il **les** lui avait transmises* – Had the ministry passed this information on to the Prime Minister? – Yes, it had passed **it** on to him
In a question, a **DO** may be introduced by *combien de* and moved from object position to initial position, thus becoming a PDO	***Combien de candidats** a-t-on interviewés?* *(On a interviewé **combien de candidats**? (DO))* – **How many candidates** have they interviewed?
In a similar case, *quel* introduces a PDO	***Quelles autorités** avez-vous consultées?* – **Which authorities** have you consulted?
In a relative clause (see **4.27**), *que* refers back to a noun and takes the number and gender of that noun. In the example, *la voiture* is feminine singular, so *que* is taken to be feminine singular, causing agreement.	*La voiture que les voyous avaient volée a été retrouvée quelques heures plus tard* – **The car** – **which** the thugs had stolen was found a few hours later

«Voici ta fille», dis-je.

Il eut un sursaut et me regarda.

Puis il la saisit et l'enleva dans ses bras… Il tourna vers moi sa tête baissée et me dit:

«Je **les** ai ramenés, les deux autres… Tu iras les voir dans leur maison.»

Alain-Fournier, *Le Grand Meaulnes*

Depuis l'époque gallo-romaine, l'huître est connue et appréciée de tout le monde. Certes les techniques ostréicoles ont évolué, mais les huîtres **se** sont aussi affinées.

Estival: L'été passion en Charente-Maritime

EXERCICES

A Ajoutez la terminaison qui s'impose dans les phrases suivantes.

1 J'ai cherché les diskettes et je les ai trouvé__ dans le tiroir du bureau.

2 J'ai préparé les papiers qu'il fallait et je les ai passé___ à mon chef.

3 Combien de billets a-t-on vendu___?

4 Quels livres de Giscard d'Estaing avez-vous lu__?

5 Que pensez-vous des photos que l'on a vu___ aujourd'hui?

B Faites accorder le participe passé avec le complément d'objet direct précédent.

1 Pierre a lu la lettre qu'il avait reçu ce matin-là.

2 L'ambassadeur n'a pas pu accepter les conditions que lui ont offert les autorités.

3 Combien de logiciels a-t-il acheté?

4 Quelles raisons a-t-on donné?

5 Mes enfants m'avaient demandé les nouveaux vidéos Disney et je les leur ai acheté.

C Dites **si**, **oui** ou **non**, il faut faire accorder le participe passé des phrases suivantes. Corrigez les erreurs.

1 J'avais rencontré ma sœur en ville et je lui avais **donné** les nouvelles.

2 Les nouvelles que je lui avais **donné** n'étaient pas très agréables.

3 Les deux filles se détestent. Elles se sont **dit** bonjour, mais rien de plus.

4 Combien de femmes avait-on **attendu** pour le congrès sur le féminisme au 21e siècle?

5 Quels livres avez-vous **lu** sur les philosophes comme Foucault?

6 Michel m'avait demandé mes notes sur l'Ancien Régime et je les lui ai **prêté**.

5.17 *Verbs taking* être

REFLEXIVE VERBS

With reflexive verbs, the reflexive pronoun is sometimes the direct object of the verb. In compound tenses, this PDO causes agreement on the past participle. If the reflexive pronoun is not a PDO, no agreement ensues.

Rule	Examples
Je takes the gender of the speaker. In the following example it refers to *Sylvie* and is feminine; *me* is therefore also feminine. The p.p. agrees with *me*	«*Je **me** suis couchée tard hier soir*» a dit *Sylvie* – 'I went to bed late last night,' said Sylvie
If the subject is feminine, the reflexive pronoun is feminine. Here, the PDO *se* (*s'*) refers to *Colette* and is therefore feminine. The p.p. agrees with the PDO	***Colette** s'est dépêchée vers la sortie* – Colette hurried towards the exit
As above, plural PDOs also cause agreement (*-s*, *-es*)	*Les deux garçons **se** sont enfuis* – The two boys fled *Les deux filles **se** sont tues* – The two girls fell silent
With a PDO of mixed gender, the masculine agreement is used	*Sylvie et Roger ne **se** sont levés qu'à 11 heures ce matin* – Sylvie and Roger didn't get up until 11 o'clock this morning

Rule	Examples
Feminine agreements will sometimes show up in speech	*Les trois filles **se** sont mis**es** en route* – The three girls set off

> 'Gradlon, Gradlon, si tu crains Dieu, ne garde point en croupe la fille que tant tu chéris; c'est par elle qu'Ys ta ville est ruinée et donnée à l'Océan; elle a livré son corps à tous, son âme à l'ennemi de Dieu, et Dieu **s'est lassé** d'elle, et Il l'a jugée.'
>
> Charles Guyot, *La Légende de la ville d'Ys*
>
> Depuis lundi, les Sochaliens* **se sont installés** au Domaine de Tournon dans la banlieue d'Aix-en-Provence.
>
> *France-Soir*
>
> * les Sochaliens – l'équipe de football de Sochaux

If the reflexive verb has an **indirect object pronoun**, the past participle shows no agreement in the written form:

Rule	Examples
With verbs which usually use *à* (e.g. *demander à*) the reflexive use is indirect	*Virginie **s**'est demandé s'il fallait partir ou non* – Virginie wondered whether she should leave or not
With actions done to parts of one's own body, an **indirect** reflexive pronoun is used. There is no agreement with *se* in the example	*Morgane **s**'est cassé la jambe (la jambe* is the following DO) – Morgane has broken her leg
With the reciprocal use of reflexive pronouns, there is no agreement if an IDO precedes the verb, as with *écrire à, téléphoner à, chuchoter à*	*Mes deux filles **se** sont écrit une fois par semaine tout le temps qu'elles étaient en Fac* – My two daughters wrote **to each other** once a week all the time that they were at University

EXERCICES

A   Ajoutez la terminaison qui s'impose dans les phrases suivantes.
1   Sylvie s'est levé__ et est sortie.
2   La même situation s'est reproduit__ deux mois plus tard.
3   Les deux armées se sont attaqué__.
4   Les dames se sont mis__ en route.
5   La directrice s'est montré__ favorable au projet.

Dans quelles phrases la prononciation du participe passé change-t-elle?

B   Faites accorder le participe passé avec le complément d'objet direct là où il le faut.

1   Les deux leaders se sont rencontré au congrès de Paris.

2   Le président et le chancelier allemand se sont parlé au sujet des dettes du Tiers-Monde.

3   Charlotte et Guy se sont envoyé des e-mail.

4   Juliette s'est décidé à abandonner ses études à l'Université de Strasbourg.

5   Anne et Fatima se sont pris de bec.

6   Après la boum, les gars ne se sont levé qu'à midi.

7   «J'étais si fatiguée que je me suis couché de très bonne heure hier soir», a dit Sylvie.

8   Lorsque Mme Martin s'est retrouvé dans sa ville natale, elle ne s'attendait pas à y rencontrer son ancien fiancé.

OTHER VERBS TAKING *ÊTRE*

The following verbs use *être* as their auxiliary. Those marked with an asterisk (*) may take *avoir* if they are followed by a direct object:

aller, arriver, descendre*, devenir, entrer*, monter*, mourir, naître, partir, passer*, rentrer*, rester, retourner*, sortir*, tomber, venir.

It will be noticed that most of these verbs express motion. Note however that not all verbs of motion use *être* in compound tenses, e.g. *courir.*

These verbs agree with their **subject** in the written form, **not** the preceding direct object. The agreements are those used for adjectives (see **3.11**). Note that past participles function exactly like adjectives when following *être* (cf. *La robe* est verte – *La fille* est sortie).

Rule	Examples
If the subject is feminine, the p.p. adds -*e*	*Sylvie* est arrivée hier – Sylvie arrived yesterday
If the subject is masculine plural, the agreement is -*s*	*Alain et Jean* sont partis à trois heures – Alain and Jean left at three o'clock
With a mixed gender subject, the agreement is -*s*	*La vieille dame et son mari* sont restés à Paris – The old lady and her husband remained in Paris
If the subject is masculine singular, no agreement is necessary on the p.p.	*Le Président* est revenu aujourd'hui d'Afrique – The President returned from Africa today

---

Je ne puis ni prier, ni dormir. Je suis ressortie dans le jardin sombre… Je suis rentrée pour lui écrire. Je ne peux accepter mon deuil.

André Gide, *La Porte étroite*

Les quatre bus sont arrivés à Sarajevo.

Headline, *Le Soir*

EXERCICE

Répondez aux questions suivantes selon l'exemple et en utilisant le passé composé.

Exemple: Les enfants vont sortir?

Non, **ils** sont déjà sorti**s**.

1   Les invités vont arriver cet après-midi, non?
2   Le bus en destination du Kosovo va partir demain?
3   Les étudiantes vont bientôt descendre dans les rues pour exiger l'égalité avec leurs homologues masculins, non?
4   Le facteur va passer d'un moment à l'autre?
5   Les soldats vont retourner dans leurs casernes la semaine prochaine?
6   Vos nièces vont venir vous voir, n'est-ce pas?

5.18 *Use of the perfect tense*

After the present, the perfect is the second most common tense in spoken French. In writing, it is frequently used in letters and in journalistic articles.

It is used to refer to an action performed in the past without any reference being made to its position in the sequence of a narrative. It thus expresses the fact that an action in the past is seen as completed. However the consequences of the action may remain in the present. The perfect in French thus corresponds to two separate usages in English. Examples of these two usages are: (1) **I did, I wrote**, and **I said** and (2) **I have done, I have written** and **I have said**.

1. Tu as fini ton livre? – Oui je l'ai fini la semaine dernière. (*Yes, **I finished** it last week.*)

2. Tu as fini ton livre? – Oui je l'ai juste fini. (*Yes, **I have** just **finished** it.*)

EXERCICE DE CONSOLIDATION

Réécrivez le texte suivant au passé composé.

> Cet incident **se produit** sur les locaux d'une boîte à Lille. Quand Roger Constant et sa femme y **arrivent** vers neuf heures du soir, ils **voient** un groupe de jeunes devant la porte d'entrée. L'un des jeunes **demande** du feu à M. Constant. Celui-ci lui en **offre**, et à ce moment-là, l'un des autres garçons **saisit** le sac à main de Mme Constant et **essaie** de s'enfuir. M. Constant **réagit** vite et **fait** un croche-pied au petit voyou qui **tombe** sur le trottoir, se fracturant le bras. Les autres, voyant le sort de leur ami, **se sauvent** à toutes jambes. Le manager de la boîte **appelle** la police. Trop choqués pour jouir d'une soirée en boîte, M. et Mme Constant **rentrent** à la maison.

5.19 *The pluperfect tense*

The pluperfect (*le plus-que-parfait*) is used to refer to an action in the past which preceded a second action, also in the past. It is thus similar to 'I had watched', 'I had done', etc. The **imperfect** of the auxiliary verb (*avoir* or *être*) is used with the **past participle**.

regarder	finir	vendre
j'**avais** regardé	j'**avais** fini	j'**avais** vendu
tu **avais** regardé	tu **avais** fini	tu **avais** vendu
il **avait** regardé	il **avait** fini	il **avait** vendu
etc.	etc.	etc.

Since the pluperfect is a compound tense, the past participles of reflexive verbs will agree with their **PDO**.

Those other verbs which take *être* agree with their subjects, as with the perfect.

se lever
je m'**étais** levé(e)
tu t'**étais** levé(e)
il s'**était** levé
elle s'**était** levée
nous nous **étions** levé(e)s
vous vous **étiez** levé(e)(s)
ils s'**étaient** levés
elles s'**étaient** levées

aller
j'**étais** allé(e)
tu **étais** allé(e)
il **était** allé
elle **était** allée
nous **étions** allé(e)s
vous **étiez** allé(e)(s)
ils **étaient** allés
elles **étaient** allées

5.20 *Use of the pluperfect*

Explanation	Examples
One action is completed before another in a narrative	*Elle **avait** déjà **commandé** son taxi; elle est donc sortie pour l'attendre* (2nd action) – She **had** already **ordered** her taxi, so she went outside to wait for it
In discussing a hypothesis in the past, the pluperfect may be used in the *si* clause	*Si nous n'**avions** pas **manqué** ce train, il ne faudrait pas que nous prenions un taxi maintenant* – If we **had** not **missed** the train, we wouldn't have to take a taxi now
If the pluperfect is used in a *si* clause, the main clause may contain a conditional perfect (see **5.23**) – We **would have arrived** on time	*Si nous n'**avions pas manqué** ce train, nous serions arrivés à temps* – If we **had** not **missed** that train, we would have arrived on time
The pluperfect is used in reported speech versions of the perfect	*'**J'ai acheté** une nouvelle voiture'* → *Il a dit qu'**il avait acheté** une nouvelle voiture* '**I've bought** a new car' → He said that he **had bought** a new car
Verbs using *être* use the imperfect of this auxiliary	*Je lui ai téléphoné. Elle m'a dit qu'elle **était rentrée** depuis quelques minutes* – I phoned her. She said that she **had come in** a few minutes earlier

La mariée **avait supplié** son père qu'on lui épargnât les plaisanteries d'usage.
Cependant un mareyeur de leurs cousins (qui même **avait apporté**, comme
présent de noces, un paire de soles) commençait à souffler de l'eau par le trou
de la serrure…

Gustave Flaubert, *Madame Bovary*

Luc Wintraecken habite le 129 rue des Atrébates, à Etterbeek. Dans la nuit de
samedi à dimanche, il fut parmi la trentaine de personnes évacuées à la suite
d'un affouillement de la chaussée. Au petit matin, en effet, une rupture de
canalisation d'eau **avait transformé** l'endroit en véritable champ de bataille.
De mémoire de riverains on n'**avait** jamais **connu** pareille pagaille.

Le Soir

EXERCICE

Rapportez les faits de l'incident de l'exercice de consolidation (page 119) selon l'agent qui est
venu interviewer les Constant chez eux. Ajoutez des détails plus précis.

> Selon l'agent de police, l'incident **s'était produit** sur les locaux du Perroquet Bleu, rue
> de la Huchette. M. et Mme Constant y **étaient arrivés** vers 2100 heures…

5.21 *The* passé surcomposé

Sometimes referred to as the **double perfect**, this tense replaces the pluperfect in
speech after conjunctions such as **quand**, **dès que** and **lorsque**.

Rule	Examples
The **perfect tense** of the auxiliary verb *avoir* is used before the past participle	*Quand **il a eu fini**, il a fait la vaisselle* – When **he had finished**, he did the washing up
The **perfect tense** of the auxiliary verb *être* is used before the past participle	*Quand **elle a été partie**, les autres se sont mis à pleurer* – When **she had left**, the others started to cry
The *passé surcomposé* is normally used with the verb *avoir vite fait de* to express speed	***Il a eu vite fait de** réparer la crevaison* – He quickly **repaired** the puncture

Note: In a narrative written in the past historic, examples of a similar tense called the
past anterior (*passé antérieur*) are found after conjunctions such as *quand, dès que* and
lorsque. In this tense, the auxiliary, *avoir* or *être* is placed in the past historic: *Quand il
eut fini, il sortit* – When he had finished, he went out. *Dès qu'il **fut rentré**, on
commença à préparer un repas* – As soon has he had returned, preparations for a meal
were begun.

5.22 *The future perfect*

The future perfect (*futur antérieur*) is composed of the future of the auxiliary (*avoir* or *être*), plus the past participle. It corresponds to the English form 'will have done/said/written', etc.

Rule	Examples
One action is completed in the future before another one is begun	*Nous **aurons reçu** des nouvelles dès demain. Nous **téléphonerons** alors à mémé* – We **will have received** news by tomorrow. **We'll telephone** Granny then
If one action has not yet finished, but will precede another in the future, the future perfect is used. English uses the perfect	*Peut-être que je poserai ma candidature à ce poste quand **j'aurai reçu** des détails supplémentaires* – Perhaps I'll apply for this job when **I have had** further details
Verbs using *être* require the future of this auxiliary	*Je t'en parlerai quand ton père **sera parti*** – I'll talk to you about it when your father's **gone**
This tense is used to express 'may have' when one incident precedes another	*L'avion **aura** peut-être **fait** escale à Réunion avant de disparaître* – The aeroplane **may have called** at Réunion before it disappeared

EXERCICES

A   Joignez les deux phrases en utilisant le futur antérieur.

> **Exemple:** Tout d'abord les autorités feront une enquête sur cette affaire. Plus tard elles en publieront les résultats.
>
> Quand les autorités **auront fait** une enquête sur cette affaire, elles en publieront les résultats.

1   M. Dufour finira le manuscrit de son livre. Puis il le remettra à la maison d'édition.

2   Nous lirons toutes les lettres de candidature. Après cela nous dresserons une liste des candidats à interviewer.

3   Le groupe va enregistrer une douzaine de chansons. Plus tard ils mixeront le tout dans leur studio suisse.

4   Je vais finir de faire cette traduction. Puis je la faxerai au client.

5   Je réussirai mon examen de conduite. Mon père m'achètera une voiture.

B Faites des phrases d'après l'exemple en respectant l'ordre des événements.

Exemple: (1) lire (2) parler

Quand j'**aurai** tout **lu**, je t'en **parlerai**

a	(1) rentrer	(2) téléphoner
b	(1) visiter	(2) revenir
c	(1) finir	(2) donner
d	(1) payer	(2) acheter
e	(1) avoir	(2) écrire

5.23 *The conditional perfect*

This tense (*le conditionnel passé*) is formed using the conditional of the auxiliary (*avoir* or *être*) and the past participle. It corresponds to the English '*would have done*', and is thus often used for hypothetical situations.

Rule	Examples
The **conditional perfect** replaces the **future perfect** in reported speech	«Je **serai** déjà **partie**»→ Elle a dit qu'elle **serait** déjà **partie** 'I **shall** already **have left**' → She said that she **would** already **have left**
In reported speech, if one action has not yet finished, but will precede another in the future, the **conditional perfect** is used. English uses the **pluperfect**	Il a dit qu'il poserait sa candidature à ce poste quand **il aurait reçu** encore des détails – He said that he would apply for this job when he **had had** further details
The **conditional perfect** of *aimer* may be used to express an unfulfilled wish	Elle **aurait** bien **aimé** visiter les États-Unis (mais elle n'a pas pu le faire) – She **would have liked** to visit the United States (but she was unable to do so)
In newspaper and media reports the **conditional perfect** is used to express uncertainty or to imply hearsay. No guarantee of truth is given	Selon les témoins de cet incident, les deux escrocs **seraient partis** à bord d'un avion volé. On en attend des confirmations – According to witnesses of this incident, the two criminals **fled** aboard a stolen aircraft. We are awaiting confirmation
The moral notion of 'ought to have' is expressed by the use of the **conditional perfect** of *devoir* (= should have)	J'**aurais dû** aller voir mon père plus souvent. Malheureusement il est mort maintenant – I **ought to have** gone to see my father more often. Unfortunately he's dead now

Topaze: Sais-tu ce que je dirais à mes élèves?… à notre époque le mépris des proverbes, c'est le commencement de la fortune. Si tes professeurs avaient eu la moindre idée des réalités, voilà ce qu'ils t'**auraient enseigné**, et tu ne serais pas maintenant un pauvre bougre.

Marcel Pagnol, *Topaze*

(Après l'attentat contre le *Rainbow Warrrior*) La seconde campagne **aurait permis** de sauver directement une centaine de baleines et indirectement plus de 1 300 autres…

Réponse à tout

EXERCICES

A Complétez les phrases suivantes en utilisant *le plus-que-parfait* et **le passé du conditionnel**

Exemple: Si vous (*lire*) tous les livres de ce savant, vous (**comprendre**) ses théories.

Si vous *aviez lu* tous les livres de ce savant, vous **auriez compris** ses théories.

1 Si les ministres (*discuter*) de tous ces dossiers, ils (**comprendre**) les problèmes qui en résulteraient.

2 Si ma copine (*avoir*) le temps, elle (**aller**) en ville.

3 Nous (**pouvoir**) nous baigner, s'il (*fait*) plus chaud.

4 Je me (**acheter**) une nouvelle maison, si je (*gagner*) le Gros Lot.

5 Si Nicolas (*passer*) plus de temps en Grèce, il (**visiter**) Delphi.

B Le monde vécu autrement. Comment aurait été le monde d'aujourd'hui si les événements suivants ne s'étaient pas produits? Utilisez le passé du conditionnel. Voir la clé (page 245) pour des solutions possibles.

Exemple: Si Adolf Hitler n'était pas né, la seconde guerre mondiale **ne se serait pas produite**.

1 Si Alexander Fleming n'avait pas découvert la pénicilline…

2 Si Saddam Hussein n'avait pas enhavi le Koweit…

3 Si Neil Armstrong n'avait jamais aluni…

4 Si l'Internet n'avait pas été inventé…

5 Si Nelson Mandela n'avait pas été libéré…

6 Si John F. Kennedy n'avait pas été assassiné…

7 Si Mère Thérèse n'était pas née…

8 Si l'URSS ne s'était pas effondrée…

PARTICIPLES

5.24 *The present participle*

The basis of the **present participle** is the *nous* form of the present. The ending *-ons* is replaced with *-ant*. The three exceptions to this rule are:

Infinitive	Present participle
avoir	**ayant**
être	**étant**
savoir	**sachant**

5.25 *Use of the present participle*

For the purposes of Exercise B, the various uses are numbered.

Explanation	Examples
1. **An ongoing activity** undertaken by the subject is described	*Il nettoya tout – il passa en trombe par la maison* ***époussetant**, **lavant**, **polissant*** – He cleaned everything. He went through the house like a whirlwind, **dusting**, **washing** and **polishing**
2. The present participle may express cause or reason when used in a phrase without a finite verb (**As** the tank **was** rapidly **emptying**...)	*La citerne **se vidant** rapidement, il fallait fermer le robinet* – **As** the tank **was** rapidly **emptying**, we had to turn off the tap
3. If it is used as an **adjective**, the present participle must agree with its noun	*Selon certains, la violence serait sur une **pente descendante*** – According to some people, violence is **on the decrease**
4. The participle may replace a relative clause which would begin with *qui*. This construction is often used after verbs of perception	*Je les ai vus/entendus **montant** l'escalier (qui montaient...)* – I saw/heard them **coming up** the stairs
5. It may be used as a noun with the appropriate article	***Les survivants** ont été hospitalisés* – **The survivors** were taken to hospital *Les enfants ont souvent peur **des revenants*** – Children are often afraid of **ghosts** (i.e. **returning** spirits)
6. If introduced by *en*, the present participle may express 'by ...ing' (e.g. By refusing ...). This form is known as a **gerund**	***En refusant** de se présenter au Tribunal, il s'est rendu passible d'une amende* – **By refusing** to appear in court, he rendered himself liable to a fine
7. A second use with *en* expresses 'while ...ing' or 'on ... ing' (While reading the newspaper...)	***En lisant** le journal, j'ai trouvé un article sur mon grand-père* – **While reading** the newspaper, I found an article about my grandfather

Explanation	Examples
8. The gerund can only refer to the subject of the main clause	*En sortant* de la bibliothèque, *il* a vu Marie – **As he came out** of the library, **he** saw Marie
9. One use of *tout en* + **present participle** stresses the simultaneity of actions	*Tout en feuilletant* le livre, il jetait des regards furtifs par la fenêtre – **All the while flicking** through the book, he cast furtive glances out of the window
10. A further use of *tout en* + **present participle** expresses 'although' or 'while'	*Tout en paraissant* honnête, Pierre a un côté sournois – **While appearing** honest, Pierre has a sly side to him
11. The present participle may be used to form a compound tense gerund. This may be used when the main clause is in the past	*En ayant assisté* au congrès, il s'était fait connaître de plusieurs gens d'influence – **By attending** the conference, he had made himself known to a number of influential people
12. French sometimes uses an infinitive where English uses a present participle	*Raisonner* avec lui n'était pas facile – **Reasoning** with him wasn't easy Note the reverse translation: Il n'était pas facile de *raisonner* avec lui – It wasn't easy **to reason** with him

Il sortit lentement du fossé et se mit en route, courbé, craintif, le cœur **battant**, vers le château lointain, **préférant** entrer là-dedans plutôt qu'au village qui lui semblait redoutable comme une tanière pleine de tigres.

Guy de Maupassant, *L'Aventure de Walter Schnaffs*

Depuis ce coup d'éclat, le bruit **rassurant** des bétonneuses ne s'est pas arrêté.

L'Étudiant

EXERCICES

A Donnez la forme du participe présent des verbes suivants.

avoir – boire – dire – devoir – être – faire – mettre – pouvoir – prendre – savoir – vouloir

B Décidez de quel emploi du participe présent il s'agit. Utilisez le numérotage du tableau ci-dessus.

Exemple: Tout en entretenant une image de générosité envers les pauvres, le gouvernement essaie de bloquer de nouveaux crédits = 10

1 **Prendre** une telle décision était vraiment difficile = ?

2 **Les étudiants** ont pris possession d'un amphi flambant neuf et climatisé = ?

3 On avait vu une forme obscure **se faufilant** entre les bâtiments = ?

4 Il faut avouer qu'il s'agit d'une pièce vraiment **passionnante** = ?

5 En **ayant commis** une telle gaffe, Latour s'est fait exclure de la société académique = ?

6 **En rentrant** chez moi, j'ai trouvé une note de la part de Sylvie = ?

C Traduisez en français.

1 *Working with Eleanor was very difficult.*

2 *She lost her job by quarrelling with the boss.*

3 *Having made this error, she looked for another job.*

4 *Looking through the newspaper, she saw an advertisement.*

5 *She phoned the office, all the while keeping her fingers crossed.**

6 *While talking to the manager, she realised that she knew him.*

* *to keep one's finger's crossed* = faire une petite prière

5.26 *The past participle*

For the formation of the **past participle**, see **5.13**. Its uses are as follows:

Explanation	Examples
The past participle is used to form **all** compound tenses	*Elle a/avait/aura/aurait tout **fini*** – She has/had/will have/would have **finished** everything
If the past participle is used as an adjective, it agrees with its noun in number and gender	*Les **clés perdues** ont été retrouvées* – The **lost keys** have been found
It may be used in an independent phrase to refer to the subject of the main clause. This applies to verbs of motion (e.g. *partir, arriver*) and participles such as *couché, assis*	***Une fois partis**, **nous** avons pu nous détendre un peu = Une fois **que nous** étions partis, nous…* – **Once on our way**, **we** were able to relax a little
It may be used as a noun with the appropriate article	***Les invités** ont commencé à arriver plus tôt que l'on ne s'y attendait* – **The guests** started to arrive earlier than we expected

Sur le siège, en effet, une femme en bonnet blanc, **penchée**, semblait guetter dans la cour quelqu'un qui vînt lui ouvrir. Le petit Claude, à côté d'elle, un vieux chapeau de paille noircie **abaissé** sur les yeux, grelottait…

Alain-Fournier, *Le Miracle de la fermière*

Les 25 000 victimes de Mitch, en Amérique centrale, nous rappellent dramatiquement que les hommes ne naissent pas tous égaux face aux cyclones. Quand vient la mauvaise saison, ce sont toujours les pauvres habitants des régions subtropicales qui trinquent. Mal **placés** sur le globe, ils essuient toujours tourbillons ravageurs et pluies diluviennes.

Marianne

EXERCICES

A Donnez les définitions suivantes en utilisant le participe passé sous la forme d'un substantif.
Exemple: ceux qu'on **invite** = les **invités**
1   les femmes qu'on **traite** mal = les mal_____
2   ceux qu'on emmène à l'**hôpital**
3   ceux dont on **abuse**
4   ceux qu'on **blesse**
5   celui qu'on **élit**
6   quelqu'un qu'on **ne connaît pas**
7   ceux qui **viennent de mourir**
8   celles qui ont pris la **retraite**

B   Utilisez la forme du participe passé qui convient. N'oubliez pas les accords.

Exemple: (Appuyer) au mur, les soldats fumaient en attendant de partir.

Appuyés au mur, les soldats fumaient en attendant de partir.

1   (Arriver) sur les lieux de l'attaque, les sauveteurs ont été étonnés de voir qu'il n'y avait pas de morts.

2   (Percher) sur le sommet de la montagne, le petit monastère tibétain est le dernier refuge de ces moines bouddhistes.

3   (Monter) sur de grands chevaux forts, les cavaliers passèrent en trombe à travers le camp.

4   (Coucher) dans un hamac, Sylvie sommeillait sous les rayons du soleil.

5   (Asseoir) derrière les tables, les jeunes filles attendaient l'arrivée de la directrice.

THE PASSIVE VOICE

The passive voice is the form of the verb which is used to show that an action happens or happened to the subject of the sentence, i.e. the subject receives or undergoes the action of the verb, e.g. The man (subject) **was hit** by the car.

Only transitive verbs (those having an object) may be made passive. So an active sentence – The car hit the man – may be made passive because it has an object, and so becomes – The man was hit by the car.

The passive may be used in any tense, but is often found in the perfect tense in reports of accidents and natural disasters, in which people are the victims of various actions by man and nature.

5.27 *Formation of the passive*

The passive consists of an appropriate tense of *être* (depending on the sense of the narrative) and the **past participle** of the verb required. Here are some examples:

Subject	être	(Tense)	Past participle
L'accusé	est	(present)	condamné
The accused	*is*		*sentenced*
Quelques prisonniers	ont été	(perfect)	libérés
Some prisoners	*have been*		*freed*
Les champs des fermiers	avaient été	(pluperfect)	inondés
The farmers' fields	*had been*		*flooded*
Les maisons des paysans	seront	(future)	emportées
The peasants' houses	*will be*		*swept away*

Subject	*être*	(Tense)	Past participle
L'opération de sauvetage *The rescue operation*	aura été *will have been*	(future perfect)	effectuée *carried out*
Le spectacle *The show*	aurait été *would have been*	(conditional perfect)	remis *postponed*

Note that in all compound tenses, *été* remains invariable.

5.28 *Use of the passive*

Explanation	Examples
In the written form, the past participle of the verb agrees in number and gender with the subject	***Trois jeunes Américains*** ont été kidnapp**és** – Three young Americans have been kidnapped
If the agent of the action is human, it is generally introduced by *par*	*Le premier ministre suédois a été assassiné **par** un inconnu* – The Swedish Prime Minister was assassinated **by** an unknown killer
If a verb of emotion is involved, the human agent is introduced by *de*	*Elle est aimée **de** tout le monde* – She is loved **by** everybody
The instrument of the action is usually introduced by *avec*	*Il a été blessé **avec** un couteau* – He was injured **with** a knife
If the instrument of the action is abstract, i.e. not an individual solid or tangible object, it is usually introduced by *par* or *de*	*Plusieurs ouvriers ont été brûlés **par** l'explosion* – Several workers were burned **by** the explosion *Notre marché est envahi **de** productions étrangères* – Our market is being invaded **by** products from abroad

Brusquement arriva par le travers du bourg un vent de tempête… Les monts d'Azergue, qui devenaient rapidement invisibles, **furent déchirés** par le fracas, **lacérés** par des lueurs, **tronqués** par des explosions géantes.

Gabriel Chevalier, *Clochemerle*

Le gang des bureaux de tabac… Outre 27 Roumains déjà visés par des arrêtés d'expulsion, une quinzaine de membres du réseau **ont été interpellés**… **Une partie** du butin **était** régulièrement **expédiée** par colis en Roumanie. Mais les cigarettes, les timbres fiscaux, les tickets de jeux et les cartes de téléphone volées chez les buralistes **étaient écoulés** par des complices.

Le Point

EXERCICES

A Complétez les phrases suivantes avec le temps indiqué du verbe **être.**

1 Plusieurs milliers d'hectares de bananiers (être: *perfect*) détruits par l'ouragan.

2 Si ce vent terrible avait continué de souffler, les maisons des habitants des îles (être: *conditional perfect*) emportées.

3 Des centaines de travailleurs (être: *future perfect*) dépourvus de travail.

4 Les autorités (être: *pluperfect*) averties de l'approche du cyclone.

5 Les survivants (être: *present*) actuellement logés dans des écoles et des collèges.

B Écrivez les phrases suivantes au passif. Faites attention au temps du verbe.

Exemple: Le premier ministre lui-même **abordera** ce dossier.

Ce dossier **sera abordé par** le premier ministre lui-même.

1 Des troupes ennemies ont attaqué les villages limitrophes de la frontière.

2 La société Computo-Tec installera les nouveaux ordinateurs la semaine prochaine.

3 Les agents de police ont fermé la ligne ferroviaire en raison d'une alerte à la bombe.

4 L'armée ennemie a entouré les défenseurs de la ville.

5 Selon les rapports qu'on a reçus, l'ouragan aurait dévasté toute cette région.

C Transformez ces titres de journaux en phrases passives au passé composé.

Exemple:

Fermeture du Théâtre National → Le Théâtre National a été fermé.

Ouverture de la nouvelle ligne R.E.R.

Installation d'une nouvelle centrale nucléaire

Augmentation de l'impôt sur le revenu

Distribution des cadeaux aux pauvres

Prévision d'une croissance économique

5.29 *Avoiding the passive*

The passive is more frequently found in English than in French. The following are ways of avoiding the passive.

Rule	Examples
A reflexive verb may be used instead of a passive. This is used with such verbs as *dire*, *voir*, *faire*, *vendre*	*Cela ne **se dit** pas en français* – That **isn't said** in French *La coiffe ne **se voit** que rarement en Bretagne* – The coiffe **is** only rarely **seen** in Brittany
On followed by an active verb may be substituted for the passive. This is often used if the subject is vague	***On croit** que Verlaine habitait ici* – **It is believed** that Verlaine lived here (i.e. by certain unspecified people)
Se voir + **infinitive/past participle** may be used. This construction is often used when an action is seen from a personal viewpoint rather than from outside	*Rousseau **s'est vu** emprisonner/emprisonné* – Rousseau was imprisoned
Faire + **infinitive** may be used to give a passive sense. This corresponds to the English construction 'to get something done'	*Il faut du temps pour **faire accepter** l'art moderne* – It takes time to **get** modern art **accepted**

EXERCICE

Trouvez d'autres moyens d'exprimer le sens des phrases suivantes en évitant d'utiliser le passif.

1 L'Irak a été exclu des pourparlers internationaux.
2 La musique traditionnelle anglaise est rarement entendue à la radio aujourd'hui.
3 Un nouveau ministre sera nommé cet après-midi.
4 Tous les documents ont été distribués aux avocats ce matin.
5 Votre cas a déjà été abordé.

5.30 *Verbs which may not be used in the passive*

Rule	Examples
Verbs which are followed by *à* cannot be used in the passive (*demander à*, *dire à*, etc.). *On* is used with the active voice	He **was asked** if he could attend – ***On** lui **a demandé** d'assister* He **was told** to stay there – ***On** lui **a dit** d'y rester*
Verbs which are followed by *de* cannot be used in the passive (*se moquer **de***, *rire **de***, etc.)	He **was made fun of** – ***On s'est moqué de** lui* She **was laughed at** – ***On a ri d'**elle*

Rule	Examples
An impersonal verb beginning with *il* may be used with an indirect object	He/She **is not allowed to** go out – *Il lui **est défendu** de sortir*
The verbs *obéir*, *désobéir* and *pardonner* are used with *à*. They may, however, be used in the passive	*Cette commande **fut** immédiatement **obéie*** – This order was instantly obeyed *Elle **fut** rarement **désobéie*** – She was rarely disobeyed *Les trois criminels **auraient été pardonnés*** – The three criminals **are supposed to have been pardoned**

THE INFINITIVE

The infinitive:

- is the **name** of the verb, e.g. *faire.*
- is the form which means 'to do something', e.g. *faire* = **to** do.
- has no subject. The word 'infinitive' suggests that the verb is not limited in time or restricted to a particular grammatical subject (cf. 'infinite').

Rule	Examples
The **infinitive** may be used as the subject of a sentence. English uses a present participle	***Subir** une opération de ce genre peut être dangereux* – **Undoing** an operation of this type can be dangerous
The **infinitive** may replace the imperative in instructions, directions, recipes and guides	***Éviter** tout contact avec les yeux* – **Avoid** all contact with the eyes ***Couper** les courgettes en rondelles de 2mm* – **Cut** the courgettes into 2mm slices
Faire followed by an **infinitive** gives the sense of 'getting someone to do something'	*Julie **s'est fait couper** les cheveux* – Julie **had** her hair **cut** (i.e. she got somebody to do it for her)
Laisser takes an infinitive when used in the sense of 'to allow'	*Mon père me **laissait aller** à la pêche le samedi* – My father **would allow me to go** fishing on Saturdays
An infinitive may follow a verb of perception (e.g. *écouter*, *entendre*, *voir*)	*Je l'ai vu **sortir*** – I saw him **go out** *Marie les a écoutés **chanter** dans la grande salle* – Marie listened to them **singing** in the hall
The conditional of *pouvoir* + **infinitive** is used to mean 'might'	*Cela **pourrait** bien faire l'affaire* – That **might** do the trick
Verbs expressing beginning or ending use *par* (= by) before infinitives	*Il a **commencé par** me **dire** mes quatre vérités* – He **started by telling** me a few home truths

Rule	Examples
An infinitive may replace a noun clause after verbs of believing, thinking, stating and fearing, e.g. *croire, penser, dire, craindre de*	*Il **croit pouvoir** tout faire* – He **thinks that he can** do everything (= *Il **croit qu'il peut**…*) *Marie **a dit se sentir** beaucoup mieux* – Marie **said that she felt** much better (= *Marie **a dit qu'elle se** sentait…*)
An **infinitive** is used after *il est possible de/ amusant de/ennuyeux de*, etc.	*Il **est possible d'**y arriver en moins de deux heures* – **It's possible to** get there in under two hours *Il **est amusant de** se faire hypnotiser* – **It's entertaining** to be hypnotised
Expressions such as 'The main thing is to/The most important thing is to' are followed by *de* + **infinitive**	*L'essentiel, c'est **de s'amuser*** – The main thing is to enjoy oneself *Le plus important, c'est **de faire** de son mieux* – The most important thing is to do one's best
If the infinitive is negative, *ne pas* precedes and the two elements remain together	*J'ai décidé de **ne pas aller** à Lyon* – I've decided **not to go** to Lyon *Il est possible de **ne pas passer** par Rennes* – It's possible **not to go through** Rennes

EXERCICES

A   Appariez les symboles avec les consignes données. Trouvez et soulignez les infinitifs.

Exemple:

Comburant
Le produit peut dégager une forte chaleur en présence de substances inflammables. Ne jamais mélanger avec un produit inflammable.

Xi

Irritant
Éviter tout contact. Se protéger lors de l'utilisation. Peut provoquer une réaction inflammatoire par contact avec la peau ou les muqueuses.

O

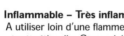

Inflammable – Très inflammable
A utiliser loin d'une flamme, éviter toute étincelle. Ce produit peut s'enflammer rapidement.

N

Nocif
Éviter de respirer ce produit trop longtemps. Risques d'accidents de faible gravité.

T – T+i

Corrosif
A manier avec la plus grande précaution. Éviter toute projection et contact avec la peau et les yeux. Peut détruire les tissus vivants.

E

Dangereux pour l'environnement
Ne jamais déverser dans l'égout. Peut causer des effets irréversibles à long terme dans l'environnement aquatique.

F – F+

Toxique – Très Toxique
Se protéger avec un masque, des gants et un tablier. Peut entraîner des risques graves, aigus ou chroniques par inhalation, ingestion ou pénétration cutanée. Ne jamais avaler, respirer ou toucher.

Xn

Explosif
A manier avec précaution. Ce produit peut exploser sous l'effet d'une flamme ou d'un choc.

C

B Substituez l'infinitif dans les phrases suivantes

Exemple: Le maire croit **qu'il est** à même de résoudre la situation.

Le maire croit **être** à même de résoudre la situation.

1 Les jeunes de la ville pensent **qu'ils peuvent** trouver les moyens de faire construire un terrain de jeux.

2 Les habitants de la cité de Sarcelles disent **qu'ils ont** moins peur de sortir qu'il y a quelques années.

3 Je ne crois pas **que je puisse** convaincre le directeur de ce qui s'est passé.

5.31 *Verbs followed by infinitives*

The verbs below require **no preposition** before an infinitive which follows. Verbs marked with an asterisk are dealt with in the notes below.

affirmer – *to state*	falloir - *to be necessary*
aimer – *to like, to love*	se figurer – *to imagine*
aimer autant – *to like... as much*	s'imaginer – *to imagine*
aimer mieux* – *to prefer*	laisser – *to allow, to let*
aller – *to go, to be going to*	oser – *to dare*
assurer – *to assure*	paraître – *to appear*
avoir beau – *to do... in vain*	partir – *to leave*
avouer – *to confess, to admit*	penser – *to think*
compter – *to intend*	pouvoir – *to be able*
courir – *to run*	préférer – *to prefer*
croire – *to believe*	prétendre – *to claim*
déclarer – *to declare*	reconnaître – *to recognise*
descendre – *to go down*	regarder – *to watch*
désirer – *to want*	savoir – *to know*
devoir – *to have to*	sembler – *to seem*
dire* – *to say*	sentir – *to feel*
écouter – *to listen*	souhaiter – *to wish*
entendre – *to hear*	soutenir – *to maintain*
envoyer – *to send*	valoir mieux* – *to be better*
espérer – *to hope*	venir* – *to come*
faillir – *almost to do...*	voir – *to see*
faire – *to make, to cause*	vouloir – *to want*

Examples:

- Alain **aime mieux aller** au cinéma – *Alain prefers going to the cinema*
- J' **aime lire** – *I like reading*
- Nous **allons rester** ici – *We're going to stay here*
- Nous **comptons assister** aux noces – *We're intending to go to the wedding*
- Je **dois finir** ceci – *I must finish this*
- Tu **espères partir** en vacances? – *Are you hoping to go away on holiday?*
- Il **faut partir** – *We've got to go*
- Je **pense aller** en Suisse cet été – *I'm thinking of going to Switzerland this summer*
- Il **vaut mieux passer** par Amiens – *It's better to go through Amiens*
- Mon beau-père **est venu voir** ses petits-enfants – *My father-in-law came to see his grandchildren*

Notes:

(1) *Aimer mieux* and *valoir mieux*, if followed by two infinitives, require *de* before the second infinitive

- *J'**aime mieux aller** en montagne que **d'aller** à la plage* – I prefer going to the mountains to going to the beach
- *Il **vaut mieux travailler** en province que **de faire** la navette entre Paris et les faubourgs* – It's better to work in the provinces than to commute between Paris and the suburbs

(2) *Dire* requires *de* if used in the sense of 'to order someone to do something'

- *Je lui **ai dit de** venir me voir* – I told him to come and see me

(3) *Venir* uses *de* for the sense of 'to have just done something'

- *Les invités **viennent d'** arriver* – The guests have just arrived

5.32 *Verbs requiring* à *before an infinitive*

These include the following. The list is not exhaustive.

aboutir – *to end*	aider – *to help*	s'attacher – *to be keen*	commencer – *to start*
accoutumer – *to accustom*	s'amuser – *to enjoy oneself*	s'attendre – *to expect*	se consacrer – *to devote oneself*
s'accoutumer – *to get used to*	apprendre – *to learn*	se borner – *to limit oneself*	continuer – *to continue*
s'acharner – *to work hard at*	s'apprêter – *to prepare oneself*	chercher – *to try*	contribuer – *to contribute*

se décider – *to make up one's mind*	hésiter – *to hesitate*	prendre plaisir – *to enjoy*	rester – *to remain*
se déterminer – *to determine*	s'intéresser – *to be interested in*	se prendre – *to start*	réussir – *to succeed*
s'efforcer – *to try*	se lasser – *to tire oneself*	se préparer – *to prepare oneself*	servir – *to be used for*
s'engager – *to commit oneself*	se mettre – *to start*	recommencer – *to recommence*	songer – *to think of*
s'ennuyer – *to be bored*	s'obstiner – *to persist in*	se réduire – *to be reduced*	tarder – *to be slow in*
exceller – *to excel enjoy*	parvenir – *to succeed*	renoncer – *to give up*	tenir – *to be keen on*
s'exercer – *to practise*	persévérer – *to persevere*	répugner – *to be reluctant*	travailler – *to work to*
se fatiguer – *to tire oneself*	persister – *to persist in*	se résigner – *to resign oneself*	trouver – *to find*
s'habituer – *to get used to*	se plaire – *to enjoy*	se résoudre – *to resolve*	viser – *to aim at, be aimed at*

Examples:

- Je me **suis accoutumé à me lever** à six heures – *I got used to getting up at six o'clock*
- Les hommes politiques **se bornent a révéler** le moins de vérités possibles – *Politicians only reveal the minimum of truth that they can*
- Jacques **s'est fatigué à construire** la muraille du jardin – *Jacques tired himself out building the garden wall*
- Henri à **réussi à avoir** son permis de conduire au troisième essai – *Henri managed to pass his driving test at the third attempt*
- Ma mère **prend plaisir à tricoter** – *My mother enjoys knitting*
- Ces mesures **visent à réduire** le taux de chômage – *These measures are aimed at reducing the unemployment rate*

5.33 *Verbs with a direct object and* à *+ infinitive*

The following verbs have a direct object and *à* before a following infinitive. The list is not exhaustive.

aider – *to help*	condamner – *to condemn*	entraîner – *to train*
amener – *to lead*	contraindre – *to compel*	exhorter – *to exhort*
assigner – *to assign*	encourager – *to encourage*	forcer – *to force*
autoriser – *to authorise*	engager – *to commit*	inciter – *to incite*

| inviter – *to invite* | pousser – *to encourage* | provoquer – *to provoke* |
| obliger – *to oblige, to force* | préparer – *to prepare* | surprendre – *to surprise* |

In the following examples, the direct object is shown in ***bold italics***.

- Tu peux **aider *ton père* à ranger** le hangar? – *Can you help your dad to tidy the shed?*
- Ces événements ***m*'ont amené à changer** d'avis – *These events led me to change my mind*
- Je veux **encourager *ma fille* à aller** en fac – *I want to encourage my daughter to go to university*
- On ne peut pas **forcer *les enfants* à faire** ce qu'ils ne veulent pas – *You can't force children to do things that they don't want to do*
- Mes parents ***m*'ont poussé à faire** mon droit – *My parents encouraged me to do law*
- **J'ai surpris *Jacques* à faire** sa valise – *I surprised Jacques packing his case*

5.34 *Verbs requiring* de *before the infinitive*

The following verbs require *de* before an infinitive. The list is not exhaustive.

s'agir – *to be a question of*	s'étonner – *to be astonished*	parler – *to speak, talk*
arrêter – *to stop*	éviter – *to avoid*	se permettre – *to allow oneself*
s'aviser – *to take it into one's head*	faire bien – *to do well*	prendre garde – *to take care not to*
avoir honte – *to be ashamed*	faire mieux – *to do better*	projeter – *to plan*
avoir peur – *to be afraid*	faire semblant – *to pretend*	promettre – *to promise*
cesser – *to stop*	feindre – *to pretend*	refuser – *to refuse*
choisir – *to choose*	finir – *to finish*	regretter – *to regret*
se contenter – *to restrict oneself*	se hâter – *to hurry*	résoudre – *to resolve*
craindre – *to fear*	menacer – *to threaten*	rire – *to laugh*
se dépêcher – *to hurry*	offrir – *to offer*	seoir (il sied) – *to be suitable*
désespérer – *to despair*	omettre – *to omit*	tâcher – *to try*
détester – *to hate*	oublier – *to forget*	tenter – *to try*

Examples:

- Il **s'agit de refaire** tout ce que l'on a déjà fait – *It's a question of redoing everything that we've already done*
- Nous **avons peur de voir** disparaître les institutions qui nous sont chères – *We're afraid of witnessing the disappearance of institutions that we cherish*
- Je **me suis étonnée de** la **voir** dans un tel état – *I was astonished to see her in such a state*

- Les gens de droite **ont menacé de voter** avec l'opposition – *Right-wingers have threatened to vote with the opposition*
- Alain **a oublié d'assister** au concours aujourd'hui – *Alain forgot to sit the exam today*

5.35 *Verbs with a direct object and* de *+ infinitive*

The following verbs have a direct object, and require *de* before the following infinitive. Those marked with an asterisk often use a **perfect infinitive**. See below **5.37**.

accuser* – *to accuse*	convaincre – *to convince*
avertir – *to warn*	dissuader – *to dissuade*
blâmer* – *to blame*	féliciter* – *to congratulate*
charger – *to charge*	implorer – *to implore*
consoler* – *to console*	persuader – *to persuade*

In the following examples, the direct object is shown in ***bold italics***.

- J'ai **convaincu *Philippe* d'aller** tout dire à sa mère – *I convinced Philippe that he should go and tell his mother everything*
- Nous n'avons pas pu **dissuader *Eric* d'acheter** cette vieille bagnole – *We didn't manage to dissuade Eric from buying that old banger*
- Les directeurs **ont félicité *le nouveau gérant* d'avoir triplé** le bénéfice en moins d'un an – *The directors congratulated the new manager on having tripled the profits in under a year*

5.36 *Verbs with an indirect object and* de *+ infinitive*

The following verbs have an indirect object (*à* + noun) and require *de* before the infinitive. Note that the sense of these verbs involves communication. The list is not exhaustive.

chuchoter – *to whisper*	dire – *to tell*	pardonner – *to forgive*
commander – *to order*	écrire – *to write*	permettre – *to allow*
conseiller – *to advise*	enjoindre – *to enjoin*	proposer – *to suggest*
déconseiller – *to advise against*	interdire – *to forbid*	recommander – *to recommend*
défendre – *to forbid*	offrir – *to offer*	suggérer – *to suggest*
demander – *to ask*	ordonner – *to order*	téléphoner – *to phone*

Examples:

- Mes parents **m**'ont conseillé **de m'inscrire** en classes du soir – *My parents advised me to go to evening classes*
- Le directeur a dit **aux élèves de sortir** immédiatement – *The headteacher told the pupils to go out immediately*
- J'ai offert **à ma cousine de l'accompagner** à Paris – *I offered to accompany my cousin to Paris*
- Madeleine **m**'a recommandé **d'aller voir** un homéopathe – *Madeleine recommended me to go and see a homœopath*
- Les autorités ont interdit **aux étudiants de se rassembler** dans les locaux de la Faculté – *The authorities forbade the students to assemble on university premises*

5.37 *The perfect infinitive*

The perfect infinitive consists of the infinitive of the auxiliary verb and the past participle, e.g. *avoir regardé, avoir fini, avoir rendu; être arrivé; s'être dépêché.*

Rule	Examples
The perfect infinitive occurs after *après* to express 'after doing/having done'. In such cases, the implied subject of both parts of the sentence is the same	***Après avoir fini*** *cette tâche, elle est repartie* – **After finishing** this task, she left ***Après être tombée*** *dans l'escalier, elle a été hospitalisée* – **After falling downstairs**, she was taken to hospital ***Après s'être levé***, *le roi s'occupait toujours de son courrier* – **After getting up**, the king always busied himself with his mail
The perfect infinitive may be used to express 'because'. This use follows *pour*	*Au dernier siècle, on battait les petits Bretons* ***pour avoir parlé*** *breton à l'école* – In the last century, young Bretons were beaten **for speaking** Breton in school
The passive voice has its perfect infinitive	*Aucun bâtiment ne semble* ***avoir été construit*** *pour magnifier la lumière naturelle, à la différence de la cathédrale de Chartres* – No building seems **have been built** to magnify natural light, unlike Chartres cathedral
The perfect infinitive may replace a noun clause after verbs of saying/thinking	*Elle dit* ***avoir été victime*** *d'une aggression = Elle dit qu'elle a été victime d'une aggression* – She says **she has been the victim** of an attack

EXERCICE

Transformez les phrases suivantes en utilisant le passé de l'infinitif.

Exemple: Henri a sillonné la France pendant toute sa vie active. Il est revenu dans son village natal.

Après avoir sillonné la France pendant toute sa vie active, Henri est revenu dans son village natal.

1   Les gangsters ont fait du racket dans ce petit quartier. Ils se sont installés en plein Paris.
2   Les paperazzi ont pris des photos de la voiture écrasée. Ils se sont enfuis.
3   Pierre s'est installé à son compte. Il a fait fortune.
4   Ma mère est tombée dans l'escalier. Elle a décidé d'acheter un petit bungalow.
5   Les manifestants se sont installés dans les locaux du journal. Ils ont invité le rédacteur à venir leur parler de la situation.

EXERCICE DE CONSOLIDATION

Indiquez le temps qui est utilisé dans les phrases suivantes.

Exemple: Pierre **avait décidé** de ne plus boire d'alcool = *Pluperfect*

1   Les deux voyageurs **sortirent** en catimini du motel.
2   La construction **sera** finie d'ici deux mois.
3   J'**aurai reçu** des nouvelles de mon ami dès demain.
4   Si nous **avions eu** le temps de le faire, nous l'**aurions fait**.
5   A cette époque-là on **avait** moins de moyens financiers.
6   Sophie **a dit** qu'elle **viendrait** nous voir.
7   Les ordinateurs **deviennent** de plus en plus sophistiqués.
8   Dès que le sénateur **eut fini** de parler, il **descendit** de l'estrade.
9   Quand Mickaël **a eu fini** son travail, il **est sorti.**
10   Si nous **pouvons** le faire, nous **acquerrons** cet argent de façon ou d'autre.

IMPERSONAL CONSTRUCTIONS

Impersonal constructions are those which are used only in the *il* form. They exist in all tenses and moods.

Type	Examples
Weather expressions, e.g. 'It's raining'	**Il pleut**, *mais **il fera** beau plus tard* – It's raining, but it will be fine later
Expressions of possibility, probability	**Il est possible que** *le spectacle soit annulé* – It's possible that the show will be cancelled **Il est probable qu**'*on y ira demain* – It's probable that we'll go there tomorrow

Type	Examples
Expressions of necessity	**Il est essentiel que** *vous soyez là* – It's essential that you should be there
Expressions of judgement	**Il vaudrait mieux** *attendre* – It would be better to wait
'It is time to…/It is time that…' **NB** *C'est le moment/l'heure de*	**Il est temps de** *sortir*/**Il est temps que** *vous sortiez* – It's time to go out/It's time that you went out
'There is, there are…/There was, there were…'	**Il y a/avait** *de quoi rire* – There is/was something to laugh about
'It's a question of…'	**Il s'agit de** *la sécurité nationale* – It's a question of national security

Mes bouquins refermé sur le nom de Paphos,

Il m'amuse d'élire avec le seul génie

Une ruine, par mille écumes bénie

Sous l'hyacinthe, au loin, de ses jours triomphaux

Stéphane Mallarmé, *Poésies*

Car enfin, **il faut** d'abord mesurer à leurs vraies nuisances les nouveaux perturbateurs de l'antique harmonie scolaire: l'immense cohorte des parents démissionnaires…

Le Point

EXERCICE

Traduisez en anglais.

1 Il y aura certainement des répercussions.
2 Il est primordial que les parents acceptent leur responsabilité en matière de scolarité.
3 Il est grand temps que ce problème se résolve.
4 Il vaut mieux ne rien dire à ce sujet.
5 Il s'agira de se débrouiller.

THE SUBJUNCTIVE MOOD

All the forms of the verb dealt with up to this point have been in the **indicative mood**.
These are the forms of the verb which are used to make statements of fact and to ask
questions. The **subjunctive mood** is a set of forms of the verb which is used for other
purposes, such as to express an attitude to what is being said or to express a doubt. Its
many uses are dealt with below, **5.43–5.60**.

Although there are four tenses in the subjunctive, only two tenses of this mood are in
current use in modern spoken French: the present and the perfect. The imperfect is
very rare, even in modern literature, and the pluperfect is confined to certain restricted
uses in literature and upper-register written French.

5.38 *Forms*

All verbs except *avoir* and *être* have the following endings in the **present** tense of the subjunctive:

Subject	Ending	Subject	Ending
je	**-e**	nous	**-ions**
tu	**-es**	vous	**-iez**
il, elle, on	**-e**	ils, elles	**-ent**

5.39 *The present tense of the subjunctive*

There are four groups of verbs in the present of the subjunctive.

Group 1. This includes the vast majority of verbs in the language. The subjunctive is formed from the third person plural (*ils/elles*) of the present tense of the indicative. Examples of regular and irregular verbs that follow this pattern are given below.

Infinitive	*ils* present indicative	*je* subjunctive	*nous* subjunctive
regarder	ils regardent	je regarde	nous regardions
finir	ils finissent	je finisse	nous finissions
rendre	ils rendent	je rende	nous rendions
dire	ils disent	je dise	nous disions
écrire	ils écrivent	j'écrive	nous écrivions
mettre	ils mettent	je mette	nous mettions
rire	ils rient	je rie	nous riions
suivre	ils suivent	je suive	nous suivions

Group 2. Three verbs have an irregular *je* form in the subjunctive from which all other forms follow:

Infinitive	*je* subjunctive	*nous* subjunctive
faire	je fasse	nous fassions
pouvoir	je puisse	nous puissions
savoir	je sache	nous sachions

Group 3. In this group, the *nous* and *vous* forms are identical to those of the **imperfect indicative**. The *je* form may or may not be irregular. Even if it is irregular, *je, tu, il/elle,*

and *ils/elles* follow the regular pattern for endings. The following table shows how *ils/elles* return to the *je* pattern.

Infinitive	*je* subjunctive	*nous* subjunctive	*vous* subjunctive	*ils/elles* subjunctive
aller	j'aille	nous allions	vous alliez	ils aillent
boire	je boive	nous buvions	vous buviez	ils boivent
croire	je croie	nous croyions	vous croyiez	ils croient
devoir	je doive	nous devions	vous deviez	ils doivent
envoyer	j'envoie	nous envoyions	vous envoyiez	ills envoient

See the Irregular verb tables (pp. 274–279) for *acquérir, mourir, mouvoir, percevoir, prendre, recevoir, renvoyer, tenir, venir, voir, vouloir.*

Group 4. The verbs *avoir* and *être.* These are completely irregular and must be learned individually.

avoir	être
j'aie	je sois
tu aies	tu sois
il/elle ait	il/elle soit
nous ayons	nous soyons
vous ayez	vous soyez
ils/elles aient	ils/elles soient

EXERCICE

Donnez la forme de la troisième personne du singulier (**il/elle**) et de la première personne du pluriel (**nous**) du subjonctif des verbes suivants.

aller – attendre – avoir – conduire – devoir – dire – être – faire – finir – mettre – suivre – venir – vivre

5.40 *The perfect tense of the subjunctive*

The present subjunctive of *avoir* and *être* are used to form the **perfect tense** of the subjunctive, just as the present tense of the indicative is used to form the perfect in the indicative. All reflexives require the present subjunctive of *être*, as do the verbs listed on page 117. All other verbs require the present subjunctive of *avoir*. Thus:

Conjugation with *avoir*	Conjugation with *être*	Conjugation with *s'être*
j'aie regardé	je sois allé(e)	je me sois assis(e)
j'aie fini	je sois arrivé(e)	je me sois réveillé(e)
j'aie rendu	je sois descendu(e)	je me sois levé(e)
j'aie reçu	je sois retourné(e)	je me sois baigné(e)
j'aie mis	je sois rentré(e)	je me sois promené(e)
j'aie été	je sois tombé(e)	je me sois couché(e)
etc.	etc.	etc.

5.41 *The imperfect subjunctive*

This tense of the subjunctive is little used today, particularly in speech, though it will be found in examples of very formal writing (essays, polemics, laws, literature). It is based on the *tu* form of the past historic. The forms which are most seen are the third person singular (*il*) of the verbs *avoir* (*il eût*), *être* (*il fût*), *faire* (*il fît*) and *devoir* (*il dût*). For a detailed treatment, see Hawkins, R. and Towell, R. – *French Grammar and Usage*. London: Arnold.

5.42 *The pluperfect subjunctive*

This tense is formed from the imperfect subjunctive of *avoir* or *être*, plus the past participle (e.g. *il eût dit, elle fût partie*). It is confined to literature and other formal styles of writing. In meaning, it is sometimes equivalent to the pluperfect of the indicative and sometimes to the conditional perfect. For a detailed treatment, see Judge, A. and Healey, F.G. (1985) *A Reference Grammar of Modern French*. London: Arnold.

5.43 *Use of the subjunctive*

When a speaker is stating matters of fact, he/she uses the indicative forms of the verb, i.e. all the forms of the verb in this grammar which precede this section on the subjunctive.

Example:

Gérard **habitait** à cette époque dans une petite maison près de Paris. Un jour il **a décidé** de tout vendre et de partir. Maintenant il **est** sans domicile fixe. Il ne **peut** pas trouver de logement.

A listener hearing sentences such as these with indicative verbs in them will understand that reference is being made to reality and to matters of fact. The subjunctive, however, is the mood that shows that things are not necessarily real to the speaker, but may perhaps only be possible.

Example:

Il est possible que Gérard **puisse** trouver un logement un de ces jours.

The speaker may also use the subjunctive to pass an opinion on a fact, thus giving a particular emotional nuance to the sentence. The subjunctive is the mood of the speaker's world, not that of the real world.

* *Fact:* Les autorités ne **font** rien pour lui.
* *Opinion:* Cela me choque que les autorités ne **fassent** rien pour lui.

In essence, *the indicative is the mood of reality*, *the subjunctive is the mood of attitude*.

5.44 *The subjunctive in attitudinal subordinate clauses*

In certain types of compound sentence in which **the subject of the subordinate clause is not the same as that of the main clause**, the subordinate verb is put into the subjunctive.

MAIN CLAUSE		SUBORDINATE CLAUSE		
Alain	veut	que	Philippe	**vienne** le voir
Subject			*Subject*	

Note: If the subject of the two clauses is the same, an infinitive construction is usually used, e.g. *Alain **veut venir** nous voir.*

5.45 *The subjunctive after verbs of emotion*

The use of the subjunctive is triggered by the presence in the main clause of a **verb with a particular emotional nuance**. Thus the subjunctive is used as follows:

Trigger	Examples
Verbs expressing **liking, loving** or **preferring** – *aimer que, adorer que, aimer mieux que, préférer que*	*J'adore que mes amis* ***viennent*** *dîner chez nous* – I love my friends coming to dinner with us *Je préférerais que tu ne* ***sois*** *pas là* – I would prefer that you weren't there
Verbs expressing a **wish**, such as – *vouloir, souhaiter, désirer, aimer*	*Je voudrais qu'elle* ***soit*** *là* – I'd like her to be there *Notre professeur souhaite que nous* ***travaillions*** *plus dur* – Our teacher wishes that we'd work harder *Le ministre désire qu'on lui* ***remette*** *le dossier* – The minister would like the issue to be put in her hands
Verbs expressing an emotion, such as: **Happiness**: *être content que, être heureux que, être ravi que, se réjouir que* **Sorrow**: *être désolé que, être navré que, regretter que, être triste que* **Surprise**: *être surpris que, s'étonner que* **Anger**: *être furieux que* **Hate**: *détester que* **Opinion**: *Il est bon que/mauvais que*	*Je suis content que tu* ***puisses*** *venir* – I'm glad that you can come *Suzanne est ravie que sa mère* ***aille*** *mieux* – Suzanne is delighted that her mother is better *Nous regrettons que vous ne* ***soyez*** *pas en mesure de régler cette facture* – We regret that you are unable to settle this invoice *Mon père est furieux que tu* ***aies*** *fait cela* – My father is furious that you did that

– A quoi tu penses, Bel Gazou?

– A rien, maman.

– «A rien, maman». Il n'est pas mauvais que les enfants **remettent**, de temps en temps, avec politesse, les parents à leur place.

Colette, Le Curé sur le mur

J'ai failli être prêtre, puis militaire. Mais ça m'a fait peur; je ne voulais pas que ma vie **soit** toute tracée, alors je suis venu en France, où j'ai découvert l'amour du théâtre…

VSD

Les vœux et les émotions. Complétez les phrases suivantes en mettant le verbe entre parenthèses au subjonctif.

a Verbes réguliers

1 Ma mère ne veut pas que nos parents (**arriver**) la veille des noces.

2 Mon fils n'aime pas que sa petite sœur (**se coucher**) à la même heure que lui.

3 Je préférerais que mes enfants ne (**regarder**) pas les émissions de télévision qui contiennent des éléments violents.

4 Céline préfère que sa fille (**finir**) toutes ses corvées de ménage avant de sortir.

5 A vrai dire, je souhaiterais que vous me (**rendre**) tout ce que je vous ai prêté.

b Verbes irréguliers

1 Je déteste qu'on me (**faire**) attendre chez le dentiste.

2 Vous préféreriez que votre fils n'(**avoir**) pas accès à l'Internet.

3 Les teenagers n'aiment pas que les parents (**être**) là quand on fait une boum.

4 On est ravi que la princesse de Monaco (**pouvoir**) assister au festival de Cannes.

5 Nous nous étonnons que la municipalité ne (**être**) pas en mesure de résoudre ce problème.

5.46 *The subjunctive after verbs of fearing*

Verbs of **fearing** are followed by a subjunctive.

Trigger	Examples
Verbs of **fearing**: *avoir peur que, craindre que, redouter que* **Note**: in formal French, *ne* is required before the subjunctive if the main verb is affirmative	*J'ai peur qu'il ne **soit** malade* – I'm afraid that he's ill *On craint que le meurtrier **ne puisse** s'échapper* – It is feared that the murderer will be able to escape BUT *On ne craint pas que le meurtrier **puisse** s'échapper* – There is no fear that the murderer will be able to escape

Jeudi 18 février: Je suis parti pour l'attendre dans le grand vent qui charrie la pluie… Je crains qu'il **ne pleuve**: une averse peut l'empêcher de venir.

Alain-Fournier, *Le Grand Meaulnes*

EXERCICE

La crainte. Transformez les phrases en utilisant '**Je crains que**' ou '**J'ai peur que**'. N'oubliez pas d'insérer **ne** avant le verbe au subjonctif dans les phrases affirmatives.

Exemple: Le président **est** mort.

Je crains que le président **ne soit** mort.

1   Nous **sommes** en retard.
2   Le train **est** déjà parti.
3   On **a** perdu nos bagages.
4   Jean ne nous **attend** pas.
5   Les autorités **peuvent** refuser notre demande.

5.47 *Orders, permission, prevention and forbidding*

Trigger	Examples
Verbs expressing a **command** – *dire que, ordonner que, commander que, exiger que*	*L'officier a ordonné que tous les civils **sortent** de la maison* – The officers ordered all civilians to leave the house *L'état ne peut pas exiger que l'on **fasse** son service militaire* – The State cannot demand that people undertake military service
Verbs of **allowing**, **asking**, **forbidding**, **preventing**	*Mon père a permis que mes copains **viennent** coucher chez nous* – My father allowed my friends to stay with us *La Croix Rouge a demandé que l'on **envoie** des couvertures et des médicaments* – The Red Cross has requested that one should send blankets and medicine *Les autorités ont interdit que les civils **sortent** la nuit* – The authorities have forbidden people to go out at nuit *Les inondations ont empêché que les événements se **déroulent** comme prévus* – The floods have prevented events from going off as they should

Je veux, j'ordonne, je souhaite, je désire qu'on **obéisse**.

Prosper Mérimée, *Colomba*

Exiger que l'on **apprenne** la liste des départements, préfectures et sous-préfectures peut être discuté, mais que penser des manuels scolaires d'histoire ou de géographie qui ont supprimé les résumés des leçons?

Le Figaro

EXERCICE

Complétez les phrases suivantes avec le subjonctif d'un des verbes pris dans la liste qui suit.

1 L'ONU a exigé que le général rebelle _____ tous ses armes aux forces de l'ordre.

2 Les autorités ont interdit que les camions transportant la nourriture aux rescapés de la violence _____ la frontière.

3 La dévastation a empêché que les œuvres de secours se _____.

4 Les soldats envahisseurs ont commandé que les villageois _____ la région en moins de 24 heures.

5 Le commandant des forces a permis que chaque individu _____ un seul sac et de la nourriture.

prendre – poursuivre – franchir – quitter – rendre

5.48 *Expectation and intention*

Trigger	Examples
Verbs expressing **expectation** or **intention** – *s'attendre à ce que* – to expect that *compter que, avoir l'intention que* – to intend that	*Je m'attends à ce que tous ses amis **assistent** au vin d'honneur* – I'm expecting all his friends to attend the reception *J'ai l'intention qu'il se **présente** à 9 heures* – I'm intending that he should be here at 9 o'clock

EXERCICES

A Choisissez la bonne forme du verbe.

1 Tu t'attends à ce que ton amie (vient/vienne) aujourd'hui?

2 Je compte qu'il y (ait/a) assez de place pour tout le monde.

3 Vous avez l'intention que le groupe (part/parte) à midi?

4 Je ne m'attends pas à ce que ce poste vous (soit/est) proposé.

5 Frédéric ne compte pas que ses collègues (savent/sachent) les détails de cette affaire.

B Traduisez en français.

1 I'm expecting that everybody will be there.

2 You are expected to be at the meeting (*On s'attend...*).

3 I'm intending that people should know the truth.

4 Are you expecting Stéphane to come?

5 I'm intending that he should come, at any rate (*en tout cas*).

5.49 *Verbs of saying and thinking used negatively*

The subjunctive is used after verbs of **saying**, **thinking** and **believing** when they are used negatively, i.e. the speaker's attitude is one of denial. If they are used positively in statements, the indicative is used. This affects such verbs as *dire, affirmer, penser, croire, trouver, se figurer, imaginer, supposer.* The verb *nier* (to deny) must, logically, always have a subjunctive. Similarly *rien ne prouve que* has a negative sense.

Positive statement	Negative statement
Je pense qu'il **peut** nous aider – *I think that he can help us*	Je ne pense pas qu'il **puisse** nous aider – *I don't think that he can help us*
Le gouvernement croit que la crise **est en** train de se résoudre – *The government believes that the crisis is resolving itself*	Le gouvernement ne croit pas que la crise **soit** en train de se résoudre – *The government doesn't believe that the crisis is resolving itself*
Le directeur trouve que votre plan **a** de bons points – *The manager thinks that your plan has some good points*	Le directeur ne trouve pas que votre plan **ait** de bons points – *The manager doesn't think that your plan has any good points*
Le rédacteur du journal a affirmé que 20 personnes **ont** trouvé la mort – *The newspaper's editor stated that 20 people had died*	Le rédacteur du journal a nié que 20 personnes **aient** trouvé la mort – *The newspaper's editor denied that 20 people had died*

– Je sais, les mesures anti-inflation et tout. Tout de même, nous n'en avons besoin que pour deux semaines et…

– Je ne pense pas que nous **puissions** discuter de cela au téléphone, n'est-ce pas?
J.-P. Berman, M. Marchetueau et M. Savio, *L'anglais économique et commercial*

Rien ne prouve que le gouvernement **soit** en mesure de distraire de son budget les sommes qui serviraient aux prêts dont vous parlez.
Bernard Cresson, *Introduction au français économique*

5.50 *Verbs of saying and thinking used interrogatively*

The subjunctive also follows verbs of **saying**, **thinking** or **believing** when they are used interrogatively, i.e. in questions.

Positive statement	Interrogative
Le premier ministre pense que le taux du chômage **doit** baisser d'ici deux mois – *The Prime Minister thinks that the unemployment rate will fall in two months' time*	Le premier ministre pense-t-il que le taux du chômage **doive** baisser d'ici deux mois? – *Does the Prime Minister think that the unemployment rate will fall in two months' time?*

Positive statement	Interrogative
On peut bien se figurer que l'affaire **peut** se résoudre sans problèmes – *We can well imagine this matter resolving itself without any problems*	Peut-on se figurer que l'affaire **puisse** se résoudre sans problèmes? – *Can we imagine this matter resolving itself without any problems?*
Moi, je suppose qu'il **est** absent – *I suppose he's absent*	Et toi, penses-tu qu'il **soit** là? – *Do you think that he's here?*

Note: The indicative mood may sometimes be used instead of the subjunctive. The indicative in the subordinate clause of the question suggests or hopes that the answer will be 'Yes'. The use of the subjunctive suggests or hopes that the answer will be 'No'.

5.51 *Expressing doubt*

Since doubt is essentially a negative way of thinking or expressing oneself, verbs following expressions of doubt take the subjunctive.

Trigger	Examples
Verbs expressing **doubt** – *douter que, ne pas être certain/sûr que*	*Doutez-vous qu'il **ait** suffisamment d'argent?* – Do you doubt that he has enough money? *Corinne n'est pas sûre que son amie **puisse** l'aider dans cette affaire* – Corinne isn't sure that her friend can help her in this matter

Je doute, je nie, je conteste qu'il **ait** raison!

Édouard Estaunié, *L'Appel de la route*

Note: Some **impersonal** expressions are used to express doubt, e.g. *il est **douteux** que*. See below, **5.52.**

EXERCICE

Répondez aux affirmations suivantes en exprimant le doute. Utilisez le subjonctif du verbe dont il s'agit.

Exemple: On dit qu'Henri Laforgue va se présenter aux élections municipales.

Moi, je doute qu'il se **présente**.

1   On dit que les résultats sont tout à fait prévisibles.
2   On dit que Laforgue a de grandes ambitions.
3   On dit qu'il pourra renouveler la politique du parti.
4   On dit qu'il veut devenir député à l'Assemblée Nationale.
5   On dit qu'il sait manipuler les idéologues du parti.

5.52 *Impersonal expressions*

The subjunctive is used in *certain* impersonal expressions, i.e. expressions which begin with *il*. These expressions may express **necessity**, **possibility**, **impossibility**, **improbability**, **doubt**, **uncertainty**, **untruth**, **importance**, **preference** or an **impression**.

Category	Examples
Necessity: *il faut que, il est nécessaire que, il est essentiel que, il est primordial que*	*Il est essentiel que tous les candidats soient là de bonne heure* – It is essential that all candidates should be there early *Il faut que nous fassions la vaisselle* – We must do the washing up
Possibility: *il est possible que, il se peut que*	*Il est possible que tu puisses venir avec nous* – It's possible that you'll be able to come with us
Impossibility: *il est impossible que, il n'est pas possible que*	*Il est impossible que nous soyons là avant 9 heures* – It's not possible for us to be there before 9 o'clock
Improbability: *il est peu probable que, il n'est pas probable que*	*Il est peu probable que les Socialistes aient suffisamment d'influence sur les députés révoltés* – It is unlikely that the Socialists have enough influence over the rebel MPs
Doubt: *il est douteux que, il est à douter que*	*Il est douteux que l'affaire se résolve à temps* – It's doubtful that the matter will resolve itself in time
Uncertainty: *il n'est pas certain que, il n'est pas sûr que*	*Il n'est pas sûr que le suspect ait été sur les lieux en ce moment* – It isn't certain that the suspect was on the premises at the time
Untruth: *il n'est pas vrai que, il est faux que*	*Il n'est pas vrai que les étudiants aient occupé les locaux de la Faculté* – It isn't true that the students occupied University premises
Importance: *il est important que, il est d'importance que*	*Il est important que l'on examine tous les résultats de cette expérience* – It is important that we should examine all the results of this experiment
Preference: *il vaut mieux, il vaudrait mieux*	*Vous avez dit qu'il faut prendre le train. A mon avis il vaudrait mieux que l'on prenne l'avion* – You said that we should take the train. In my opinion it would be better to fly.
Impression: *il semble que* **NB** In a statement *Il me semble que* is followed by the indicative, in a question or a negative statement, by the subjunctive	*Il semble que l'argent ait disparu* – It seems to me that the money has disappeared BUT *Il me semble que l'argent a disparu* – It seems to me that the money has disappeared (cf. *Il ne me semble pas que l'argent ait disparu* – It doesn't seem to me that the money has disappeared)

Mais il n'est pas vrai que je **veuille** taxer le logement et les résidences principales, il n'est pas vrai que je me **propose** d'augmenter les droits de succession en ligne directe.

François Mitterrand, *Discours du 8 mai 1981*

EXERCICE

Complétez les phrases suivantes avec une expression impersonnelle qui convienne au sens.

1 _____ que la population de la France soit plus importante que celle de l'Angleterre.

2 _____ que nous fassions de notre mieux pour réduire la pollution.

3 _____ que le conflit entre les protestants et les catholiques en Irlande du Nord puisse se résoudre de notre vivant.

4 Je n'en suis pas sûr, mais _____ que le directeur soit sur le point de démissionner.

5 _____ qu'un homme puisse survivre sur Vénus à cause de la gravité et de l'atmosphère d'acide sulphurique.

5.53 *Conjunctions*

The subjunctive is used after the following conjunctions, which fall into various categories.

Category	Examples
Concession – *bien que, quoique, encore que, malgré que*	*Bien que la violence* **soit** *en augmentation, il faut voir le côté positif des choses* – Although violence is increasing, we have to look on the bright side of things *Il a décidé de partir, encore qu'il n'***ait** *pas d'argent* – He decided to leave, although he has no money
Purpose – *pour que, afin que*	*Il faudra commander plus de chaises, pour qu'il y* **ait** *suffisamment de places pour tous* – We must order more chairs so that there are enough places for everybody
Time – *avant que*, après que* (spoken French), *jusqu'à ce que**, que* (= *jusqu'à ce que*) as in *en attendant que* * Requires *ne* in formal French **Only takes subjunctive if there is a sense of purpose	*Vous devez lui parler avant qu'il (ne)* **parte** – You must speak to him before he leaves *Restez là jusqu'à ce que vous vous* **sentiez** *mieux* – Stay there until you feel better *On va rester ici en attendant que les autres* **arrivent** – We'll stay here until the others arrive
Fear – *de peur que, de crainte que* **NB** The verb has an expletive *ne* with it	*On a évacué le théâtre de peur que la bombe* **ne soit sur** *le point d'exploser* – The theatre was evacuated for fear that the bomb was about to explode
Condition – *pourvu que, à condition que, à moins que* (+ *ne*)	*Pourvu qu'on me* **paie**, *on y ira samedi* – Provided that I'm paid, we'll go on Saturday *A moins que le Ministre* **ne démissionne**, *cette crise ne peut pas se résoudre facilement* – Unless the Minister resigns, this crisis will not easily resolve itself
Negation – *non que, loin que, ce n'est pas que, sans que*	*Il ne sait pas faire les maths – non qu'il* **soit** *stupide* – He can't do maths – not that he's stupid *Loin que l'on* **dispose** *des fonds nécessaires, les coffres sont vides* – Far from our having the necessary funds available, the coffers are empty *Elle est sortie, sans que je* **puisse** *lui dire «au revoir»* – She went out without my being able to say 'Goodbye' to her

Category	Examples
Limitation – *pour peu que, si peu que*	*Pour peu que vous* **croyiez** *qu'on est capable de l'être, tout le monde peut être violent* – However little you think we may be so, everybody is capable of being violent
Alternatives – *soit que, que... ou que*	*Soit qu'il* **ait** *commis ce crime, soit qu'il* **soit** *innocent, il faut attendre voir* – Whether he committed this crime or whether he's innocent, we shall have to wait and see *Qu'il* **puisse** *le faire ou qu'il ne* **puisse** *pas le faire, cela m'est égal* – Whether he can do it or whether he can't, I don't care
Description – *tel que*	*Il faut trouver un abri tel que les sans-domicile n'***aient** *pas à subir les intemperies de l'hiver* – We must find a shelter so that the homeless won't have to endure the bad weather this winter
Supposition – *supposé que, en supposant que, à supposer que, en admettant que, en cas que* **NB** *Si* (if) **always** takes the indicative	*Supposé que l'avion* **soit** *déjà parti, qu'est-ce qu'on va faire?* – Suppose the plane's already gone, what are we going to do?

Il faut qu'elle [une communication] soit importante et urgente **pour que** vous n'**ayez** pas crainte de vous aventurer jusqu'ici.

Claude Vautel, *Mon curé chez les riches*

«**Qu'**il **pleuve**, qu'il **vente** ou qu'il **neige**, Paul devait pousser la grosse femme sur sa chaise roulante» … raconte un cafetier.

VSD

EXERCICES

A Choisissez la conjonction qui convient dans les phrases suivantes.

Exemple: Josyane a décidé d'aller à Paris _____ elle aille mal. (avant qu'/bien qu')

Josyane a décidé d'aller à Paris **bien qu'**elle aille mal.

1 Je dois verser de l'argent à mon compte en banque _____ je ne sois pas à découvert. (avant que/pour que)

2 Il faut que tout soit prêt _____ le maire et les notables arrivent. (tel que/avant que)

3 L'ONU continuera avec ses pourparlers _____ on en arrive à une solution. (jusqu'à ce qu'/pour peu qu')

4 _____ tous les conseillers démissionnent. Qui va les remplacer? (supposons que/sans que)

5 Nous pourrons payer le loyer de salle polyvalente, _____ toutes les places soient vendues ce soir. (en admettant que/à condition que).

B Concession. Transformez les phrases suivantes en utilisant **bien que**, (ou **quoique** ou **encore que**), selon l'exemple.

Exemple: Le ministre de la culture compte ouvrir la nouvelle bibliothèque, même si la construction n'en est pas terminée.

Le ministre de la culture compte ouvrir la nouvelle bibliothèque, **bien que** la construction n'en **soit** pas terminée.

1 Dans les institutions éducatives, il y a de plus en plus de paperasse, même s'il n'y a pas suffisamment de fonds pour qu'on achète les livres dont on a besoin.

2 Même si les CD ne coûtent presque rien à produire, les fabricants font un énorme bénéfice avec eux.

3 Même si on a à soutenir un fils en fac, on ne bénéficie d'aucune baisse des impôts.

4   En Europe on mange bien, même si le Tiers-Monde meurt de faim.

5   Même si la littérature du dix-neuvième siècle se lit de moins en moins, elle a encore un message à transmettre à notre société de consommation.

5.54 *Use of* que *to replace* si *in co-ordinated clauses*

As has been noted above, *si* is always followed by the indicative. If two clauses expressing supposition are co-ordinated, however, the second may be replaced by a clause introduced by *que*, followed by a verb in the subjunctive. This is particularly true of written French.

Examples:

Si M. Lefèvre a suffisamment de supporters et **qu**'il se **présente** aux élections, il fera un admirable maire – *If M. Lefèvre has enough supporters and if he stands in the election, he will make an admirable mayor*

Si vous avez le temps et **que** vous ne **soyez** pas occupé, venez me voir – *If you have the time and you're not busy, come and see me*

5.55 *Purpose and result*

The expressions *de sorte que/en sorte que* may express either purpose or result, much like the English 'so that' – 'He worked hard so that he would be able to go to University' (purpose) v. 'He worked hard, so that he finally obtained the results that he needed' (result).

The expression *de manière à ce que* expresses purpose, but *de telle manière que* expresses result. The expression *de façon à ce que* expresses purpose, *de façon que*, result.

In the following pairs, the subjunctive is used to express **purpose**, the indicative to express **result**. Sentences expressing **result** are, of course, often in a past tense.

Purpose (subjunctive)	Result (indicative)
Il m'a donné une carte de façon à ce que je **puisse** y aller en voiture – *He gave me a map so that I could get there by car*	J'avais bien préparé la route de façon que j'y **suis arrivé** sans problèmes – *I carefully prepared the route with the result that I got there without any problems*
Il a arrangé le dîner de manière à ce que tout le monde **se plaise** – *He arranged the dinner so that everybody should enjoy themselves* **NB** de manière à ce que *is found in speech*	Il avait arrangé le dîner de telle manière que tout le monde **s'est plu** – *He arranged the dinner in such a way that everybody enjoyed themselves*

Purpose (subjunctive)	Result (indicative)
Il m'a prêté ses notes de sorte que je **sois** à même de réussir l'examen – *He lent me his notes so that I should be able to pass the exam*	J'avais bien étudié, de sorte que je **suis** sorti majeur de la classe – *I studied hard, with the result that I came top of the class*

Ils s'arrangent de façon à ce qu'il n'en **soit** pas ainsi à la maison.

Jules Vallès, *Les Réfractaires*

EXERCICE

Choisissez soit l'indicatif, soit le subjonctif, selon le sens et la structure de la phrase.

1   Si vous pouvez venir – et si vous (**vouliez/voulez**) venir – téléphonez-moi le plus tôt possible.

2   Si André arrive à temps à Londres et qu'il (**a/ait**) réservé une chambre d'hôtel, il n'aura pas de problèmes.

3   Moi, je vais réserver deux places pour le congrès, de sorte que nous (**pourrons/ puissions**) être sûrs de pouvoir y assister.

4   Tout s'est bien déroulé, de telle manière que nous (**avons/ayons**) décidé de répéter cette expérience.

5   Les portes du théâtre sont barrées de manière à ce que les fans ne (**puissent/peuvent**) pas entrer pendant le concert.

5.56 *The subjunctive in clauses beginning with* que

Que may be used in the sense of **whether** and introduce a clause, as shown above (**5.53**). If a clause which is the equivalent of a noun phrase begins a sentence, then the verb in that clause must be in the subjunctive.

Introductory phrase	Examples
Que…	**Qu**'il soit **saoûl** ne m'étonne pas – *That he's drunk doesn't surprise me*
Le fait que…	**Le fait que** son entreprise **ait** fait faillite ne semble pas le déranger – *The fact that his business has gone bankrupt doesn't seem to bother him*
L'idée que…	**L'idée que** l'homme **puisse** survivre sur la lune est ridicule – *The idea that man can survive on the moon is ridiculous*

Introductory phrase	Examples
La notion que…	**La notion que** l'être humain **soit** une machine biologique est tout à fait démodée – *The notion that a human being is a biological machine is completely out-dated*

> [Les teenagers] sont occupés, essentiellement, à vivre au présent… Que, ce faisant, ils se **préparent** des lendemains qui grincent… peu en conviennent.
>
> Maurice T. Maschino, *Vos enfants ne m'intéressent plus*

5.57 *The subjunctive in clauses following indefinite expressions*

Indefinite expressions such as *whatever* and *whoever* contain the idea that what is under discussion is not totally real. French therefore uses the subjunctive in such cases.

Expression	Meaning	Examples
quoi que	*whatever*	**Quoi qu'il dise**, je sais qu'il ment – *Whatever he says, I know that he's lying*
qui que	*whoever*	**Qui que** vous **voyiez**, ne dites rien à ce sujet – *Whoever you see, say nothing about this matter*
où que	*wherever*	**Où que** vous **soyez,** n'oubliez pas de me téléphoner – *Wherever you are, don't forget to phone me*
quel que + *verb* + *noun* **NB** quel *must agree in number and gender with its noun*	*whatever*	**Quels que soient** les résultats de ce test, il ne faut pas s'en inquiéter – *Whatever the results of this test may be, we mustn't worry*
quelque + *noun* **NB** quelque *agrees in number with its noun*	*whatever*	**Quelques** propositions qu'on **puisse** vous faire, n'oubliez pas ce que je vous ai dit – *Whatever suggestions are made to you, don't forget what I've told you*
quelque + *adjective* (*also*: si/pour/aussi + *adj.*) **NB** quelque *is invariable*	*however*	**Quelque** attirant que **soit** le salaire, je ne suis pas tenté – *However attractive the salary may be, I'm not tempted* **Si** riche qu'il paraisse, il n'a pas vraiment beaucoup d'argent – *However rich he may appear to be, he really hasn't any money*

> [La création artistique et le renouveau de l'expression culturelle] Tout cela a
> d'autant plus de chance de s'épanouir que la tutelle est moins pesante et
> l'autorité plus libérale, **à quelque** niveau qu'elles s'**exercent**.
>
> H. Krier et L. Ergan, *Bretagne de 1975 à 1985*

EXERCICE

Traduisez en anglais.

1 Que les jeunes en soient conscients ou pas, le danger que représente l'abus de
   drogues et d'alcool est omniprésent.

2 Quoi que vous pensiez d'Angélique, elle a vraiment de bonnes intentions.

3 Où que vous rencontriez des abus de ce genre, il faut en faire rapport à la police.

4 Quelles que soient les raisons qu'on ait données, ce qui est sûr, c'est qu'on essaie
   de cacher cette affaire.

5 Le fait que le directeur ait tout nié n'a aucune importance.

6 Quelles que soient les allégations qu'on ait faites contre elle, Margot est innocente.

5.58 *The subjunctive after superlatives*

The subjunctive is used after the relative pronouns *qui, que, dont* or the adverb *où*
preceded by a superlative or by expressions such as *le premier, le dernier, le seul,
l'unique.* This use of the subjunctive suggests the idea of 'absoluteness' – absolutely the
first, the best, the last, etc.

Type	Examples
superlative – le plus grand	C'est le plus grand camion qui **soit** – *It's the largest lorry in existence*
superlative – le meilleur	C'est la meilleur amie qu'elle **ait** – *She's the best friend that she has*
le premier	C'est la première machine qui **soit** munie d'un moteur à particules – *It's the first machine to be fitted with a particle-drive*
le dernier	C'est la dernière personne du village qui **ait** survécu aux bombardements – *He was the last person in the village to survive the bombing*
le seul	Thomas Pynchon est le seul lauréat dont on ne **sache** presque rien – *Thomas Pynchon is the only prize-winner about whom we know virtually nothing*

Type	Examples
l'unique	Knock est l'unique site irlandais où on **ait vu** de telles choses – *Knock is the only site in Ireland where such things have been seen*

°EXERCICE

Mariez les débuts et les fins des phrases.

Exemple:

Molière est le seul des trois grands dramaturges classiques…

Molière est le seul des trois grands dramaturges classiques **qui n'ait pas été membre de l'Académie Française.**

Molière est le seul des trois grands dramaturges classiques	est la seule qui me donne des frissons quand je l'entends.
Le Général Charles de Gaulle	est la seule grande ville où je puisse vivre.
La Renault Twingo	qui n'ait pas été membre de l'Académie Française.
Paris	était le plus brillant soldat qui ait vécu.
Les peintures de Picasso	est le seul véhicule moderne qui me plaise.
La musique de Jean-Michel Jarre	sont les dernières qui aient vraiment choqué le monde.

5.59 *The subjunctive after a negative antecedent*

The subjunctive is used after the relative pronouns *qui, que, dont* or the adverb *où* preceded by the words *personne, rien, peu* and *aucun* used in a negative sense, or by any other negative antecedent.

Type	Examples
personne	Je ne connais personne qui **puisse** vous donner une réponse – *I don't know anyone who can give you an answer*
rien	Il n'y a rien qui **serve** à soulager une telle détresse – *There is nothing which will serve to relieve such distress* Rien que j'**aie** vu ne compare à cela – *Nothing that I have seen compares to that*
peu	Il y a peu de choses dont on **sache** moins que la question de l'existence de Dieu – *There are few things about which one knows less than the existence of God*

Type	Examples
aucun	Il n'y a aucun terrain plat où un avion **puisse** atterrir – *There's no flat site where an aircraft could land*
pas de	Il n'y a pas de machine qui **soit** mieux adaptée à ces fins – *There is no machine which is better adapted to these ends*

5.60 *The subjunctive in clauses expressing a desired quality*

Take the sentence 'I'm looking for someone who can drive a lorry'. This can mean two things:

1) There is, in fact, someone who can drive a lorry, and I'm looking for him/her.
2) It's possible that there's someone round here who can drive a lorry, and if so, I'd like to find him/her.

The first meaning would translate as: *Je cherche quelqu'un qui **sait** conduire un camion.*

The verb *savoir* is in the indicative mood (*sait*) because a fact is being reported.

The second meaning would translate as: *Je cherche quelqu'un qui **sache** conduire un camion.*

The verb *savoir* is in the subjunctive (*sache*) because this is not a question of fact. It's a question of a **desired quality** in the person sought.

The subjunctive is used after the relative pronouns *qui, que, dont* or the adverb *où* if the sense of the relative clause expresses a **desired quality** in the noun to which the relative pronoun refers.

Relative pronoun	Examples
qui	Je cherche quelqu'un qui **puisse** porter ces paquets – *I'm looking for someone who can carry these packages*
que	Je dois trouver une robe que ma femme **puisse** porter au bal – *I have to find a dress which my wife can wear to the ball*
dont	Il faut trouver une firme dont on **soit** certain – *We need to find a firm that's trustworthy*
où	Nous voulons trouver un appartement où il n'y **ait** pas de voisins chahuteurs – *We want to find a flat where there are no noisy neighbours*

> Emmanuel Garcia: Il me semble qu'un travail personnel des élèves qui **fasse** appel à beaucoup plus de lecture doit être encouragé.
>
> *Libération*

EXERCICE

Choisissez la bonne forme du verbe.

1   Nous avons embauché une secrétaire qui (est/soit) forte en informatique.

2   Nous voulons embaucher un cadre qui (connaisse/connaît) l'Europe.

3   J'ai trouvé une maison qui (correspond/corresponde) exactement à mes souhaits.

4   Mon père cherche un emploi qui (n'est/ne soit) pas si exigeant.

5   Ma mère a un emploi qui lui (convient/convienne) parfaitement.

6

Adverbs

An adverb is a word which makes the sense of a verb, a phrase or a sentence more precise. It may modify a verb by making reference to the time, the place or the manner in which the action is carried out.

Adverbs and adverbial expressions of all types fall into three categories.

Category 1:	Single words	e.g. *alors, là, simplement*
Category 2:	Compound words (those linked by an apostrophe or hyphen)	e.g. *là-haut, avant-hier, d'ailleurs*
Category 3:	Invariable phrases	e.g. *tout à fait, dans la suite, en particulier*

Note: In the tables that follow, these categories will be listed as 1, 2 and 3.

6.1 *Adverbs of time*

Category	Adverb	Meaning
1	actuellement	*at the moment, currently*
	alors	*then, at that time*
	après	*after*
	auparavant	*previously*
	aussitôt	*immediately*
	autrefois	*formerly*
	bientôt	*soon*
	cependant	*meanwhile*
	déjà	*already*
	demain	*tomorrow*
	depuis	*since, for*
	dernièrement	*recently*

Category	Adverb	Meaning
	désormais	*henceforth, from now on*
	dorénavant	*henceforth, from now on*
	encore	*still, yet*
	enfin	*at last, finally*
	hier	*yesterday*
	jamais	*ever*
	longtemps	*a long time, for a long a time*
	lors	*at that time*
	maintenant	*now*
	naguère	*recently*
	parfois	*sometimes*
	puis	*then, next*
	quand	*when*
	quelquefois	*sometimes*
	récemment	*recently*
	sitôt	*immediately*
	soudain	*suddenly*
	soudainement	*suddenly*
	souvent	*often*
	tard	*late*
	tôt	*early*
	toujours	*still, always*
2	après-demain	*the day after tomorrow*
	aujourd'hui	*today*
	l'avant-veille	*the day before the day before*
	d'abord	*at first*
	jusqu'ici	*until now*
	jusqu'alors	*until then*
3	à présent	*now*
	à temps	*in time*
	avec le temps	*in the course of time*
	au fil des années	*as the years go/went by*
	cet après-midi-là	*that afternoon*
	ce jour-là	*(on) that day*

Category	Adverb	Meaning
	ce matin-là	*that morning*
	de bonne heure	*early*
	dès lors	*from then on*
	de temps en temps	*from time to time*
	en retard	*late*
	le lendemain	*the following day*
	le surlendemain	*the day after the following day*
	sur-le-champ	*immediately*
	tantôt... tantôt...	*now... now...; at one moment... at the next...*
	tout de suite	*immediately*
	la veille	*the day before*

6.2 *Position of time adverbs*

Rule	Examples
Adverbs may **not** be placed between subject and verb	*Je vais* **souvent** *à Caen* – I **often** go to Caen NOT *Je* **souvent** *vais à Caen*
Single word time adverbs are placed immediately after the verb in a simple tense	*On part* **demain** – We're leaving **tomorrow** *Nous attendons* **toujours** *le facteur* – We're **still** waiting for the postman
Time adverbs are placed between auxiliary and past participle in a compound tense	*Il est* **enfin** *parti* – He finally left *On avait* **longtemps** *attendu le facteur* – We had waited for the postman **for a long time**
In a compound tense, *aujourd'hui, autrefois, demain, hier, tard* and *tôt* may only be placed before or after the complete verb, never between auxiliary and past participle	*Il est parti* **hier** – He left **yesterday** **Aujourd'hui**, *il est parti* – **Today**, he has left *Elle était sortie* **tôt** – She had gone out **early**
With compound tenses, longer expressions may follow the past participle... or be placed at the beginning of the sentence	*Il est parti* **le lendemain** – He left **the following day** **Le lendemain**, *il est parti* – **The following day**, he left
It is common to place adverbial expressions of time at the beginning of the sentence, as this sets the action in time	**En 1789**, *ce fut la Révolution* – **In 1789**, the Revolution broke out **Ce matin-là**, *tout était calme* – **That morning**, everything was quiet

Rule	Examples
An adverbial expression of time in an initial position may link the sentence to the one that precedes it	*Anatole sort de la cabane, ferme la porte à clé et va se promener sur les falaises. **Deux jours plus tard** un pêcheur trouve son cadavre au pied des rochers* – Anatole went out of the hut, locked the door and went for a walk on the cliffs. **Two days later**, a fisherman found his body on the rocks below.
Since *alors* can mean 'well', it is best to place it within the sentence to give it a temporal sense	*Nous habitions **alors** à Dunkerque* – At that time we were living in Dunkirk
Depuis is used to show that an action commenced earlier continues or continued (see **5.2, 5.10**)	*J'attends cette lettre **depuis** une semaine* – I have been waiting for this letter **for** a week *Alain attendait les résultats de l'examen **depuis** un mois* – Alain had been waiting for his exam results **for** a month

Le jour était loin encore, mais **déjà** une moitié de la nuit, plus claire que la nuit, divisait le ciel.

Colette, *Le Blé en herbe*

EXERCICE

Insérez l'expression adverbiale là où il le faut dans les phrases suivantes. Dans certains cas, il y a plusieurs possibilités.

1 Nous comptons partir. (**demain**)
2 Marianne et les autres étaient sortis. (**la veille**).
3 On a dû attendre une heure, mais Céline est descendue de sa chambre. (**enfin**)
4 On m'a dit que Beauchamp était arrivé. (**la veille au soir**)
5 Il ne se passait rien de spécial. (**ce matin-là**)
6 Les femmes n'avaient pas la possibilité d'aller en fac. (**autrefois**)
7 Paul était sorti à dix heures du matin. Il n'était pas encore rentré. (**douze heures plus tard**)
8 Il est revenu. (**tard**)
9 C'était 1940. On n'avait pas beaucoup à manger. (**alors**)
10 On a attendu l'arrivée du nouveau prêtre. (**longtemps**)

6.3   *Adverbs of place*

Category	Adverb	Meaning
1	ailleurs	*elsewhere*
	dedans	*inside*
	dehors	*outside*
	derrière	*behind*
	dessous	*underneath*
	dessus	*above*
	devant	*in front*
	ici	*here*
	là	*there*
	loin	*far*
	où	*where*
	partout	*everywhere*
	y	*there*
2	au-delà	*beyond*
	là-bas	*over there*
	là-dedans	*inside*
	là-dessous	*underneath*
	là-dessus	*above*
	par-dessus	*over*
3	à gauche	*on the left*
	à droite	*on the right*
	autre part	*elsewhere*
	çà et là	*here and there*
	côte à côte	*side by side*
	d'un côté... de l'autre côté	*on the one side... on the other side*
	de toutes parts	*on all sides*
	en amont	*upstream*
	en arrière	*backwards*
	en aval	*downstream*
	en avant	*forwards*
	en bas	*below, downstairs*
	en dehors	*outside*

Category	Adverb	Meaning
	en haut	*above, upstairs*
	n'importe où	*anywhere*
	par ci, par là	*here and there*
	par dessus	*over and above*
	par devant	*in the front*
	quelque part	*somewhere*
	tout droit	straight on

6.4   *Use of adverbs of place*

Rule	Examples
Adverbs of place are usually placed close to their verb	*Il y a **partout** des exemples de miracles naturels* – There are examples of natural miracles **everywhere**
If the adverb is stressed, it occurs at the beginning or the end	***Là-bas** on voit se dresser de vieux moulins* – **Over there** one can see the outlines of old windmills *Il y a un petit café **là-bas*** – There's a little café **over there**
Ici, là, ailleurs and *partout* may not stand between auxiliary and past participle	*Mon oncle avait voyagé **partout*** – My uncle had travelled **everywhere** *Elle n'a pas trouvé ce qu'elle cherchait, donc elle est allée **ailleurs*** – She didn't find what she was looking for, so she went **elsewhere**
Où may be used as a relative pronoun of place or time (see **4.27**)	*Je l'ai rencontrée dans la ville **où** j'habite* – I met her in the town in **which/where** I live *Le jour **où** il est parti, j'ai pleuré à chaudes larmes* – The day **that** he left, I wept buckets
Par-dessus contains the idea of 'on top of'	*Mets un pull **par-dessus** ta chemise* – Put a pullover on **over** your shirt ***Par-dessus** le marché, il est parti sans rien dire* – **On top of** all that, he left without saying anything

Elle… voulut s'enfuir pour ne pas être remarquée par les autres femmes qui s'enveloppaient de riches fourrures. Loisel la retenait:

– Attends donc. Tu vas attraper froid **dehors**. Je vais appeler un fiacre.

Guy de Maupassant, *La Parure*

[Luc Alphand – champion de ski] – Pendant que le sang vous bat les tempes, lui, il file en souplesse. Fluide et aérien, il effleure la poudre d'un sillage léger. «A l'entraînement, on ne va jamais **tout droit**…»

Le Nouvel Observateur

6.5 *Adverbs of quantity*

Category	Adverb	Meaning
1	assez	*enough*
	autant	*as many/as much*
	beaucoup	*much, many*
	bien (des)	*much, many*
	combien	*how much/how many*
	davantage	*more*
	encore	*some more*
	force	*many*
	moins	*less*
	peu	*little*
	plus	*more*
	que…!	*what a lot of…!*
	si	*so*
	tant	*so much*
	tout	*entirely, quite*
	trop	*too much, too many*
	un peu	*a few, a little*
3	la plupart de	*the majority of*
	la plus grande partie de	*most of*

6.6 *Use of adverbs of quantity*

Rule	Examples
Adverbs of quantity used with the infinitive are always placed before the infinitive	*Je ne veux pas **trop** travailler* – I don't want to work **too** much
Assez is regularly used with adjectives and adverbs. It precedes them	*Mon frère est **assez** grand* – My brother is **fairly** tall *Les réfugiés étaient **assez** bien nourris* – The refugees were **fairly** well nourished
In simple tenses, *assez* follows the verb. In compound tenses, it is placed between auxiliary and past participle	*Je ne pense pas que mon fils dorme **assez** la nuit* – I don't think that my son sleeps **enough** at night *J'ai décidé que j'avais **assez** travaillé* – I decided that I'd worked **enough**
Assez de means 'enough (of)'	*Vous avez **assez d'argent** pour y aller?* – Have you got **enough** money to go there?
Beaucoup is normally followed by *de*	***Beaucoup de** jeunes s'entendent bien avec leurs parents* – **Many** young people get along well with their parents
Bien is usually followed by *des*	***Bien des habitants** se sont enfuis devant l'éruption volcanique* – **Many inhabitants**… cf. *Beaucoup **des** habitants* = Many **of the** inhabitants…
Before a noun, *combien* requires *de*	***Combien de** Français ont une résidence secondaire?* – **How many** French people have a second home? ***Combien de** temps faudra-t-il?* – **How long** will it take? (lit. How much time…?)
Davantage can only modify verbs. Unlike *plus*, it cannot have *de* or *que* after it. *davantage* often occurs at the end of its phrase	*Mon grand-père doit avoir quatre-vingt ans ou **davantage*** – My grandfather must be eighty or **more** *Alain est très doué, mais sa sœur l'est encore **davantage*** – Alain is very intelligent but his sister is even **more so**
La plupart des or *la majorité des* is used with countable nouns	***La plupart des** professeurs en ont assez des chahuteurs* – **The majority of teachers** are fed up with disruptive pupils
La plus grande partie de is used with mass nouns	*Après les inondations, **la plus grande partie de** la farine était inutilisable* – After the floods, **most of** the flour was unusable
Plus is followed by *de* if a quantity is envisaged	*Il y avait **plus de** dix agents dans la salle* – There were **more than** ten policemen in the room

Rule	Examples
Plus que is used for a true comparative	*Il produit **plus que** les autres* – He produces **more than** the others
Autant and *tant* may be used in comparatives, *autant* for **positives** and *tant* for **negatives**	*Il apprécie la musique **autant** que moi* – He likes music **as much** as I do *Elle n'apprécie pas la musique **tant** que moi* – She doesn't like music **as much** as I do
With *autant* and *tant* used as adverbs of quantity, the same distinction applies	*Croyez-vous qu'il y ait ici **autant de** gens qu'on le dit?* – Do you think that there are **as many** people here as they say? *Je ne crois pas qu'il y ait ici **tant de** gens qu'on le dit* – I don't think that there are **as many** people here as they say
Tant may be equivalent to 'because... so' or 'because... so many'	*Il a dû s'arrêter, **tant** il était fatigué* – He had to stop, because he was **so** tired *La firme a fait faillite, **tant** elle avait de dettes* – The firm went bankrupt, because it had **so many** debts
Tout (quite, completely, entirely) is invariable, except before a feminine adjective beginning with a consonant or *h* aspirate. It then becomes *toute*	*En sortant du tunnel, les rescapés étaient **tout** noirs* – When they came out of the tunnel, the escapees were **completely** black *À la fin de la journée, Marie était **toute** fatiguée* – At the end of the day, Marie was **completely** worn out
Trop may modify an adjective or a verb	*Il est **trop** petit pour être pompier* – He's too small to be a firefighter *Nous avons **trop** donné à cet ingrat* – We gave **too much** to this ingrate
Before a noun, *trop* requires *de*	*Il y a toujours **trop de** travail à faire!* – There's always **too much** work to do!

6.7 Adverbs of manner

Many adverbs of manner are formed by adding *-ment* to the feminine form of the adjective, but there are other forms as well.

Rule	Examples
The adverb is usually formed by adding *-ment* to the feminine of the adjective	*sportif → sportive → sportive**ment*** *facile → facile → facile**ment*** *généreux → généreuse → généreuse**ment***
For adjectives ending in *-i*, use the masculine form to create the adverb	*vrai → vrai**ment*** *poli → poli**ment*** Exception: *gai → **gaiement** or **gaîment***

Rule	Examples
Some adjectives ending in *-e* take an accute accent before the ending	*aveugle* → *aveugl**ément*** *commode* → *commod**ément*** *conforme* → *conform**ément*** *énorme* → *énorm**ément*** *immense* → *immens**ément*** *opiniâtre* → *opiniâtr**ément***
Some adjectives change the mute *-e* of the feminine into an *-é* before the ending	*commun* → *commune* → *commun**ément*** *confus* → *confuse* → *confus**ément*** *exprès* → *expresse* → *express**ément*** *importun* → *importune* → *importun**ément*** *obscur* → *obscure* → *obscur**ément*** *précis* → *précise* → *précis**ément*** *profond* → *profonde* → *profond**ément*** *profus* → *profuse* → *profus**ément***
Adjectives ending in *-ant* change to *-amment*	*constant* → *const**amment*** *abondant* → *abond**amment***
Adjectives ending in *-ent* change to *-emment*	*apparent* → *appar**emment*** *prudent* → *prud**emment*** Exception: *lent* → **lentement** *présent* → **présentement** *véhément* → **véhémentement** (rare)
Some adverbs ending in *-u* require a circumflex on the *-u* in the adverb. **NB** The masculine form is modified, not the feminine	*assidu* → *assid**ûment*** *congru* → *congr**ûment*** *continu* → *contin**ûment*** *cru* → *cr**ûment*** *dû* → *d**ûment*** *nu* → *n**ûment***
The following have irregular *-ment* formations	*bref* → **brièvement** *gentil* → **gentiment** *impuni* → **impunément** *traître* → **traîtreusement**
The following adjectives have related but irregular forms	*bon* → **bien** *mauvais* → **mal** *meilleur* → **mieux** *petit* → **peu** *pire* → **pis**
The following have no modern adjectival form. The adjective existed in Old French	**notamment** – especially **nuitamment** – nightly **précipitamment** – precipitately **sciemment** – knowingly

Victorieusement fui le suicide beau

Tison de gloire, sang par écume, or, tempête!

Stéphane Mallarmé, Plusieurs Sonnets

Faut-il remonter à Alain Gerbaud, évoquer Alain Colas ou simplement rappeler que tout a commencé un jour de juin 1964 à Newport, en Nouvelle Angleterre, quand un jeune officier nommé Eric Tabarly a vengé la France de tous ses Trafalgar? En tout cas depuis trente ans, l'exploit en solitaire est devenu un label **parfaitement** tricolore.

Le Nouvel Observateur

EXERCICES

A Donnez la forme de l'adverbe de manière qui est basée sur les adjectifs suivants.
actif – difficile – malheureux – impoli – aveugle – profond – courant – violent

B Choisissez parmi les adverbes ainsi formés ceux qui conviennent aux phrases suivantes.
1   Jacques Chirac parle _____ l'anglais.
2   Mon mari n'a pas pu assister au concert. _____, il était malade.
3   J'ai toujours du mal à réveiller mon fils – il dort _____.
4   Sans savoir exactement où il allait, Jean continua à pénétrer _____ dans la jungle.
5   Il faut décourager _____ ce genre de conduite.

6.8   *Adjectives for adverbs*

Some adverbial expressions use the adjectival form, not the adverb, especially in set expressions.

jeter **bas** – to throw down	couper **court** – to cut short	parler **fort** – to speak loudly
parler **bas** – to speak softly	s'arrêter **court** – to stop short	parler **haut** – to speak loudly
l'échapper **belle** – to have a narrow escape	marcher **droit** – to walk straight	chanter **juste** – to sing in tune
sentir **bon** – to smell good	travailler **dur** – to work hard	voir **juste** – to understand
tenir **bon** – to hold firm	chanter **faux** – to sing flat	raisonner **juste** – to reason correctly
coûter **cher** – to cost a lot	couper **fin** – to cut thinly	s'arrêter **net** – to stop short
voir **clair** – to see clearly	frapper **fort** – to hit hard	couper **ras** – to cut close

NB *vite* (quickly) is an adverb of manner, although it looks like an adjective.

6.9 *Position of adverbs of manner*

Rule	Examples
In simple tenses, the adverb follows the verb	*C'est **vraiment** nul!* – That's really rubbish! *Sarah travaille **bien**, mais sa sœur travaille **mieux*** – Sarah works **well** but her sister works **better**
In compound tenses, the adverb is usually placed between auxiliary and past participle	*Il avait **immédiatement** acheté la maison* – He had **immediately** bought the house *Il y avait devant lui un pilier et il a **mal** entendu ce qui se passait* – There was a pillar in front of him and so he couldn't hear what was happening
Bien, mal, mieux and *trop* are placed between a verb and any infinitive that they govern	*Il ne faut pas **trop** dire* – We must not say **too much** *Il vaudrait **mieux** rester ici* – It would be **better** to stay here
If the adverb is very long (polysyllabic) it often follows the past participle in a compound tense	*Elle a répondu **inconsciemment*** – She replied **without thinking** (i.e. **unconsciously**)
Adverbs which modify the whole sentence often occur at the beginning or end	***Malheureusement**, il est mort* – **Unfortunately**, he's dead *Il est mort, **malheureusement*** – He's dead, **unfortunately**

Mania a **beaucoup** travaillé – et **très bien** travaillé… Mais… Mania devient **subitement** indolente… elle découvre **constamment** de nouvelles beautés à la terre polonaise…

Eve Curie, *Madame Curie*

Enfin des champions écossais, **spécialement** venus à l'occasion du match France-Écosse du tournoi des Cinq Nations ont effectué une démonstration de lancer de poutre.

Le Nouvel Observateur

EXERCICE

Insérez l'adverbe dans les phrases suivantes.
1. Henri a réagi (**violemment**).
2. On serait tenté de croire que la société va s'écrouler (**facilement**).
3. Hier soir, je me suis amusé (**beaucoup**).
4. Anne est captivée par le charme de ce jeune homme (**complètement**).
5. Je ne cesse d'être étonné par les découvertes de la science (**constamment**).

6.10 *Comparison of adverbs*

Adverbs of manner may be compared in a similar way to that in which the comparatives of adjectives are formed, using *plus* (more) and *moins* (less). The French equivalent of 'as' or 'than' is *que*.

Inferiority	Equality	Superiority
Anne travaille **moins vite que** Paul – *Anne does not work as quickly (as fast) as Paul*	Isabelle travaille **aussi vite que** Paul – *Isabelle works as quickly (as fast) as Paul*	Sandrine travaille **plus vite que** Paul – *Sandrine works more quickly (faster) than Paul*

The following adverbs have irregular comparatives.

Adverb	Comparative
bien – *well*	mieux – *better*
mal – *badly*	pis – *worse* (*only used in set expressions* – plus mal *is more common*)

Je ne sais rien de **plus proprement** breton que ce grand service de mon vieux fermier Guillaume Guerveno que nous célébrâmes un jour d'octobre.

Yves de Boisboissel, *Bretagne, ma mère bien-aimée*

La contradiction ligne-couleurs… Matisse la résoudra et l'on comprend **mieux,** après cette exposition, le sens de l'interjection de Moreau à son élève: «Vous simplifierez la peinture». L'on saisit **mieux** aussi les limites des expositions monographiques, si réussies soient-elles…

Le Point

6.11 *Superlatives of adverbs*

Unlike adjectives, adverbs in their superlative form use only the article *le*.

Examples:

Anne et Isabelle travaille **vite**, mais Sandrine travaille **le plus vite**.

Anne et Isabelle travaille **bien**, mais Sandrine travaille **le mieux**.

6.12 *Adverbs of affirmation*

Category	Adverb	Meaning
1	absolument	*absolutely*
	assurément	*assuredly, certainly*
	aussi	*so*
	bien	*indeed*
	certainement	*certainly*
	certes	*certainly (concessive)*
	exactement	*exactly*
	oui	*yes*
	précisément	*precisely*
	si	*yes*
	soit	*so be it*
	voire	*even*
	volontiers	*willingly*
	vraiment	*really*
2	d'accord	*agreed, OK*
3	en vérité	*in truth*
	pour sûr	*for certain*
	sans doute	*no doubt*

6.13 *Use of adverbs of affirmation*

Rule	Examples
Oui is used to answer a question which does not contain a negative	*Est-ce que les marchandises sont arrivées?* – **Oui** – Have the goods arrived? – **Yes**
Si is used in answer to a question containing a negative	*Philippe n'est pas déjà parti?* – **Si** – Philippe hasn't left already, has he? – **Yes**
Soit confirms a wish or intention. The final *-t* is pronounced	*Vous voulez y aller?* **Soit.** *Mais moi, je ne vais pas vous y accompagner* – You want to go there? **Fine.** But I'm not going with you
Voire reinforces what has been said	*Au dix-neuvième siècle,* **voire** *au début du vingtième, l'écrit occupait la place d'honneur* – In the nineteenth century, **and even** at the beginning of the twentieth, the written word occupied the place of honour

Rule	Examples
Sans doute never quite loses the sense that there is, in fact, some doubt!	*Il n'est pas encore arrivé? Il est **sans doute** en route* – Hasn't he arrived yet? **No doubt** he's on his way

6.14 *Adverbs of doubt*

Category	Adverb	Meaning
1	apparemment	*apparently*
	probablement	*probably*
	vraisemblablement	*probably*
2	peut-être	*perhaps, maybe*
3	sans doute	*no doubt, doubtless*

6.15 *Use of adverbs of doubt*

Rule	Examples
Peut-être may follow the verb (the auxiliary in a compound tense)	*Maman est **peut-être** dans le jardin* – **Perhaps** Mum's in the garden *Elle est **peut-être** sortie* – She has **perhaps** gone out
If *peut-être* stands at the head of the clause or sentence, *que* must be added	***Peut-être que** maman est dans le jardin* – **Perhaps** Mum's in the garden ***Peut-être qu'**elle est sortie* – **Perhaps** she's gone out
An alternative to adding *que* is to invert the verb and its pronoun subject. This is often found in writing	***Peut-être** le roi **était-il** déjà mort* – **Perhaps** the king was already dead ***Peut-être n'avait-il** pas pu s'échapper* – **Perhaps** he had been unable to escape
Inversion takes place if *sans doute* begins the sentence	***Sans doute** les conservateurs **seront-ils** au pouvoir d'ici dix ans* – **No doubt** the Conservatives **will be** in power in ten years' time

C'est **peut-être** l'an prochain qu'elle tombera à ses pieds et qu'elle lui dira des paroles de femme «Phil, ne sois pas méchant…»

Colette, *Le Blé en herbe*

«Dans la splendeur des lis» est un des romans les plus brillants d'Updike, et **peut-être** le plus désenchanté: tout un siècle passe au filtre de son regard triste.

Le Point

EXERCICE DE CONSOLIDATION

Traduisez en français.

1 – *Does that programme start at 7 o'clock?*

– *Yes.*

2 – *Your radio doesn't work, does it?*

– *Yes.*

3 *If you want to leave home, so be it.*

4 *Perhaps the train is late.*

5 *No doubt we shall be able to find a hotel.*

NEGATION

This is the process by which the sense of a sentence is made negative. Negation is often clearly marked by the presence of *ne*, but this is not always the case.

6.16 *Non*   No, not

Rule	Examples
Non is used to negate an entire statement, question or imperative	– *Amsterdam est la capitale des Pays-Bas*
	– ***Non**, c'est faux. C'est La Haye*
	– Amsterdam is the capital of the Netherlands
	– **No**, that's wrong. It's the Hague
	– *Tu vas au cinéma ce soir?*
	– ***Non***
	– Are you going to the cinema tonight?
	– **No**
	– *Viens ici!*
	– ***Non!***
	– Come here!
	– **No!**

Rule	Examples
Non may be used in reported speech after *que*	*Il a dit que **non*** – He said **no** *Elle a répondu que **non*** – She replied **not**
Non may be used after *espérer que*	– *Il va pleuvoir?* – *J'espère que **non*** – Is it going to rain? – I hope **not**
Non may be used to seek another speaker's agreement	*Philippe va être là ce soir, **non**?* – Philippe's going to be there tonight, **isn't he**? *Les vêtements sont chers en France, **non**?* – Clothes are expensive in France, **aren't they**?
Non may be used before phrases to negate their sense	*Sabine habite **non loin de** chez moi* – Sabine lives **not far from** me
Non may be used in place of an entire clause	*Lui veut partir, moi **non*** (= *je ne veux pas partir*) – He wants to leave, I **don't** (want to leave)
Non is often used to replace a clause after the use of *si* (if)	*Je ne sais pas **si** elle veut nous accompagner ou **non*** (= *ou si elle ne veut pas nous accompagner*) – I don't know if she wants to come with us or **not**
Non may replace a clause in a written sentence where spoken French would use *pas*	*Le sommet des ministres du G8 a eu lieu, mais **non** dans les circonstances qu'on aurait souhaitées* (= *ce n'était **pas** dans les circonstances...*) – The summit of G8 ministers took place, but **not** in the circumstances that one would have wished
Non may form half of a two-part contrast with *mais*. It may be reinforced with *pas*	*M. Dufour a acheté cette maison, **non** pas pour y vivre, **mais** pour qu'elle lui serve d'investissement* – M. Dufour bought this house, **not** to live in, but as an investment
A contrast may be made by using a positive infinitive and an infinitive introduced by *non* (*pas*)	Valère: *Il faut manger pour vivre, et **non pas** vivre pour manger* Harpagon: *Il faut vivre pour manger, et **non pas** manger pour vi... Non ce n'est pas cela!* (Molière, *L'Avare*) Valère: We must eat to live and **not** live to eat. Harpagon: We must live to eat and **not** eat to... No that's wrong!
A contrast may be expressed by *non seulement... mais aussi*	***Non seulement** les rebelles ont brûlé l'hôpital, **mais aussi** ils ont tué les médecins* – **Not only** did the rebels burn the hospital, but they **also** killed the doctors
Non may be used before adjectives to negate their sense	*Il avait un album plein de photos **non montées*** – He had an album full of **unmounted** photos

Rule	Examples
In a few rare cases, the *non* is attached to a present participle to form an adjective or adverb	*Malgré les circonstances, il arborait un air* **nonchalant** – Despite the circumstances, he was wearing an **indifferent** air *La gravité du cas* **nonobstant**, *il faut faire la part de l'accusé* – **Notwithstanding** the seriousness of the case, we must make allowances for the accused
A clause expressing cause may be introduced by *non que* (or *ce n'est pas que*). The verb is in the subjunctive	*Mon père a décidé de prendre sa retraite.* **Non** **qu**'*il ne veuille plus travailler, mais il est malade* – My father has decided to retire. **Not that** he doesn't want to work any more, but he's ill.

6.17 *Ne… pas* Not

Rule	Examples
Pas may not stand alone – it must always have a complement to complete its sense	**Pas** *un* – **Not** one **Pas** *du tout* – **Not** at all
Ne… pas is the regular way of negating a verb. In compound tenses, place *pas* after the auxiliary verb. Shorten *ne* to *n'* before a vowel	*Les cyniques* **ne** *croient* **pas** *que ce problème puisse se résoudre* – Cynics don't believe that this problem can be solved *Jusqu'à maintenant, on* **n**'*a* **pas** *été en mesure de le résoudre, c'est vrai* – So far, we haven't been able to solve it, it's true
Ne… pas may **not** be combined with *jamais, plus, point, rien*. But see below, **6.31**, for permissible combinations	*Je n'y irai plus jamais* NOT *Je n'y irai* **pas** *plus jamais* – I'll never go there again
Adverbs such as *heureusement, malheureusement, certainement, seulement, cependant, peut-être* and *même* may be placed between the verb and *pas*	*Les résultats de cette élection n'étaient* **certainement pas** *prévisibles* – The results of this election were **certainly not** predictable *Le pilote n'avait* **cependant pas** *su s'orienter dans les ténèbres* – The pilot had **not**, **however**, been able to get his bearings in the dark
Ne pas usually precedes the infinitive	*Cécile craint de* **ne pas** *réussir* – Cécile is afraid of **not** succeeding
If the infinitive is in the perfect, *ne pas* usually precedes *avoir* or *être* cf. *ne… jamais* (**6.20**)	*J'ai toujours regretté de* **ne pas avoir eu** *l'occasion de visiter l'Australie* – I've always regretted **not having had** the opportunity to visit Australia *Les agents prétendaient* **ne pas être** *arrivés à temps* – The police claimed **not to have arrived** in time

Rule	Examples
Ne and *pas* may frame the auxiliary in written French cf. *ne... jamais* (**6.20**)	*Ce qu'il regrettait, c'est de **n'avoir pas** assez fait pour son père qui mourait* – What he regretted was **not having** done enough for his dying father
Ne and *pas* frame an inverted verb	***N'est-il pas** vrai qu'il ait tout avoué?* – **Isn't it** true that he confessed everything?
Un, une and partitives (*du, de la, de l', des*) become *de* after *pas*	*Il y a du pain? – Non, il n'y **pas de** pain, mais il y a des gâteaux* – Is there any bread? No, there's no bread, but there are some cakes
Pas un(e) means 'not a single (one)'. The verb requires *ne* before it	*Il attendit une réponse. **Pas une** voix **ne** se fit entendre* – He waited for a reply. **Not a single voice was heard** *Les juges l'attendaient. **Pas un ne** parla* – The judges were waiting for him. **Not a single one** spoke
Pas alone may negate (1) a noun, (2) an adjective, (3) an adverbial	(1) *J'ai trouvé tous les couteaux mais **pas les cuillers*** – I've found all the knives **but not the spoons** (2) *Il est lent, mais **pas stupide*** – He's slow, **but not stupid** (3) *Sophie habite à Paris, **pas loin** des Invalides* – Sophie lives in Paris, **not far** from the Invalides
Pas may stand for part of a sentence in which the verb has been omitted, particularly in speech	***Pas vrai!*** (= *Ce n'est **pas** vrai*) – **Not true** (= It's **not true**)
Ne... pas... ne pas: this construction is used with an infinitive to give emphasis (e.g. You can't not... = You must...) or to imply a subtle nuance of meaning	*Vous **ne** pouvez **pas ne pas** nier cette accusation! Ce serait terrible!* – You **can't not** deny this accusation! That would be terrible! (i.e. You must deny this accusation)
Similarly *ne... pas... ne... pas* may give a certain nuance of doubt	*Je **ne** prétends **pas** que ce **ne** soit **pas** vrai* – I'm not saying that it isn't true (but...)
The following are useful idioms involving *pas*	***pas** du tout* – not at all ***pas** mal de* – a lot of ***pas** encore* – not yet ***pas** que je sache* – not that I'm aware of
In spoken French, *ne* is often dropped	*Ben, je sais pas, moi* – Well, **I don't know**, myself

> «Ce **n'**est **pas** nous qu'il a maudits; c'est le roi, **n'**est-ce **pas**… c'est le pape…
> C'est Nogaret…»
>
> Maurice Druon, *Le Roi de fer*
>
> «On **ne** peut **pas** avoir un discours sur l'anti-racisme sans avoir des Arabes à la
> tête du parti, ou sur la pauvreté sans avoir de chômeurs.»
>
> *Le Monde*

EXERCICE

Transformez les phrases suivantes en utilisant **ne**… **pas** avec les éléments **en gras**.

Exemple: Les terroristes **avaient téléphoné** pour prévenir les autorités qu'ils avaient posé
une bombe.

Les terroristes **n'avaient pas téléphoné** pour prévenir les autorités qu'ils avaient
posé une bombe.

1 Nous **avons pu** attendre l'arrivée de Jules pour commencer.
2 Les exclus **peuvent** s'offrir des vacances.
3 Nous avons décidé d'**acheter** la maison que nous avons vue la semaine dernière.
4 J'ai toujours regretté d'**avoir assisté** à cette série de conférences.
5 Dans ce collège-là, les élèves semblent **devoir** être obéissants.

6.18 *Ne… point*   Not

Rule	Examples
Ne… point is used in literary language and regional dialects. It is generally considered to be more emphatic than *ne… pas*	*Philippe n'a **point** réussi à retrouver sa mère* – Philippe had **no** success in locating his mother *Les immigrés croates n'ont **point** d'argent* – The Croat immigrants have **no** money (at all)
Ne… point may only be used if the verb has a complement, i.e. if there is more of the sentence to follow	*Je ne crois **pas**!* NOT *Je ne crois **point**!* – I don't think so! *Je ne crois **point** qu'il puisse le faire* – I **don't** believe that he can do it
When used with an infinitive, *ne point* is used	*Ils ont pris une autre rue pour **ne point** devoir passer devant le commissariat* – They took another street so as **not to** have to pass the police station

> Elles mangeaient d'une manière délicate, en tenant l'écaille sur un mouchoir fin et en avançant la bouche pour **ne point** tacher leurs robes.
>
> Guy de Maupassant, *Mon oncle Jules*

6.19 *Ne... plus*   No longer, no more

Rule	Examples
Plus can never stand alone	*Il n'y va **plus*** – He **no longer** goes there ***Plus** jamais!* – Never **again!**
Ne... plus can mean 'no... longer'	*André **ne** va **plus** au club* – André **no longer** goes to the club *Les autorités **ne** sont **plus** prêtes à supporter ce genre de conduite* – The authorities are **no longer** prepared to tolerate this type of behaviour
In compound tenses, *ne... plus* in this sense frames the auxiliary	*Il **n'**y avait **plus** pensé* – He had stopped thinking about it (i.e. had **no longer** thought about it)
Ne... plus may combine with certain other negatives (see **6.31**)	*Je n'y avais **plus jamais** pensé* – I'd **never** thought about it **again** *De la maison et du garage, il ne restait **plus rien** –* **Nothing** was **left** of the house and garage
Like *pas*, *plus* requires *de* before a noun or noun phrase	*Il n'y a **plus de** lait dans le frigo* – There's **no more** milk in the fridge
Plus un(e) means 'not a single (one)'	*Du gâteau que j'avais préparé, il **ne** restait **plus une** miette* – Of the cake I'd made, **not a single** crumb remained *Les cambrioleurs avaient pris tous les tableaux. Il **n'**en restait **plus un*** – The burglars had taken all the paintings. **Not a single one** remained
Non may combine with *plus* to mean 'neither'	*Je ne vais pas au club ce soir. Moi **non plus*** – I'm not going to the club tonight. **Neither am I**

Il se rassit, désespéré. Sa situation lui paraissait sans issue. La nuit était tout à fait venue, la nuit muette et noire. Il **ne** bougeait **plus**, tressaillant à tous les bruits inconnus…

Guy de Maupassant, L'Aventure de Walter Schnaffs

Un militant de Créteil attrape le micro baladeur et y lance, ironique: «D'entendre ça, ça me rassure. Parce que avec nos réunions de cellules désertiques et nos camarades qui **n'**osent **plus** militer c'est pas tout à fait ce que j'entends et ce que je rencontre».

Le Monde

EXERCICE DE CONSOLIDATION

Le présent (**5.1**) et *ne… plus* (**6.19**). Comment le monde a changé! Expliquez ce qui se passe maintenant.

Exemple: En 1950 on lisait beaucoup de livres.

On **ne** lit **plus** beaucoup de livres. Maintenant il y a la télévision et l'Internet.

1 En 1900 on voyageait à cheval et en carosse.
2 En 1910 on respectait les aristocrates.
3 En 1920 on écoutait beaucoup de jazz.
4 En 1940 on allait souvent au cinéma.
5 En 1960 les collégiens se conduisaient bien.

6.20 *Ne… jamais*   Never

Rule	Examples
Jamais may stand alone	*Tu dois l'épouser!* – You must marry him! *Jamais!* – Never!
Ne… jamais frames the verb in simple tenses, the auxiliary in compound tenses	*Il y des clients qui **ne** paient **jamais** à temps* – There are some customers who never pay on time *Mon grand-père **n'avait** jamais **passé** un examen de conduite* – My grandfather **had never taken** a driving test
Without *ne*, *jamais* means 'ever' in a direct or indirect question	*Vous avez **jamais** été en Espagne?* – Have you **ever** been to Spain *Le juge voulait savoir si l'accusé avait **jamais** volé une auto* – The judge wanted to know if the accused had **ever** stolen a car

Rule	Examples
Jamais in initial position in the sentence does not require inversion of subject and verb, unlike the English 'never'	*Jamais victoire ne fut plus complète* – **Never** was a victory more complete. **NB** (1) *une* is omitted in French; (2) in English, subject and verb are inverted
Jamais may combine with certain other negatives (see **6.31**)	*Il n'avait **jamais rien** vu de pareil* – He had **never** seen **anything** like it

– Et vous avez découvert à quelle ceinture était pendu ce poignard?

– Hélas! Non, répondit d'Artois. J'ai cherché, mais j'ai perdu la trace. Nos belles sont habiles. Je **n'**ai **jamais** couru cerfs* dans mes forêts de Conches qui s'entendissent mieux à brouiller la voie…»

Maurice Druon, *Le Roi de fer*

*courir cerfs = *to hunt stags*

[Jean Carmet] «Des inconnus m'invitaient à leurs fêtes de famille. On m'a même emmené en vacances, des gens que je **n'**avais **jamais** vus»

Le Nouvel Observateur

EXERCICE

Du jamais vu! Complétez les phrases suivantes pour indiquer ce que l'Homme n'a pas été capable de faire… jusqu'à maintenant! Voir la clé (page 255) pour des solutions modèles.

Exemple: Jusqu'à maintenant, les scientifiques…

   Jusqu'à maintenant, les scientifiques **n'**ont **jamais** clôné un être humain.

   1   Jusqu'à maintenant, les astronautes…

   2   Jusqu'à maintenant, les hommes politiques…

   3   Jusqu'à maintenant, les mères…

   4   Jusqu'à maintenant, les hommes…

   5   Jusqu'à maintenant, les ordinateurs…

6.21 *Ne … rien*   Nothing, not anything

Rule	Examples
Rien may stand alone	*Qu'est-ce que tu as acheté? **Rien*** – What did you buy? **Nothing**
In simple tenses, *ne… rien* frames the verb	*On lui pose des questions, mais il **ne** dit **rien*** – People ask him questions but he says **nothing**

Rule	Examples
In compound tenses, *ne… rien* frames the auxiliary (like *ne… pas*)	*Les policiers avaient fouillé le suspect, mais ils **n'avaient rien** trouvé* – The police had searched the suspect but had found **nothing**
If *rien* is the subject of its sentence, the order is *rien ne…*	***Rien ne** va plus!* – No more bets! ***Rien ne** vaut la cuisine lyonnaise* – Nothing is equal to Lyonnais cooking
Rien may combine with certain negatives (see **6.31**)	*Je n'ai **plus rien*** – I've got **nothing left** *Il n'avait **jamais rien** vu de la sorte* – He'd **never** seen **anything** like it
Rien requires *de* before a following adjective. This also applies if the adjective is in the comparative (*plus…, moins…*)	*Il n'y avait **rien d'intéressant** à faire* – There was **nothing interesting** to do ***Rien de plus relaxant** que d'aller à la pêche* – There's **nothing more relaxing** than going fishing
Before an infinitive, the order is *ne rien*	*Estelle avait décidé de **ne rien acheter*** – Estelle had decided **not to buy anything** (i.e to buy **nothing**)
With modal verbs such as *devoir, pouvoir, savoir* and *vouloir* used with an infinitive, *ne… rien* frames the modal, even if it is an infinitive itself	*Je **ne veux rien** faire ce soir* – I don't want to do **anything** this evening *Les autorités se plaignaient de **ne pouvoir rien** faire* – The authorities were complaining of **being unable** to do **anything**
Pas does not normally combine with *rien* but note the following idiom	*Ce **n'est pas rien!*** – It's important! (i.e. It **isn't nothing!**)

> Mon père appela le domestique et lui dit d'aller voir… Quand l'homme revint, il affirma qu'il **n'**avait **rien** vu.
>
> Guy de Maupassant, *Mademoiselle Perle*
>
> [Sur la bourse de Moscou] «Il **ne** se passe **rien**, c'est la journée la plus calme de l'année», a commenté Gary Kinsey, Courtier de la maison Brunswick Warburg.
>
> *Le Monde*

6.22 *Ne... personne* Nobody, no one, not... anybody

Rule	Examples
Personne may stand alone	*Qui est-ce que tu as vu?* **Personne** – Who did you see? **Nobody**
In simple tenses, *ne... personne* frames the verb	*Pauline vient de déménager. Elle **ne** connaît **personne** dans cette rue* – Pauline has just moved house. She does **not** know **anybody** in this street
In compound tenses, *ne... personne* frames both the auxiliary and the past participle auxiliary	*Les policiers avaient cherché partout, mais ils **n'**avaient trouvé **personne*** – The police had searched everywhere but had found **no one**
If *personne* is the subject of its sentence, the order is *personne ne...*	***Personne ne** sait ce qui se passe* – **Nobody** knows what's happening ***Personne n'**a avoué avoir commis le vol* – **Nobody** has admitted to committing the theft
Personne may combine with certain negatives. It will maintain its regular position in relation to the verb (see **6.31**)	*Il n'y a **plus personne*** – There's **nobody left** here *Il n'avait **jamais** vu **personne** sur ce chemin* – He'd **never** seen **anybody** on that road
Used with an adjective *personne* requires *de*	*Il n'y a **personne de qualifié** ici* – There's **nobody qualified** here
Before an infinitive, the order is *ne* + infinitive + *personne*	*On a décidé de **n'interviewer personne*** – We have decided **not to interview anybody**
With modal verbs such as *devoir, pouvoir, savoir* and *vouloir* used with an infinitive, *ne...* precedes the modal, and *personne* follows the infinitive	*Je **ne veux voir personne** ce soir* – I **don't want to see anybody** this evening *Les autorités se plaignaient de **ne pouvoir arrêter personne*** – The authorities were complaining of **being unable** to arrest **anybody**
personne may follow a preposition	*Elle **n'**était accompagné de **personne*** – She **wasn't** accompanied by **anybody**

EXERCICE DE CONSOLIDATION

Répondez aux questions suivantes en utilisant **ne... pas**, **ne... jamais**, **ne... plus**, **ne... rien**, **ne... personne** ou **personne ne...**

Exemple: Vous êtes **jamais** allé en Turquie?

      Non, je **n'**y suis **jamais** allé.

1   Le cambrioleur a été vu de **quelqu'un**?

2   Vous aimez la musique de Berg?

3   Votre sœur va **toujours** à Perros-Guirec faire un cure de thalassothérapie?

4   Les scientifiques ont **jamais** vu **quelque chose** qui puisse les convaincre de l'existence des OVNIs?

5   **Quelqu'un** vous attendait à la gare?

6   Il y a **quelque chose** à manger dans le placard?

6.23 *Ne... guère*   Hardly

Rule	Examples
In simple tenses, *ne... guère* frames the verb	*Moi, je **ne** sais **guère** que dire* – I **hardly** know what to say
In compound tenses, *ne... guère* frames the auxiliary	*Le prisonnier **n'**avait **guère** touché à son repas* – The prisoner had hardly touched his meal

> La Tour, dans le passé, **n'**avait **guère** servi que de corps de garde ou de resserre. C'était Marguerite qui, récemment, avait décidé d'y faire installer des pièces de séjour…
>
>   Maurice Druon, *Le Roi de fer*

6.24 *Ne... aucun*   Not one, not any, none at all

Rule	Examples
Aucun(e) may stand alone, in which case it is a pronoun referring to a previously mentioned noun	*Il y avait des meubles là? – **Aucun*** Was there any furniture there?– **None at all** *Tu as des idées là-dessus? – **Aucune*** Have you got any ideas about it? – **None at all**
Aucun(e) used as an adjective is attached to a noun and requires *ne*	***Aucune** trace **n'**a été trouvée* OR *On **n'**a trouvé **aucune** trace* – **No** trace has been found

Rule	Examples
Aucun may combine with certain other negatives (see **6.31**)	*Je n'achèterai **plus jamais aucun** disque de lui* – I'll **never** buy **another** record of his **again** *Aucune évidence ne s'est jamais produite* – **No** evidence was **ever** produced

6.25 *Nul*   No

Rule	Examples
Ne... nul(le) frames the verb in simple tenses, the auxiliary and the past participle in compound tenses	*Il n'y a **nulle** raison de faire cela* – There is **no** reason to do that *On n'avait trouvé **nulle** façon de le faire* – **No** way to do it had been found
Aucun must be used in place of *nul* if a preposition follows	***Aucun de** ses collègues n'était là* (NOT ***Nul de** ses collègues*) – **None of** his colleagues was there

6.26 *Ne... aucunement, ne... nullement*   Not at all, in no way

Rule	Examples
Ne... aucunement is equivalent to 'not ... in any way'. It is found only in the written language	*L'accusé n'était **aucunement** coupable de ce qui s'était passé* – The accused was **in no way** responsible for what had happened
Ne... nullement is equivalent to 'not at all' and, like *ne... aucunement*, it is found in written language	*Il ne m'a **nullement** dérangé dans mon travail* – He didn't disturb me **at all** when I was working

6.27 *Nulle part*   Nowhere, not anywhere

Rule	Examples
In simple tenses, *ne... nulle part* frames the verb	*Je **ne** trouve **nulle part** les papiers que cherche* – I **can't** find the papers that I'm looking for **anywhere**
In compound tenses, *ne... nulle part* frames the auxiliary and the past participle	*Eliane **n'avait** trouvé **nulle part** une robe qui lui aille* – Eliane had**n't** found a dress to suit her **anywhere**
If combined with other negatives, *nulle part* usually appears last	*Il a disparu dans la nature et on **ne** l'a **plus jamais** revu **nulle part*** – He disappeared into the country and was **never again** seen **anywhere**

6.28 *Ni... ni...*   Neither... nor...

Rule	Examples
A single *ni* may be used to follow *pas*. The verb is preceded by *ne*	*Il n'y a **pas** de farine, **ni** de beurre* – There isn't any flour, there isn't any butter **either** OR..., **nor** is there any butter
If *ni* is repeated, *pas* may not be used. The verb is preceded by *ne*	*Il n'y a **ni** farine **ni** beurre* – There's **neither** flour **nor** butter
Ni... ni... may be used with the joint subjects of the sentence. The verb is preceded by *ne*	***Ni** les blancs **ni** les noirs **ne** sont prêts à accepter ce genre de violence* – **Neither** the blacks **nor** the whites are prepared to accept this type of violence
Ni... ni... may precede infinitives. The verb is preceded by *ne*	*Les enfants **ne** veulent **ni** sortir **ni** s'amuser tranquillement* – The kids **neither** want to go out **nor** to amuse themselves quietly
Ni may be used with a conjoined pair of nouns after *sans*	*Ils étaient partis **sans** argent **ni** vêtements* – They had left **without** money **or** clothes

> La preuve que c'était un fantôme, c'est que, quand il a ouvert la porte, il n'y avait plus rien. **Ni** berger, **ni** fantôme, **ni** RIEN.
>
> Marcel Pagnol, *Le Château de ma mère*

6.29 *Ne* used alone

In dependent clauses:

Rule	Examples
Ne is used in dependent clauses expressing a suggested negative with reference to past time with phrases such as *il y a... que, voilà... que, depuis... que*	*Voilà longtemps que je **ne** l'ai vu* – It's a long time since I've seen him OR I have **not** seen him for a long time *Il y a longtemps qu'elle **ne** nous a écrit* – She has not written to us for a long time
Ne is used with a clause following a comparative adjective	*Philippe est plus grand que je **ne** m'y attendais* – Philippe is bigger than I expected i.e. I was **not** expecting Philippe to be so big
Ne is used after verbs of fearing such as *avoir peur que, craindre que, redouter que*	*On craint que tous les passagers du vol 234 **ne** soient morts* – It is feared that all the passengers on flight 234 are dead *J'ai peur que les autres **ne** soient là* – I'm afraid that the others will be there

Rule	Examples
If *douter, nier* or *désespérer* are used negatively or interrogatively, *ne* is added to the verb of the subordinate clause	*Je **ne doute pas** qu'il **ne** soit riche* – I don't doubt that he's rich ***Niez-vous** que ce **ne** soit vrai?* – Are you denying that it's true?
With verbs which have the sense of 'prevent' or 'avoid', *ne* is added to the verb of the subordinate clause	*Il faut **empêcher** que ces prédictions **ne** se réalisent* – We must **prevent** these predictions from coming true ***Prenez garde** que votre enfant **ne** s'éloigne du jardin* – **Make sure** that your child **doesn't stray** out of the garden
In the written language, *ne* is used after *avant que* (before) and *à moins que* (unless), *il s'en faut que* (far from) and *peu s'en faut que* (almost). In the spoken language, *ne* is often dropped	*Il faut avoir tout fini avant qu'il **n'arrive*** – We must have finished everything before he arrives *On sortira, à moins qu'il **ne** pleuve* – We'll go out unless it rains
Sans que does not normally require *ne*, but if the main clause is negative, *ne* will appear before the verb	***Rien ne** se passe dans son entreprise sans qu'il **n'en** soit informé* – **Nothing** happens in his firm without his being informed of it
If the subordinate clause contains *personne, rien, jamais* or *aucun*, *ne* will apppear before the verb	*André a pris la décision sans que **personne n'en** soit informé* – André took the decision without **anybody** being informed of it
If a sentence has a negative main clause and a negative subordinate clause introduced by *qui* or *que*, the verb in the subordinate clause uses only *ne*	*Il **n'y** a **personne** qui **ne** puisse comprendre cela* – There's **nobody** who **can't** understand that *Il **ne possède pas** un seul disque que je **n'aie** entendu* – He **doesn't own** a single record that I **haven't** heard

In main clauses:

Rule	Examples
With the verbs *pouvoir, savoir, oser, cesser, bouger, pas* is frequently omitted, particularly in the written language	*Je **ne saurais** vous donner une idée de l'importance de ces révélations* – I **couldn't** begin to tell you how important were these revelations *Il **ne pouvait** s'en souvenir* – He **couldn't** remember
In certain fixed expressions and constructions, usually found only in formal written styles	*A Dieu **ne** plaise!* – God forbid! *Si je **ne** me trompe* – If I'm not mistaken *Il **n'a** garde de le perdre* – He'll take care not to lose it *Que **ne** me l'aviez-vous dit?* – **Why** had you **not** told me?

Rule	Examples
With *importer* in certain expressions: *n'importe* – it doesn't matter *n'importe quoi* – anything *n'importe où* – anywhere *n'importe quand* – some time *n'importe lequel* – any one	– *Le PDG n'est pas là.* **N'importe** – The MD isn't there? **It doesn't matter** – *Qu'est-ce que tu veux manger?* – ***N'importe quoi!*** – What do you want to eat? – **Anything!** – *Quand est-ce qu'il faut que je te rende ton livre?* – ***N'importe quand*** – When shall I give you your book back? – **Some time** – *Passez-moi un livre.* **N'importe lequel** *fera l'affaire* – Pass me a book. **Any one** will do

6.30 *Ne... que* Only

Ne... que is not a true negative. It restricts the sense of the sentence, clause or phrase and is equivalent to 'only'.

Rule	Examples
The *que* is placed before the element to be restricted	*Francine* **ne** *boit* **que** *du vin rouge* – Francine drinks **only** red wine
In compound tenses, *ne... que* frames both auxiliary and past participle, and may include other elements	*Céline* **n'a** *mangé* **que** *quelques biscuits* – Céline ate **only** a few biscuits *Olivier* **n'avait** *entendu les nouvelles* **que** *la veille au soir* – Olivier had heard the news **only** the previous evening
Ne... que may be compounded with *pas*, to mean 'not only' – thus, *ne... pas que*	*Il* **n'y** *a* **pas que** *les animaux qui souffrent dans de telles circonstances* – It's **not only** the animals who suffer in such circumstances
If it is the sense of the **verb** which is being restricted, then *ne faire que* must be used	*Je* **ne** *fais* **que** *répéter ce que les autres ont dit* – I'm **only repeating** what the others said

– Donne de l'argent à Joseph pour qu'il aille payer ces huîtres à présent. Il **ne** manquerait plus **que** d'être reconnus par ce mendiant.

Guy de Maupassant, *Mon oncle Jules*

Le tabagisme **n'**a pas **que** des conséquences néfastes sur la santé. Il semble bien qu'il porte aussi atteinte au décor des restaurants.

Paris, Nº 24

6.31 *Combining negatives*

Ne… pas may only combine with *que*.

Examples:

Il **ne** veut **pas** exprimer **que** ses regrets – *He does **not only** want to say that he's sorry.*

Dufour **n**'avait **pas** acheté **que** ce qu'il fallait en ce moment – *Dufour had **not** bought **only** what he needed at that time.*

If negatives are combined they retain the position with regard to infinitives and past participles as outlined above. The usual order of negatives in combination is as follows.

ne	plus	jamais	rien/personne	que	aucun	nulle part

→

Examples:

- Je **ne** vais **plus jamais** faire cela – *I shall **never** do that **again***
- Je **n**'ai **plus rien** trouvé – *I did **not** find **anything else***
- Je **n**'ai **jamais** vu **personne** dans la maison – *I **never** saw **anyone** in the house*
- Je **n**'ai vu **plus personne** – *I saw **no one else***
- Je **n**'ai **plus jamais rien** trouvé de ce genre – *I **never again** found **anything** of that type*
- Je **n**'ai **plus jamais** vu **personne** qui lui ressemble – *I **never again** saw **anybody** who looked like her*
- Je **n**'ai **jamais** trouvé **aucune** trace de son passage – *I **never** found a **single** trace of his passing*

Louis… **n**'entendait **plus rien**, parce qu'il ne faisait que se répéter, dans un grand bourdonnement de sang qui lui bruissait aux oreilles: «Ma fille n'est pas de moi… Ma fille n'est pas de moi…»

Maurice Druon, Le Roi de fer

[Yannick Noah] «On oublie ce que le sport peut vous apporter. Ce **n**'est **plus qu**'une douleur…»

Le Nouvel Observateur

EXERCICE

Complétez les phrases suivantes avec un minimum de **deux** éléments négatifs.

Exemple: On a cherché encore des survivants, mais…

>   On a cherché encore des survivants, mais on n'a trouvé **plus personne**.

1   Duhamel est revenu encore une fois pour revoir ses enfants, mais après cela…

2   J'ai trouvé une fois dans une brocanterie un petit tableau de Derain, mais depuis…

3   J'ai essayé le saut à élastique. Une fois, ça suffit! Je…

4   La plage était déserte. Au loin, j'ai vu un pêcheur, mais à part lui, pendant toute la journée…

5   La police a cherché en vain des indices de ce crime, mais le voleur avait été très habile. On…

EXERCICE DE CONSOLIDATION

Les négatifs. Traduisez en anglais.

1   Hakim habite non loin de la boulangerie où il travaille.

2   Le gouvernement n'était certainement pas au courant de cette affaire.

3   On ne croit plus que la science puisse résoudre tous nos problèmes.

4   Jamais inondation ne fut si dévastatrice.

5   Rien de plus terrible que la mort d'un bien-aimé.

6   Personne n'est prêt à assumer la responsabilité.

7   La femme qu'on avait sortie des décombres n'était guère consciente de ce qui se passait.

8   Je n'avais vu André nulle part.

9   Il n'y avait ni radio ni télévision dans la maison.

10   On voulait jouer au foot, mais on n'avait que dix joueurs.

7

Prepositions

Prepositions serve to indicate the position of one thing in relation to another and to link together expressions within the same sentence.

There are two types, simple and compound. Some simple prepositions such as *à* and *de* are used to form verbal constructions, e.g. *demander* **à** *quelqu'un* **de** *faire quelque chose.*

7.1 Simple prepositions

Preposition	Meaning	Preposition	Meaning
à	*to, at*	excepté	*except*
après	*after*	hors, hormis	*except*
avant	*before (temporal)*	malgré	*despite, in spite of*
avec	*with*	outre	*besides*
chez	*at the house of, among*	par	*by, through*
concernant	*concerning*	parmi	*among*
contre	*against*	pendant	*during*
dans	*in, into*	pour	*for*
de	*of, from*	sans	*without*
depuis	*since*	sauf	*except*
derrière	*behind*	selon	*according to*
dès	*from, by (temporal)*	sous	*undor*
devant	*in front of*	suivant	*according to*
durant	*during, throughout*	sur	*on, onto*
en	*in, into*	touchant	*concerning*
entre	*between*	vers	*towards (place)*
envers	*towards (emotional)*		

> L'aspect **de** la ville, surtout **à** cette époque, augmentait encore l'impression causée **par** la solitude **de** ses alentours. Nul mouvement **dans** les rues…
>
> Prosper Mérimée, *Colomba*
>
> Pour avoir une chambre **dans** un foyer, il est recommandé **d**'en faire la demande **avant** le mois **de** mai, ou **au** plus tard **avant** les vacances d'été.
>
> *L'Étudiant*

EXERCICE

Choisissez dans le tableau à la page 199 une préposition qui puisse compléter le sens des phrases suivantes.

1 Alors, vous voyez là la boulangerie et le café? Eh bien, l'entrée de l'appartement est située _____ les deux.

2 J'ai été très soulagé de revoir Delphine, car elle avait été absente _____ plus de trois heures.

3 _____ le début, j'ai su que ce métier me plairait.

4 Quelle émotion peut-on éprouver _____ un homme de ce genre?

5 Évidemment le directeur était en colère, et il est sorti _____ mot dire.

6 _____ tous les efforts des chirurgiens, on n'a pas pu sauver la vie à cette victime.

7 _____ 1997, Aurélie habite rue d'Anvers.

8 Tous mes amis étaient à la boum, _____ Karen, qui était malade ce jour-là.

9 _____ les tabloïdes, le ministre des affaires étrangères aurait eu une affaire de cœur avec sa secrétaire.

10 _____ dix ans, tous ceux qui se sont battus à la première guerre mondiale seront morts.

7.2 *Compound prepositions and prepositional phrases*

Only a few of these are linked by hyphens. The list is not exhaustive.

Preposition	Meaning	Preposition	Meaning
à cause de	*because of*	à moins de	*unless, without*
à côté de	*beside, next to*	à propos de	*about*
à force de	*by dint of*	à travers	*through*
à l'égard de	*as regards*	au travers de	*through*
à l'exception de	*except*	au-dehors de	*outside*
à l'intention de	*for*	au-delà de	*beyond*

Preposition	Meaning	Preposition	Meaning
au-dessous de	*under, below*	en avant de	*in front of*
au-dessus de	*above*	en dépit de	*despite, in spite of*
au-devant de	*in front of*	faute de	*for want of*
au lieu de	*instead of*	grâce à	*thanks to*
auprès de	*near to, compared with*	jusqu'à	*until, as far as*
au sujet de	*about*	le long de	*along*
autour de	*around*	lors de	*at the time of*
d'après	*according to*	pour ce qui est de	*as regards*
d'avec	*(separated) from*	près de	*near*
de la part de	*on behalf of, from*	quant à	*as for*
en arrière de	*behind*	vis-à-vis de	*opposite to*

La veille de son départ, **au lieu d'**aller à la chasse, Orso proposa une promenade **au bord du** golfe (***by** the bay*).

Prosper Mérimée, *Colomba*

Dans l'un des cinq cents foyers regroupés **au sein de** (*within*) l'UFJT (Union des foyers des jeunes travailleurs)… vous aurez à payer entre 2 300 et 3 000 F par mois.

L'Étudiant

EXERCICE

Choisissez dans le tableau ci-dessus une préposition qui puisse compléter le sens des phrases suivantes.

1 Maria voulait savoir ce qu'il y avait (au-dessus/au-dessous/au delà) des montagnes qui fermaient la vue de la maison.

2 (Au lieu/Auprès/Au dehors) d'aller en prison, il a pu payer une amende.

3 (Grâce à/En dépit d'/Faute d') argent, nous n'avons pas pu aller en vacances.

4 Vous continuez (autour du/jusqu'au/vis-à-vis du) carrefour, et là il faut prendre à gauche.

5 Tous les ministres ont assisté à cette réunion extraordinaire, (en dépit/à l'égard/à l'exception) de M. Lenoir, qui était en Russie à ce moment-là.

6 Tu as bien raté le coup. Ta note est (au-dessous/à l'intention/au travers) de la moyenne.

7 Tout l'après-midi, nous avons marché (à travers/au devant du/le long du) canal, et vers le soir on est arrivés à l'écluse qu'on cherchait.

8 Mon fils a pu assister au cours (faute de/grâce à/auprès de) sa grand'mère qui a payé ses frais.

9 (Lors de/A force de/A propos de) travailler, nous avons pu nous procurer plus de trente mille francs.

10 (En arrière/En avant/Lors de) la Révolution, notre ville n'était qu'un tout petit hameau.

7.3 *Time and place*

Two of the principal uses of prepositions are to express concepts of time and place.

TIME

Many prepositions express a relationship of **time**, though this may not be their exclusive use.

Preposition	Examples
à	Il arrivera **à** deux heures – *He'll arive **at** two o'clock* Nous habitions en Bretagne **à** cette époque-là – *We lived in Brittany **at** that time* Il ne se passe pas grand'chose **à** l'heure actuelle – *There's not much happening **at** present*
après	Philippe était arrivé **après** la fermeture du cabinet – *Philippe had arrived **after** the surgery had closed*
avant	On en discutera **avant** le dîner – *We'll discuss that **before** dinner* En 345 **avant** Jésus Christ – *In 345 **B.C.***
dans	Nous allons partir **dans** dix minutes – *We're going to leave **in** ten minutes (i.e. ten minutes from now) cf. en*
de	Cendrars y habita **de** 1912 à 1914 – *Cendrars lived there **from** 1912 to 1914*
depuis	Je ne l'ai pas vu **depuis** la Saint Sylvestre – *I haven't seen him **since** New Year's Eve* Tu la connais **depuis** longtemps? – *Have you known her long (i.e. **for** a long time)?* *(depuis translates 'for' when an action begun in the past continues into the present)*
dès	**Dès** huit heures, la salle était comble – ***By** eight o'clock the theatre was full*
durant	**Durant** tout l'automne, les pluies ne cessèrent en Inde – ***Throughout** the autumn, the rains never ceased in India (Durant stresses the idea of duration and is more emphatic than pendant = during)* Dix années **durant** elle travailla pour payer ses dettes – ***For** ten **long** years she worked to pay off her debts (Durant may be placed after the noun. This is more often found in the written language)*
en	Nous serons à Paris **en** deux heures – *We'll be in Paris in two hours (i.e. **within** two hours) cf. dans* **En** 1968 il y eut des émeutes dans les rues – ***In** 1968 there were riots in the streets*

Preposition	Examples
entre	Les voleurs avaient pénétré par effraction **entre** minuit et deux heures du matin – *The thieves had broken in **between** midnight and two o'clock*
jusqu'à	On a attendu **jusqu'à** huit heures, et puis on est partis – *We waited **until** eight o'clock and then we left* Les troupes étaient obligés d'y rester **jusqu'à** nouvel ordre – *The troops were compelled to wait there **until** further orders* (jusqu'à nouvel ordre *is a set expression*)
pendant	**Pendant** la nuit, les riverains avaient entendu des bruits étranges – ***During** the night, the locals had heard strange noises* Les voyous sont restés là **pendant** quelques minutes – *The yobs stayed there **for** some minutes* (pendant *translates 'for' in the past*)
pour	Nous allons en Angleterre **pour** deux semaines – *We're going to England **for** two weeks* (pour *translates 'for' in the future*) Le Président de la République est élu pour sept ans – *The French President is elected **for** seven years* (pour *is used for an appointment or engagement for a given length of time*)
vers	**Vers** minuit tout a commencé à se calmer – ***Towards** midnight everything began to quieten down*

Les coups de feu de Montsou avaient retenti jusqu'à Paris en un formidable écho. **Depuis** quatre jours tous les journaux de l'opposition s'indignaient, étalaient en première page des récits atroces…

Émile Zola, *Germinal*

Du 14 juillet **au** 13 août, douze concerts-promenades sont proposées en des lieux chaque fois différents.

Vacances en Pays d'Auge

EXERCICE

Traduisez en français.

1 *After the concert, everybody went home.*
2 *Breakfast will be served from 7 o'clock to 10 o'clock.*
3 *It's very quiet here during the day.*
4 *The shops began to close towards 1 o'clock.*
5 *The delegation will be in Russia for two weeks.*
6 *Wait until Monday.*
7 *I'll be there between midday and 2 o'clock.*
8 *Throughout the winter, the house is empty.*

   9   *The firefighters arrived in less than five minutes.*

   10 *From that moment on, there was no hope.*

PLACE

Many prepositions express a relationship of **place**, though this may not be their exclusive use.

Figurative usage of this type of preposition is very common. The following table shows the use of the more frequent prepositions.

Preposition	Examples
à	Les Latour habitent actuellement **à** Paris – *The Latour family are currently living **in** Paris* (à *is used with the names of villages, towns and cities*) Moi, je préférerais habiter **à** la campagne – *Personally, I'd prefer to live **in** the country*
à côté de	Le cinéma est **à côté de** la banque – *The cinema's **beside** the bank* A côté des mafiosi, lui, c'est un escroc à la petite semaine – ***Compared with** the mafiosi, he's a small-time crook* (*This usage is figurative*)
après	Les diplomates étrangers sont entrés **après** l'ambassadeur – *The foreign diplomats came in **after** (i.e. **behind**) the ambassador*
à travers, au travers de	La petite fille a passé **à travers** le bois – *The little girl went **through** the wood* La balle a passé **au travers de** la porte – *The bullet went **clean through** the door* (au travers de *suggests 'despite any obstacle'*)
au-delà de	On ne voyait rien **au delà du** capot, tant le brouillard était épais – *We couldn't see anything **beyond** the bonnet, the fog was so thick*
chez	Ces événements se seraient produits **chez** un ministre conservateur – *These events are alleged to have taken place **at the home** of a Conservative minister* Cela a moins d'importance **chez** les Français – *That is less important **to** the French*
dans	Une fois **dans** la voiture, Richard s'est décrispé – *Once **inside** the car, Richard relaxed* (**NB** dans *is more definite than* en *and requires the definite article. cf.* Il est arrivé en voiture – *He came **by** car*)
de	Ma cousine vient de rentrer **de** France – *My cousin has just returned **from** France* (**NB** *not* de la France – *the article before the names of feminine countries is dropped after* de *when it means 'from'*) On a reçu des nouvelles **du** Japon – *News has been received from Japan* (**NB** de + le *becomes* du *with the names of masculine countries*)
depuis (… jusqu'à)	Les inondations s'étendent **depuis** le Rhin **jusqu'à** l'Elbe – *The floods stretch **from** the Rhine **to** the Elbe*
derrière	La petite hutte était située **derrière** l'immeuble – *The little hut was **behind** the block of flats*
devant	La voiture noire était en stationnement **devant** la mairie – *The black car was parked **in front of** the town hall* Le prisonnier a comparu **devant** le tribunal local – *The prisoner appeared **before** the local court. cf.* avant = before (temporal)

Preposition	Examples
devant *(cont)*	**Devant** ces faits, le gouvernement a dû céder – ***Faced with*** *these facts, the government had to give in (The usage is figurative, i.e. Finding themselves **in front of** these facts…)*
entre	Le village se trouve **entre** la rivière et les montagnes – *The village is situated **between** the river and the mountains*
	Les deux jeunes gens sont tombés **entre** les mains de guérillas afghans – *The two young people fell **into** the hands of Afghan guerillas*
	Il a fallu choisir **entre** une Renault et une Peugeot – *We had to choose **between** a Renault and a Peugeot (The usage is figurative)*
par	Nous avons passé **par** la cuisine – *We went **through** the kitchen*

Dans la plaine rase, **sous** la nuit sans étoiles, d'une obscurité et d'une épaisseur d'encre, un homme suivait seul la grande route **de** Marchiennes **à** Montsou…

Émile Zola, *Germinal*

A voir: la fête du cheval **à** Cambremer les 13 et 14 août. Concours de percherons, de maniabilité et d'attelage…

Vacances en Pays d'Auge

EXERCICES

A Écrivez une description de cette maison, en utilisant des adverbes de lieu et des prépositions. Voir la clé (page 258) pour une solution modèle.

Exemple: Le salon est **en face de** la salle à manger. Dans le salon il y a un canapé qui est situé **entre** deux fauteuils…

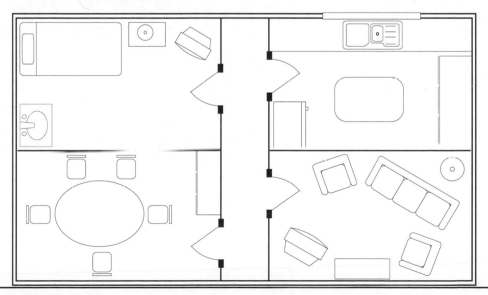

B Traduisez en anglais.

1 A côté de Nice, Marseille est peu attirante.

2 Est-il possible de faire le choix entre un mari et ses enfants?

3 Devant les forces rassemblées de l'OTAN, le dictateur a dû céder.

4 Cette agglomération hideuse s'étend maintenant depuis les montagnes jusqu'au littoral.

5 Les politiciens ne voient rien qui se situe au delà de leur mandat.

7.4 *Agents and instruments:* avec, à, de *and* par

Rule	Examples
The **instrument** of an action may be expressed using *avec*	*La jeune fille avait été tuée avec un couteau* – The girl had been killed **with** a knife
Some expressions with *coup* take *à*, some take *de*	*On avait repoussé les loups à coups de pierre* – The wolves had been beaten off **by** throwing stones *Le policier a fendu la porte d'un coup de hache* – The policeman split the door **with** a stroke of the axe
'The wherewithal' is translated by *de quoi*	*Les refugiés Kosovars n'ont pas de quoi vivre* – The refugees from Kosovo have **nothing** to eat (i.e. don't have **the wherewithal** to eat)
The agent of a passive verb is introduced by *par*. This element would be the subject in an active version of the sentence	*Deux ingénieurs ont été tués par l'explosion* – Two engineers were killed **by** the explosion, (i.e. *L'explosion a tué deux ingénieurs*)
The agent of a passive verb is expressed by *de* if the agent is emotionally involved in the action	*Céline est aimée de tout le monde* – Céline is loved **by** everybody *Il était détesté de tout un chacun* – He was hated **by** all and sundry
De is used following verbs which express such ideas as: cover, fill, surround, follow, accompany, clothe, stain	*Tout le paysage était recouvert de neige* – The whole countryside was covered **with** snow *Salvain est entré, suivi de son fils* – Salvain came in, followed **by** his son *Les maisons étaient entourées d'eau* – The houses were surrounded **by** water

Comme elle [Emma] fut longtemps avant de trouver son étui, son père s'impatienta; elle ne répondit rien, mais, tout en cousant, elle se piquait les doigts, qu'elle portait ensuite à sa bouche pour les sucer. Charles fut surpris **de** la blancheur de ses ongles.

Gustave Flaubert, *Madame Bovary*

Des centaines de cheminots, de manœuvres ont été brûlés **par** l'explosion des premières machines à vapeur.

Brigitte Friang in *Le Figaro*

EXERCICES

A Insérez dans les phrases suivantes la préposition qui s'impose.

1   Deux pompiers ont été brûlés _____ les flammes.

2   Mère Thérèse était adorée _____ tout le monde.

3   Mon père a terrassé le cambrioleur ____ un coup de poing.

4   Toute la cuisine était pleine _____ boue.

5   Le directeur de la banque avait été rattaché _____ une corde.

B Complétez les phrases suivantes avec une expression qui convient.

1   Le maire est sorti, suivi…

2   La table était couverte…

3   Les Zoulous avaient été repoussés à coups…

4   Charles fut surpris…

5   Emma était vêtue…

Conjunctions

Conjunctions are invariable words or phrases which serve to link two parts of a sentence, paragraph or text together. Conjunctions may be co-ordinating or subordinating.

8.1 Co-ordinating conjunctions

Co-ordinating conjunctions are often found in **descriptions.**

They link words, phrases, clauses or sentences, and fall into the following categories. Each section linked has equal status in the sentence.

The following conjunctions link together words and expressions which are similar in meaning or which contrast:

Type	Conjunctions	Examples
Linking	*ainsi que* – as well as *alors* – so *aussi bien que* – as well as *bien plus* – even more so *comme* – like *ensuite* – next *et* – and *mais* – but *ni* – nor *non moins que* – no less than *ou* – or *puis* – then	*Tout le cabinet était là, **ainsi que** des hauts fonctionnaires* – All the cabinet was there **as well as** some senior civil servants *Les sauveteurs ont tenté d'atteindre l'avion écrasé, **mais** ils ont été repoussés par la neige* – The rescuers tried to reach the crashed aircraft, **but** they were beaten back by the snow

The following conjunctions explain the reasons for a statement:

Type	Conjunctions	Examples
Cause	*car* – for *effectivement* – in fact, indeed *en effet* – indeed	*On a accusé le fonctionnaire de détournement de fonds. **Effectivement**, il avait volé plusieurs millions* – The civil servant was accused of embezzlement. **Indeed**, he had stolen several million

These conjunctions introduce the result of a previous statement:

Type	Conjunctions	Examples
Consequence	*ainsi* – thus *aussi* – so *c'est pourquoi* – that's why *conséquemment* – consequently *donc* – therefore *en conséquence de quoi* – in consequence of which *par conséquent* – consequently *par suite* – consequently *partant* – hence, consequently	*On n'avait plus confiance en elle, **donc** elle a démissionné* – People no longer had confidence in her, **so** she resigned *La banque a fait faillite, **en conséquence de quoi** plusieurs milliers d'employés ont perdu leur emploi* – The bank went bust, **in consequence of which** thousands of staff lost their jobs

The following conjunction eases the transition between one statement and another:

Type	Conjunctions	Examples
Transition	*or* – now	*Le cambrioleur rentra; **or**, la police l'attendait* – The burglar returned home; **now**, the police were waiting for him

These conjunctions enable one to contrast what is said in one statement with what is said in another:

Type	Conjunctions	Examples
Opposition, restriction	*au contraire* – on the contrary *au moins* – at least *cependant* – however *d'ailleurs* – moreover *mais* – but *néanmoins* – nevertheless *par contre* – on the other hand *pourtant* – however *toutefois* – however	*Le gouvernement peut présenter ses excuses, **mais** cette crise était inévitable* – The government may offer its apologies, **but** this crisis was inevitable

These conjunctions enable one to express a choice of possibilities:

Type	Conjunctions	Examples
Alternatives	*ou* – or *ou... ou...* – either... or... *ou bien* – or else *soit... soit...* – either... or...	*Il y deux possibilités – **soit** on reste, **soit** on part* – There are two possibilities – **either** we stay **or** we leave

The following conjunctions introduce further information:

Type	Conjunctions	Examples
Explanation	*à savoir* – namely *c'est-à-dire* – that is to say	*La politique, **c'est-à-dire**, le pouvoir* – Politics, **that is to say**, power

---

Je croyais connaître admirablement tous les entours de la commune; **mais** passé la ferme de la Saudraie, l'enfant me fit prendre une route où jusqu'alors je ne m'étais jamais aventuré.

André Gide, *La Symphonie pastorale*

Le poids historique et économique de l'Union européenne lui impose d'assumer un rôle politique déterminant tant au service de maintien de la paix et de la stabilité internationale que dans les grandes enceintes économiques et financières. **Mais** la force de l'Union européenne réside aussi dans son modèle social qui doit être préservé.

Tribune pour l'Europe

EXERCICE

Choisissez la conjonction qui convient pour compléter le sens des phrases suivantes.

1 Celui qui avait volé la voiture est entré dans la rue Paradis; _____, cette rue est une impasse, et on a eu vite fait de l'arrêter.

2 Le ministre des affaires étrangères _____ son homologue britannique sont en pourparlers depuis quelques heures, _____, jusqu'ici, sans issue.

3 On a nommé le nouveau chef de la Banque de France, _____ M. André Dutour.

4 Mes parents iront en Irlande _____ en Angleterre. Ça dépendra de la situation politique.

5 Laforge a été déclaré coupable du meurtre de sa fiancée; _____ les preuves ne sont pas tout à fait claires.

8.2 *Subordinating conjunctions*

Subordinating conjunctions are often found in texts of an abstract and ordered nature, e.g. a newspaper leader, an economic forecast, a political speech, an essay, a sermon.

- They serve to link a subordinate clause to the clause on which it depends. They can therefore only link clause to clause. A subordinate clause cannot stand alone.
- Conjunctions marked with an asterisk (*) in the following tables demand a verb in the **subjunctive**.

8.3 *Que*

This conjunction is used very frequently. Whether the indicative or the subjunctive follows it depends on the use.

Use	Examples
Que follows verbs such as *dire, demander, penser, croire*. **NB** *que* must be used in French even where 'that' can be omitted in English	*Mon père m'a dit* **qu'***il faut aller en Fac* – My father told me (**that**) you have to go to university *La police a demandé* **que** *le bâtiment soit évacué* – The police asked **that** the building should be evacuated
Que replaces another conjunction. The use of the indicative or the subjunctive mood of the verb depends on the nature of the conjunction replaced	*Il faut attendre* **que** *la tempête soit passée* – We must wait **until** the storm's passed (*que* replaces *jusqu'à ce que*) **Quand** *on est jeune et* **qu'***on n'a pas de soucis, le monde est très beau* – **When** you're young and (**when**) you don't have any cares, the world is a wonderful place (*que* replaces *quand*)
If *que* replaces *si*, it is always followed by the subjunctive	*Si les socialistes gagnent les législatives, et* **que** *la gauche accède au pouvoir, que se passera-t-il?* – If the socialists win the general election and (**if**) the left gets into power, what will happen?

Topaze: Je vous supplie de ne point faire entendre une voix si pure **qu'**elle rendrait ridicules les pauvres chiffres que nous allons discuter.

Marcel Pagnol, *Topaze*

On croyait **que** cela ne se passait que dans les films noirs américains. Or trois policiers marseillais, deux capitaines et un lieutenant, fort bien notés par leur hiérarchie, viennent d'être mis en examen.

Marianne

8.4 *Other types of subordinating conjunction*

The following conjunctions serve to introduce the reason for a statement:

Type	Conjunctions	Examples
Cause	*c'est que* – it's because *comme* – as *parce que* – because *puisque* – since *vu que* – seeing that	*Elle est sortie* **parce qu***'elle avait besoin d'air* – She went out **because** she needed air **Puisque** *vous insistez, nous accepterons votre version de l'incident* – **Since** you insist, we'll accept your version of the incident

The following conjunctions are used to introduce the reason for an action:

Type	Conjunctions	Examples
Purpose	*afin que** – in order that *de façon/manière à ce que** – in such a way that (see also **5.55**) *de sorte que** – so that *pour que** – in order that	*Je fais des économies* **pour que** *nous* **ayons** *de l'argent* – I'm saving **so that** we shall have some money *Je vais te prêter de l'argent* **de sorte que** *tu puisses aller à Paris* – I'm going to lend you some money **so that** you can get to Paris

The following introduce a result:

Type	Conjunctions	Examples
Consequence	*de sorte que* – with the result that (see also **5.55**) *de façon/manière que* – in such a way that *si bien que* – so that *tellement... que* – to such a degree that	*On a tout dépensé,* **de sorte** *qu'on est fauchés* – We've spent everything, **so** we're broke *Sally a* **tellement** *dansé hier soir qu'elle est tout à fait claquée ce matin* – Sally danced **so much** last night **that** she's shattered this morning

These conjunctions introduce two types of contrast:

Type	Conjunctions	Examples
Concession, opposition	*bien que** – although *quoique** – although *alors que* – whereas *tandis que* – whereas	***Bien qu'****il soit malade, il insiste pour sortir* – **Although** he's ill, he insists on going out *Les veuves peuvent bénéficier des polices d'assurance,* ***tandis que*** *les veufs ne reçoivent pas un sou* – Widows can benefit from insurance policies like these, **whereas** widowers don't receive a penny

These conjunctions enable one to express the conditions under which something might happen:

Type	Conjunctions	Examples
Condition, supposition	*à condition que** – provided that *à moins que** (+ ne)* – unless *au cas où* – if *pourvu que** – provided that *si* – if	***Pourvu qu'****il y ait suffisament de place, tout le monde viendra* – **Provided that** there's enough space, everyone will come *Si nous arrivons à temps, nous pourrons prendre une bière* – **If** we arrive in time, we'll be able to have a beer

These conjunctions situate a statement in time:

Type	Conjunctions	Examples
Time	*alors que* – when *après que* – after *aussitôt que* – as soon as *avant que** – before *depuis que* – since *jusqu'à ce que** – until *lorsque* – when *pendant que* – while *quand* – when	*Nous partirons* ***quand*** *il arrivera; s'il arrive* ***avant que*** *nous soyons prêts, offrez-lui à boire* – We'll go **when** he arrives; if he arrives **before** we're ready, offer him something to drink *Les gardes se tiendront ici,* ***jusqu'à ce que*** *le prince ait accueilli tous les invités* – The guards will stand here **until** the prince has finished welcoming all the guests

These conjunctions introduce comparisons and similarities:

Type	Conjunctions	Examples
Comparison	*ainsi que* – as well as *comme* – like, as *comme si* – as if *de même que* – just like *moins que* – less than *plus que* – more than	*Alain, **de même que** Jacqueline, est plus grand **que** son frère* – Alain, **just like** Jacqueline, is taller than his brother *Dufour était dangereux – **moins que** son frère ne l'était, peut-être, mais dangereux quand même* – Dufour was dangerous – **less** so **than** his brother, perhaps, but dangerous nevertheless

---

Topaze: Tu n'es pas un de ceux qui nourrissent la flamme, mais tu la protèges de tes pauvres mains, et j'ai la rage au cœur de les voir pleines d'engelures **parce que** tu n'as jamais pu te payer ces gants de peau grise fourrée de lapin que tu regardes depuis trois ans dans la vitrine d'un magasin.

Marcel Pagnol, *Topaze*

J: En fin de course, **si** tous ne veulent pas volontiers l'admettre, le choix entre les deux derniers postulants est bien souvent fondé sur quelque chose de subjectif.

L'Étudiant

EXERCICES

A Complétez les phrases suivantes avec la conjonction proposée.

1 On a téléphoné *but* il n'y avait personne.

2 On soupçonnait Lefèvre d'avoir commis ces vols. *Indeed*, il n'avait pas d'alibi.

3 Mon mari a oublié d'aller à la banque. *Consequently*, il n'avait pas d'argent.

4 La vieille Nancy vivait toute seule. *Now*, sa nièce habitait en Nouvelle-Zélande à cette époque-là.

5 La plupart des scientifiques s'enthousiasment pour ce projet. *However*, il y a toujours des sceptiques.

6 On ne peut pas continuer avec ces recherches *because* il n'y a pas suffisamment de fonds.

7 *Although* Josyane veuille se marier, Stéphane ne veut pas renoncer à sa liberté.

8 On sortira demain, *provided that* j'aie fini mon travail.

9 Jeanne a allumé la télé *as soon as* on est rentrés.

10 Hélène a rougi *as if* elle était coupable.

B Complétez les phrases suivantes selon le sens de la conjonction en gras.

1 Le gouvernement doit augmenter le nombre de professeurs dans les lycées **parce que**…

2 Il faudra installer plus de bancs dans la salle polyvalente **pour que**…

3 On ouvrira les portes **aussitôt que**…

4 Tout se passera bien, **à moins que**…

5 On ne paie pas suffisamment les employés, **si bien que**…

6 Cet auteur continue d'écrire, **bien que**…

7 Matthieu a cessé de jouer au foot **depuis que**…

8 Nous viendrons te voir **quand**…

9

The French sentence

9.1 *Basic word order*

In declarative sentences (those sentences that make a statement) the basic order of elements is: **subject** – **verb** – **object**.

S   V   O

André **a reçu** *une lettre*
  S   V   O

Les ministres **ont voté** *le budget*
       S   V   O

Each of these elements may, of course, be qualified or modified in sense by elements attached to them, such as adjectives and adverbs, but the essential order remains:

Le petit André **a reçu** hier *une lettre* importante de son grand'père.

Les ministres d'État **ont voté** à unanimité *le budget* sur les salaires des fonctionnaires.

9.2 *Adverbs*

It is important to keep adverbs and adverbial expressions as close as possible to the verbs that they modify (see **6.2**, **6.4**, **6.6**, **6.9** and **6.15**).

Examples: ... **a reçu** hier
         ... **ont voté** à unanimité

Time expressions may occur at the beginning of the sentence, particularly if this links the sentence to a previous one;

Example: En 1996, cette petite société s'installe dans les Bouches-du-Rhône. **Deux ans plus tard**, on s'implante à Toulouse et à Clermont-Ferrand.

Adverbial expressions of **manner** usually precede those of *place:*

Examples: Elle a passé **en trombe** *par Paris.*
         Les refugiés sont arrivés **sans bagages ni argent** *au centre de la Croix Rouge.*

9.3 *Direct and indirect objects*

Some sentences have both a direct object (DO) and an indirect object (IDO). In this case, the direct object normally precedes the indirect object:

Matthieu a prêté *de l'argent* à son ami.

DO   IDO

If the direct object is longer than the indirect object, however, the order is reversed:

Matthieu a prêté à son ami *l'argent dont il avait besoin.*

IDO   DO

9.4 *The End-weight Principle*

A sentence consists of a number of word groups, as will be seen above. In spoken French it is usually the last word in each group which bears the stress.

Examples: *Matthieu*   a *prêté*   de l'*argent*   à son *ami*

Les ministres d'*État*   ont voté à *unanimité*   le *budget*

sur les *salaires*   des *fonctionnaires*

There are also a number of short words which cannot bear stress. These include:

Articles: *le, la, les, du, des, au, aux*

Subject pronouns: *je, tu, il, on, nous, vous, ils, elles*

Object pronouns: *me, te, se, le, la, les, lui, nous, vous, les, leur*

Demonstrative adjectives: *ce, cet, cette, ces*

Possessive adjectives: *mon, ma, mes, ton, ta, tes, son, sa, ses, notre, nos, votre, vos, leur, leurs*

Adverbs: *ne, y, en*

Prepositions: *à, de, en, par, sur, etc.*

Conjunctions: *et, mais, que, si, etc.*

Now, combining these two facts, we see that short, unstressed words **precede** longer words to which they are attached in the word group.

Examples: Je la connais.

Ce bâtiment imposant

Il en est revenu.

The long, important words – the 'heavy' ones, if you like, are thus at the end of the word group. We can call this the End-weight Principle: the 'heavy' bits go at the end!

The End-weight Principle accounts for the order in sentences such as that quoted above on the reversed order of direct object and indirect object:

Matthieu a prêté à son ami *l'argent dont il avait besoin.*

          IDO   DO

Since, here, the direct object is 'heavier' than the indirect object, it comes at the end of the sentence. Technically, this building up of sentence elements and saving the most important until last is known as *cadence majeure*, or major cadence. Here's another example:

La Grande Bretagne a octroyé
à ses anciennes colonies *le privilège d'être membres du Commonwealth.*

          IDO   DO

9.5 *Triple rhythm*

One of the commonest features in French writing is the occurrence of words, phrases or clauses in threes. This is known as *rythme ternaire*, or **triple rhythm**. It may be combined with *cadence majeure*, so that the last element of the three is the longest:

Foie gras, gibier, fruits de mer, tant de mets que l'on aime à déguster.

  1   2   3

In an article on the life of the actress Simone Signoret, the writer sums her up thus:

Actrice sublime, écrivain étonnament doué, militante capable d'affronter tous les conformismes,

    1   2   3

telle fut Simone Signoret…

9.6 *Double rhythm*

As well as triple rhythm, French writers often use *rythme binaire* or **double rhythm**, that is to say, elements of the sentence occur in pairs. This is particularly useful for expressing **similarity** or **difference.**

SIMILARITY

In one type of *rythme binaire*, the first element is repeated:

Vivez léger, **vivez** organisé. (*advert for software*)

The grammar, here, is also parallel: **command** + **adjective**, and the halves are of roughly equal length. This gives a sense of balance. In an article on weather-forecasting we find:

Un front arrivera en fin de matinée sur le littoral Atlantique… Et le vent, **à combien** et **à quelle altitude**?

The similarity of content is underlined by the parallel construction: *à* + **question word** in each half.

DIFFERENCE

If we use *ou* or *plutôt que*, we introduce elements into the sentence which contrast with each other – they are alternatives. Thus:

… nous réadaptons les cartes selon les demandes de nos clients, **sur ordinateur** ou, tout simplement, **à la main**.

Although the constructions are similar (**preposition** + **noun**), the meanings are opposite.

If we set out some French sentences in a slightly unusual way, we can see how pairs of grammatically similar elements in a sentence can be made to contrast. Here the italicised elements are grammatically similar to the elements in bold, but contrast in meaning.

Il déplore que toutes les propositions formulées ont pour but

de réduire   *la souveraineté*   *nationale*

et **d'accroître**   **les pouvoirs**   **de l'Union européenne.**

Il excelle à décrire des mouvements *apparemment réguliers*

et **en fait chaotiques.**

9.7 *Double rhythm: conclusion*

Rythme binaire involves using pairs of the same part of speech (nouns, verbs, adverbs, etc.) in pairs. Where the **similarity** of meaning is stressed we find:

(1) words of similar or related meaning,

(2) the length of the elements is similar,

(3) grammatical constructions are used in parallel.

Where **contrast** is being stressed, we find that elements (2) and (3) are often common, but in (1) the words have opposite or dissimilar meanings.

Key to exercises

1   *Nouns*

PAGE 11, EXERCICE A

1. plomb

2. chef

3. pied

4. coq

5. sac

6. four

7. détail

8. vin

9. tam-tam

10. nid

PAGE 11, EXERCICE B

1. La princesse

2. Une bavure

3. une bougie

4. une algarade

5. le mot 'déesse'.

6. une grave carence

7. une grille

8. la seconde guerre mondiale

PAGE 12, EXERCICE C

1. Le progr**amme**

2. Le Roy**aume**

3. La redev**ance**

4. le privil**ège**

5. la Te**rre**

6. le part**i**

PAGE 14, EXERCICE A

amie – Juive – boulangère – paysanne – veuve – nièce – fasciste – reine – chamelle – héroïne – actrice – bru – femme – mineure – Allemande – hôtesse – chienne – étrangère

PAGE 14, EXERCICE B

copain – directeur – Parisien – cousin – pâtissier – comte – Espagnol – empereur – idiot – chat – marchand – lion – Suisse – ambassadeur

PAGE 14, EXERCICE DE CONSOLIDATION A

Le Parlement européen des jeunes regroupe des jeunes de quatorze à dix-huit ans, **une** semaine par an. Chacun des douze pays de **la** Communauté envoie **une** délégation de treize élèves de l'enseignement secondaire. L'objectif **du** Parlement européen des jeunes est de mettre au point **un** outil efficace, permettant des échanges d'idées entre les jeunes d'Europe. **Le** programme comporte deux parties: **la** première partie – deux jours en forêt de Fontainebleau vise, au travers d'activités physiques et sportives, à créer des liens entre participants. **La** seconde partie dure cinq jours. Il s'agit d'une simulation **du** Parlement qui a pour objectif de débattre de sujets d'intérêt commun: éducation, environnement, affaires sociales.

PAGE 15, EXERCICE DE CONSOLIDATION B

Masculin: commerce, management, BAC, titre, État, contrôle, marketing, entrepreneur, mois, stage, cours, cycle, établissment, enseignement, service, lecteur

Féminin: gestion, école, année, série, ouverture, science, admission, année, option, finance, vente, ressource, affaire, université, rue, scolarité, alternance, création, reprise, preparation, page

PAGE 17, EXERCICE A

1. la poste

2. un mort

3. Le solde

4. un tour; la Tour

5. la Manche; un vapeur

6. La physique

7. une critique

8. un vase

9. Ma mémoire

10. Une livre

PAGE 17, EXERCICE B

Exemples:

1. *Au café:* Monsieur! Un crème et un thé citron, s'il vous plaît.
   A la boulangerie: Un chou à la crème, s'il vous plaît.

2. Les critiques ont tapé sur le nouveau livre de Françoise Chandernagor.
   Moi, je trouve que cette critique n'est pas bien méritée.

3. Ce livre est assez difficile à lire.
   Que vaut la livre en ce moment?

4. J'ai acheté un placard en kit, mais il n'y avait pas de mode d'emploi dans le carton.
   Les vêtements sombres sont à la mode cette année.

5. Le page a devancé le roi et la reine.
   Vous trouverez la solution à la page 34.

6. Au physique il était très costaud.
   La chimie, ça va, mais la physique, je n'y comprends rien.

7. Les musulmans tiennent au droit du port du voile.
   En été, j'aime bien faire de la voile.

PAGE 18, EXERCICE A

Masculin:	passeport	Monseigneur	chef d'oeuvre	cure-dents	portemanteau
	porte-avions	ver à soie	ouvre-boîtes	pot-de-vin	beau-père
	cache-nez				
Féminin:	basse-cour	demi-bouteille	belle-mère	voiture-restaurant	

PAGE 18, EXERCICE B

abat-*jour*

casse-*noisettes*

chef-*lieu*

contre-*ordre*

demi-*heure*

grand' *mère*

petit-*fils*

vice-*président*

PAGE 20

PAGE 24, EXERCICE A

des camions-citernes	des arrière-plans	des cache-nez
des mini-jupes	des pauses-café	des qu'en dira-t-on?
des faire-part	des coups d'œil	des wagons-lits
des cerfs-volants	des grands-pères	des tasses à thé

PAGE 24, EXERCICE B

une brosse à dents	un chou-fleur
un porte-parapluie	un timbre-poste
une contre-attaque	un non-lieu
une belle-fille	un pare-brise

2 *Articles*

PAGE 26

l'enfant – les riverains – le siècle – les inquiétudes – le bout – l'alternance – les astronomes – le phénomène – l'atmosphère – le consommateur – la couche – les profondeurs – le parachute – le soleil – la lune – les planètes

PAGE 28

1. Passez-moi **le lait et le sucre** s'il vous plaît.

2. Tu as vu **les journaux** ?

3. **Les dauphins et les baleines** deviennent de plus en plus rares.

4. Vous avez visité **le Mexique ou l'Argentin**? – Non, mais j'ai visité **les États-Unis et le Canada**.

5. Vous ne parlez pas **espagnol**? – Non, je ne parle que **le français et l'anglais**.

6. Moi, je trouve que **l'été** est intolérable dans les pays humides.

7. **Le petit Philippe** est le garçon qui a **les cheveux bruns** et les **yeux verts**. Il a eu un accident **la semaine dernière**. Il s'est cassé **le bras**.

8. **Monsieur le maire, messieurs les membres du conseil municipal**, c'est avec grand plaisir que je prends la parole devant cette réunion importante.

9. C'était la liquidation. On vendait tout à des prix fous – Châteauneuf-du-pape, 20 francs **la bouteille**, du fromage à dix francs **la livre**, des fruits à 50 centimes **la pièce**!

10. **Le dimanche** on va voir mes parents d'habitude, mais **dimanche dernier**, c'était **la Saint André**, la fête de mon fils, donc **le matin** on est allés **à l'église**, et **l'après-midi** on est restés **à la maison**.

PAGE 29, EXERCICE A

un âge – un calme – une cage – un choix – une cour – un dialecte – une doctrine – une énigme – un insecte – un intervalle – un manque – un nuage – un ordre – une ombre – un principe – une sphère – un ustensile – une victime

PAGE 29, EXERCICE B

un‿aide – un hall – un héros – un homard – un‿homme – un hoquet – un‿horaire – un‿hôtel – un hublot – un‿igloo – un‿oiseau – un‿uniforme

PAGE 30

1. Qu'est-ce que c'est qu'**un** vélodrome?

2. La vague a heurté la plage avec **une** puissance inattendue.

3. Pour les maçons, il y a **des** sandwichs et **des** thermos de café.

4. Je n'ai pas vu **un** seul épisode de ce feuilleton.

5. Il me faudra **un** litre **de** lait et **une** douzaine **d**'œufs.

PAGE 32, EXERCICE A

  1. = 11
  2. = 3
  3. = 4
  4. = 7
  5. = 1
  6. = 5
  7. = 2
  8. = 8
  9. = 10
10. = 9

PAGE 32, EXERCICE B

1. Mon père est scientifique.

2. Mon arrière grand-père était **un** amiral célèbre.

3. Lui est Français, sa femme est Belge.

4. Quel beau château!

5. Alain Lecronon, député pour le Finistère, a pris la parole.

PAGE 34, EXERCICE A

1. Pour le pique-nique, il faudra **du** jambon, **des** tomates et **des** chips.

2. Il ne faut pas qu'on se fasse **des** soucis à ce sujet.

3. Y a-t-il suffisamment **de** place?

4. Elle n'a vraiment pas **de** patience.

5. Dans cette rue-là, il y a **de** grandes maisons qui appartiennent au Ministre de l'Intérieur.

6. Y a-t-il **d'**autres possibilités?

7. Moi, je n'ai plus **de** papier. Tu peux m'en prêter?

8. Il y a **des** tasses ici, mais je ne pense pas qu'il reste beaucoup **de** café.

PAGE 34, EXERCICE B

«Bon, il nous faudra **du** papier, **des** diskettes, **des** trombones, **des** crayons, **des** bics, **des** enveloppes. Pour les toilettes, **du** papier hygiénique, **du** savon, **des** serviettes en papier…» etc.

PAGE 35, EXERCICE C

1. Si, il y a **du** pain et **du** beurre.

2. Si, j'ai **des** cousins.

3. Si, il restait **des** places.

4. Si, il avait **de l'**argent.

5. Si, on m'a rendu **de la** monnaie.

PAGE 35, EXERCICE DE CONSOLIDATION A

Forme de l'article partitif	Terminaison du nom
de la	pati**ence**
de la	limon**ade**
du	plom**b**
du	ser**vice**
du	from**age**
de la	chapel**ure**
du	pai**n**
de la	far**ine**

PAGE 35, EXERCICE DE CONSOLIDATION B

1. **La** France connaît des difficultés économiques en ce moment.

2. Pendant la guerre du Golfe, les pilotes britanniques ont agi avec **un** courage incroyable.

3. **Les** éléphants sont en voie de disparition.

4. **Le** samedi je reste toujours planté devant la télé à regarder le foot.

5. Vous avez **du** papier? Je veux écrire une lettre.

3 *Adjectives*

PAGE 39, EXERCICE A

mille trois cents – mille neuf cents – trois millions – deux milliards – cinq mille six cent soixante-quinze – quatorze (virgule) sept pour cent – six mille – deux cent trois – mille treize

PAGE 39, EXERCICE B

1. vingt et un

2. quatre-vingts

3. mille soixante-dix

4. cinq mille

5. mille cinq cents

PAGE 39, EXERCICE C

1. Cinq cent soixante dix-sept 2. Mille cinq cent quatre-vingt-quatorze 3. Mille six cent trente-neuf. 4. Cinq cent vingt-deux 5. Six cent soixante-sept 6. Six cent quatre-vingt-quinze 7. Cinq cent un 8. Huit mille cinq cent soixante 9. Quinze mille cinq 10. Cent quarante 11. Trois cent trente-trois 12. Deux mille trois cent quatre.

PAGE 41, EXERCICE A

La Belgique arrive en quatrième place.

La Grèce arrive en troisième place.

L'Italie arrive en cinquième place.

La Danemark arrive en première place.

Le Royaume-Uni arrive en deuxième place.

L'Allemagne arrive en dixième place.

PAGE 41, EXERCICE B

François Premier – Philippe Deux – Louis Treize – Louis Dix-Huit – Élisabeth Première – Georges Six – Édouard Huit

PAGE 41, EXERCICE C

1. **La moitié** des élèves souhaitent avoir des professeurs plus qualifiés.

2. **Le quart** des directeurs d'entreprises ne sont pas satisfaits de la politique gouvernementale.

3. **Le tiers** des commerçants interrogés souhaiteraient avoir deux jours de congé par semaine.

4. **Trois septièmes** des voitures ont des défauts cachés.

5. **Sept dixièmes** des jeunes croient avoir de bons rapports avec leurs parents.

PAGE 44

Exemple:

André Rolin est né le 2 février 1950. **Son** père, Hubert Rolin, est mort en 1987. **Sa** mère Alice Rolin (née Laval) est née en 1931. **Son** frère, Grégoire est avocat. Il a deux sœurs. **Sa** sœur aînée, Huguette (née 1948), est peintre. **Sa** sœur cadette, Cécile (née 1949), est professeur d'art dramatique. **Son** ambition enfantine était d'être acteur. **Ses** livres les plus connus sont: *Voyage autour de mon cœur* (1987), *Un fidèle rapport* (1989), *Va, je ne le hais point* (1994). **Son** ambition actuelle est de gagner le Prix Goncourt.

PAGE 45

1. De **quel** livre est-ce que tu parles?

2. De **quels** calculs est-ce que tu parles?

3. De **quels** résultats est-ce que tu parles?

4. De **quelles** possibilités est-ce que tu parles?

5. De **quel** logiciel est-ce que tu parles?

PAGE 47, EXERCICE A

cette architecture – ces casques – ces ciseaux – cette église – ce hamster – ce journal – cette lampe – ce livre – cette possibilité

PAGE 47, EXERCICE B

1. Les actions de **ce** dictateur ont horrifié le monde.

2. Vous avez vu **cette** nouvelle dans le journal?

3. Passe-moi **cette** chemise, s'il te plaît – non, **cette** chemise-là!

4. **Cet** aéroport détient le record des retards.

5. Lesquelles est-ce que tu préfères – **ces** chaussettes-ci ou **ces** chaussettes-là?

PAGE 49

1. Battez les cartes et distribuez-les. **Chaque** joueur en reçoit sept.

2. **Plusieurs/Quelques** enfants attendaient devant le magasin – cinq ou six, peut-être.

3. Jusque-là, on n'avait reçu **aucune** nouvelle de Jules.

4. **Certaines** femmes pensent que le féminisme a déjà atteint ses buts, mais **d'autres** femmes croient qu'on en est loin de là.

5. **N'importe quel** Français vous dira que la langue anglaise l'emporte sur le français en matière de publicité.

6. **Quelles que** soient vos idées là-dessus, vous feriez mieux de vous taire à ce sujet.

7. Une **telle** idée ne m'était jamais passée par la tête.

8. Ma fille a été horrifiée. Elle portait la **même** robe que sa mère!

PAGE 52, EXERCICE A

1. un camion **hollandais**

2. des citoyens **belges**

3. la langue **allemande**

4. des refugiés **bosniaques**

5. du café **sud-américain**

6. des produits **français**

PAGE 52, EXERCICE B

Jamais chose **pareille** ne s'était produite dans ce **petit** village **tranquille**. Mme Lebec n'avait pas la réputation d'être très **discrète** et elle avait été la **première** à faire courir le bruit dans cette **petite** commune **bretonne**. Ce bruit était certainement **faux**. Danielle était tout à fait **heureuse** et n'avait aucune intention de quitter son mari **ivrogne**. Sa mère avait été la **dernière** à avoir des nouvelles de sa fille **rousse**, et en avait été très **inquiète**.

PAGE 55, IBM… FRANCE

L'insertion **professionnelle** des personnes **handicapées** dans les conditions **ordinaires** de travail est sans doute une disposition **légale**, mais aussi un enjeu **économique** et **social** pour les entreprises.

L'objectif est **clair**. **Toute** personne dans l'entreprise doit pouvoir exercer un métier ou des responsabilités sur le **seul** critère de la compétence. Cela suppose d'acquérir les connaissances et d'apprendre à se servir des outils **exigés** par la fonction.

IBM, entreprise **citoyenne**, mène cette **double** action.

PAGE 56, EXERCICE A

1. L'Amérique du Sud est **moins** grande que l'Amérique du Nord.

2. L'Amérique du Nord est **plus** grande que l'Europe.

3. L'Asie est **plus** grande que l'Afrique.

4. L'Europe est **moins** grande que l'Amérique du Sud.

5. L'Amérique du Nord est **moins** grande que l'Afrique.

PAGE 57, EXERCICE B

Exemples:

Jeanne est plus grande que Céline, mais elle est moins douée qu'elle.

Céline est plus petite que Marc, mais elle est plus douée que lui, et encore plus douée que Jeanne.

PAGE 58, EXERCICE A

le stégosaure	le dinosaure le plus stupide qui ait vécu
la girafe	le plus grand l'animal du monde
le Pacifique	l'océan le plus profond du monde
Pluton	la planète la plus froide du système solaire
Thrust SSC	la voiture la plus rapide du monde
Lockheed SR-71A (Merle)	l'avion le plus rapide du monde
Tomb Raider	le jeu-vidéo le plus vendu du monde
Coca-Cola	la boisson la plus connue du monde
le Prince Abdul Aziz Bin Fahd	le teenager le plus riche du monde
Jeanne Calment (morte 1999)	la plus vieille femme du monde

PAGE 59, EXERCICE B

Exemples:

1. *Titanic* – C'est le film le plus romantique du monde!

2. les Spice Girls – C'est le groupe le plus sexy du monde!

3. le Concours de l'Eurovision – C'est l'émission la moins intéressante du monde!

4. le Mundial – C'est le concours sportif le plus passionnant du monde!

5. une soirée sans télévision – C'est la soirée la plus ennuyeuse du monde!

PAGE 62

1. un petit homme chauve

2. la seule raison légitime

3. des mouvements frénétiques et saccadées

4. une vaste plaine nue

5. le nouveau port breton

6. une grande église élégante

7. une vie irresponsable et dissipée

8. des résultats inattendus et effrayants

9. les forces militaires orientales

10. les deux premiers prix

PAGE 64

1. le mois dernier

2. un ancien juge

3. l'évidence même

4. la seule solution

5. un enfant curieux

6. une pièce propre

7. les rares hameaux

8. certains hommes

9. un pur mensonge

10. une voiture chère

PAGE 65, EXERCICE DE CONSOLIDATION

La porte des îles anglo-normandes

Le port de Saint Quay a trouvé sa compagnie. Émeraude Lines exploite une liaison **quotidienne** avec Jersey. Dix mille passagers en deux mois. Émeraude Lines vient de faire une **belle** percée à Saint-Quay-Portrieux. La compagnie **anglo-normande** a l'habitude du trafic avec les îles **malouines**.

Le **dernier** né des ports **breton**s exprime ainsi sa **pleine** vocation. Ses promoteurs n'ont pas lésiné sur les moyens: 800 000 mètres de roches pour protéger un bassin de 17 hectares **cubes**; 10 pontons pour l'accueil de **quelque** 950 voitures; 700 places de parking pour les automobiles sur 5 hectares de terre-plein et un centre **commercial**.

Émeraude Lines a pris un **bon** départ.

4 *Pronouns*

PAGE 71, EXERCICE A

1. J'ai vu André et Marianne en ville et je **leur** ai demandé de venir à la boum.

2. Je comprends bien l'anglais, mais je ne **le** parle pas très bien.

3. J'ai une nouvelle voisine. Je **la** connais de vue, mais je ne **lui** ai pas encore parlé.

4. Il y a de très beaux rideaux dans le nouveau catalogue, mais je ne vais pas **les** acheter parce qu'ils sont trop chers.

5. J'ai un manuel pour mon ordinateur, mais je ne **le** comprends pas.

PAGE 71, EXERCICE B

1. Oui, je l'aime.

2. Oui, je l'ai acheté.

3. Oui, je la connais.

4. Oui, je vous ai téléphoné.

5. Oui, je vous ai écrit.

PAGE 73, EXERCICE A

1. DO

2. IDO

3. IDO

4. DO

5. IDO

PAGE 73, EXERCICE B

1. L'incendie s'est déclaré dans le hall.

2. Tout le monde s'est rué vers la sortie.

3. Je me suis demandé ce qu'il fallait faire.

4. Ma copine s'est plainte de ce qui se passait.

5. Elle s'est cassé la cheville.

PAGE 76, EXERCICE A

1. Il y avait des sucres d'orge dans cette petite confiserie, et j'**y en** ai acheté pour ma sœur.

2. Le ministre a demandé le dossier, et le fonctionnaire confus **le lui** a remis.

3. Le directeur m'a interrogé sur ce projet et je **lui en** ai donné des détails.

4. Mon frère m'a demandé les photos qui étaient dans le bureau, et je **les lui** ai envoyées.

5. Suzanne m'avait demandé de remettre le livre dans la bibliothèque, donc je **l'y** ai remis.

PAGE 76, EXERCICE B

1. Je **les** *lui* ai remis.

2. Marguerite **l'***y* a vu.

3. Les deux garçons *y* **en** ont trouvé.

4. Le gouvernement *leur* **en** a accordé.

5. Le fonctionnaire qui s'**en** occupait *leur* y a parlé.

PAGE 77

1. Prêtez-le-moi!

2. Passez-le-lui!

3. Donnez-nous-en!

4. Prête-lui-en!

5. Dis-le-leur!

6. Donne-m'en!

PAGE 78

1. On l'a envoyé chercher.

2. On ne peut pas la permettre.

3. Ma tante est venue les voir.

4. Les élèves doivent le finir avant de rentrer à la maison.

5. Le chef les sent brûler dans la casserole.

6. Ma mère les écoute jouer dans le jardin.

7. Nous allons les visiter tous.

8. On l'a regardé partir de Queenstown pour la première et la dernière fois.

9. Mon grand-père ne les laissait jamais écouter la radio le dimanche.

10. Je veux l'apprendre depuis longtemps.

PAGE 80, EXERCICE A

1. Les documents? Je les ai laiss**és** sur la table.

2. Catherine? Je l'ai entend**ue** dans sa chambre.

3. Les enfants? Je les ai v**us** sortir il y a quelques minutes.

4. Les données? Je les ai déjà enregistré**es**.

5. Mes clés? Je les ai oubli**ées** malheureusement.

PAGE 80, EXERCICE B

1. Marie? Oui, je lui ai écrit il y a quelques jours.

2. Les ministres? Oui, on les a interview**és** à la radio.

3. Le téléphone? Oui, je l'ai entendu sonner il y a quelques minutes.

4. Les détails? Je regrette, mais je ne les ai pas encore reçu**s**.

5. Les participants? Oui, on leur avait écrit le mois dernier.

PAGE 82

1. Henri avait apporté son pique nique, mais malheureusement, j'avais oublié **le mien**.

2. Ma mère avait immédiatement accepté de venir, mais Karine n'avait pas pu persuader **la sienne**.

3. J'avais mes documents sur moi, mais Conrad s'est rappelé qu'il avait vu **les siens** sur la table.

4. Voici mes résultats. Où sont **les tiens**?

5. Votre chambre est vraiment trop petite. On va faire la boum dans **la mienne**.

PAGE 83, EXERCICE A

1. Mon grand-père doit avoir une nouvelle canne. **Celle** dont il se servait s'est cassée.

2. Je viens d'acheter des crayons pour mon fils. **Ceux** qu'il avait étaient tout usés.

3. J'ai perdu mes clés. Je ne trouve que **celles** de Céline.

4. Tu peux m'apporter un tourne-vis, chérie? **Celui** que j'utilisais a disparu.

5. Il faut que nous nous achetions un nouvel ordinateur. **Celui** que nous avons actuellement est tout à fait démodé.

PAGE 83, EXERCICE B

1. Nous avons deux téléviseurs – celui **qui** est au coin du salon et celui **que** vous avez vu dans la salle à manger.

2. Les chambres de nos fils sont en haut. Celui **de** Pierre est à gauche et celle **de** Grégoire est à côté de la nôtre.

3. Il y a trois sœurs. Celle **dont** je vous parlais habite juste à côté.

4. Il faut que nous changions tous les fils électriques de la maison. Ceux **qui** y sont actuellement sont gainés de plomb!

5. Tu te trompes. Il y a des jumelles dans la famille. Celle **dont** tu te souviens s'appelle Marie. Celle **qui** habite toujours chez ses parents s'appelle Angéline.

PAGE 86

1. **C'est** à la FNAC qu'il faut chercher les livres dont vous avez besoin.

2. **Ce** doit être Philippe qui a fait cela.

3. **Ce sont** les Français qui ont gagné le Mundial de 1998.

4. **Ce qui** est essentiel, **c'est** d'avoir égard aux besoins d'autrui.

5. **C'est** parce que son père est malade qu'Aline ne peut pas assister au concert.

6. **Ce dont** vous avez besoin, **c'est** d'une perceuse électrique.

7. **Ce** peut certainement être le cas.

8. **Ce que** Madeleine cherche, **c'est** un homme qui soit prêt à lui acheter tout **ce qu'**elle désire.

PAGE 86

1. On dit qu'il est borgne – je n'ai jamais remarqué cela.

2. Cela fait bon de se payer un petit luxe.

3. Il faut noter ceci – cet examen sera difficile.

PAGE 88

1. Le premier chapitre **que** j'ai lu m'a vraiment choqué.

2. Je ne comprenais pas ce **dont** il parlait.

3. On peut voir dans le musée le couteau avec **lequel** il a commis ces terribles meurtres.

4. Ça, c'est le monsieur **dont** la maison a été incendiée la semaine dernière.

5. A l'époque **où** vivait Louis XIV, les aristocrates considéraient la pauvreté comme normale.

6. Il faut avoir un passeport, faute de **quoi** vous ne pourrez pas franchir la frontière.

7. Les mesures **qu'**a proposées le Sénat doivent être approuvées.

8. L'agent avec **qui** j'ai parlé m'a dit qu'il faudrait me présenter au commissariat de police.

PAGE 89, EXERCICE A

1. De **quoi** est-ce que vous parlez?

2. Il faut que tu prennes *trois* de ces disques. **Lesquels** veux-tu?

3. **Qui** va assister au concert – Éliane et Georges?

4. Il faut porter de bonnes chaussures pour faire cette promenade – **lesquelles** vas-tu porter?

5. **Qu'**est-ce qu'ils comptent faire? Du patinage?

PAGE 89, EXERCICE B

1. On est restés sur le pont sous **lequel** passaient des bateaux-mouches.

2. Mondeville est un grand centre commercial **où** j'aime bien faire des achats.

3. La banque centrale européenne pourra prendre des décisions sur **lesquelles** nous n'aurons pas d'influence.

4. Le monétarisme est une politique économique à **laquelle** je n'attache pas beaucoup d'importance.

5. Jacques Chirac et Tony Blair ont assisté à un congrès devant **lequel** chacun a prononcé un discours important.

PAGE 91

1. N'importe qui peut apprendre à jouer d'un instrument de musique.

2. Certains croient que l'an 2001 est le vrai début du nouveau millénium.

3. Il faut avoir égard aux sentiments d'autrui.

4. Deux hommes se tenaient à la porte. Chacun était armé.

5. Simenon écrivit plus de 100 livres. J'en ai quelques-uns.

6. L'un des policiers est sorti. L'autre est resté assis en face de moi.

7. Vite! Passe-moi un torchon ou quelque chose. N'importe quoi fera l'affaire.

8. Après l'accident d'avion, on a retrouvé plusieurs survivants. Plusieurs étaient très émaciés. Aucun n'avait mangé depuis plusieurs jours.

5 *Verbs*

PAGE 95

j'épelle, nous épelons – je rappelle, nous rappelons – j'achève, nous achevons – je mène, nous menons – j'espère, nous espérons – je partage, nous partageons – j'essaye/essaie, nous essayons – j'emploie, nous employons – je nettoie, nous nettoyons

PAGE 96, EXERCICE A

1. = 8

2. = 4

3. = 3

4. = 1

5. = 7

6. = 6

PAGE 96, EXERCICE B

1. De gros embouteillages se **forment** au niveau de Bourges.

2. Les disques se **vendent** à des prix plus bas chez Leclerc.

3. Le samedi, les cours **finissent** à midi.

4. J'**achète** rarement des bouquins de ce genre-là.

5. En général, c'est moi qui **nettoie** ma chambre.

6. Les politiciens européens s'**inquiètent** de la situation en Albanie.

7. J'**essaye/essaie** de persuader mes copains de m'accompagner en vacances.

8. Nos enfants s'**ennuient** à Noël.

PAGE 98, EXERCICE A

Infinitif	tu	vous	nous
donner	donne	donnez	donnons
offrir	offre	offrez	offrons
aller	va	allez	allons
faire	fais	faites	faisons
avoir	aie	ayez	ayons
être	sois	soyez	soyons
boire	bois	buvez	buvons
manger	mange	mangez	mangeons

PAGE 99, EXERCICE B

Exemples:

1. Donnez-moi les raisons de cela.

2. Offrons de l'argenterie à Suzanne comme cadeau de noces.

3. Allez tout droit.

4. Allons au ciné ce soir.

5. N'ayez pas peur!

6. Sois sage, mon petit.

7. Soyez prudents.

8. Bois ton lait, Pierre.

9. Buvons à la santé de notre hôte.

10. Allez! Mangez!

PAGE 100

j'obtiendrai – je consommerai – je comprendrai – j'annoncerai – je reverrai – je servirai – je convaincrai – j'enrichirai

PAGE 101, EXERCICE A

1. Nous **assisterons** au concert de Phil Collins au Stade National.

2. Les élections cantonales **auront** lieu le mois prochain.

3. S'il neige, mes parents ne **pourront** pas venir passer Noël chez nous.

4. Si je suis recalé à mon examen, je **devrai** me représenter l'année prochaine.

5. Si les sans-abri ne reçoivent pas de secours, plusieurs centaines **mourront** cet hiver.

PAGE 101, EXERCICE B

Bretagne, Pays-de-Loire, Basse Normandie. – Le ciel gris et pluvieux de l'Ouest breton s'**étendra** aux Pays-de-Loire l'après-midi. Il ne **fera** pas plus de 11 degrés.

Limousin, Auvergne, Rhône-Alpes. – La grisaille humide présente du Masif Central au Lyonnais le matin **laissera** passer des embellies ensoleillées l'après-midi.

Languedoc-Roussillon, Provence-Alpes Côte d'Azur, Corse. – Le soleil **parviendra** à s'imposer une bonne partie de la journée, alors qu'il **sera** davantage contesté l'après-midi en Languedoc-Roussillon. Il **fera** de 19 à 22 degrés.

PAGE 104, EXERCICE A

1. Grégoire et Stéphane ont dit qu'ils **pourraient** louer une voiture à la gare.

2. Le Président a dit que la France n'**hésiterait** pas à exercer son droit de véto contre ces mesures.

3. Le PDG a dit que la société Perma **enregistrerait** de meilleurs bénéfices l'année prochaine.

4. L'ambassadeur a dit que les terroristes ne **jouiraient** pas de la protection diplomatique.

5. Le directeur a dit que les élèves **devraient** s'accoutumer aux nouveaux programmes scolaires.

PAGE 104, EXERCICE B

Si on abattait tous les arbres du Brésil,	le monde risquerait de mourir de manque d'oxygène.
Si l'État percevait plus d'impôts,	il pourrait payer des asiles pour les SDF.
Si on brûlait moins de combustibles fossiles,	la pollution atmosphérique se réduirait.
Si les jeunes regardaient moins la télé,	peut-être qu'ils auraient plus de connaissances générales.
Si les politiciens étaient sincères,	on aurait plus confiance en eux.

PAGE 104, EXERCICE C

1. Les fonctionnaires responsables de cette bavure **seraient** actuellement absents de Paris.

2. Les autorités **souhaiteraient** mettre fin à ces abus.

3. M. Normand **posséderait** plus de 2 millions de francs.

4. Les jeunes beurs **craindraient** de sortir le soir dans les rues de la cité.

5. Les actions **risqueraient** de perdre 50% de leur valeur cette semaine.

PAGE 107, EXERCICE A

A Kerveillant, on n'**était** pas loin de l'école. Même pas trois quarts d'heure à naviguer dans la boue des chemins creux, puis les nids de poule et on **arrivait** au bourg tout de suite, malgré les vents et les pluies. L'hiver, on **partait** de nuit, on **revenait** de nuit. Nous **étions**, dit mon père, les enfants de la chandelle de résine. A midi, on **mangeait** un quignon ou une soupe dans une maison amie ou parente pour les plus chanceux, dans l'encoignure d'une porte pour les autres et c'**était** fait. Mon père étant l'aîné, ma grand'mère lui **confiait** quelques sous avec lesquels il se **chargeait** de nourrir les autres.

PAGE 108, EXERCICE B

1. Si le tribunal *libérait* ce jeune voyou, il s'**agirait** d'une vendetta entre les familles.

2. Si Florence n'*allait* pas en Fac, qu'est-ce qu'elle **ferait**?

3. Si on ne *trouvait* pas les informations dans cette encyclopédie, il **faudrait** chercher ailleurs.

4. Nous ne **pourrions** pas aller à Paris si la voiture n'*était* pas réparée à temps.

5. Bon nombre de gens **risqueraient** de perdre de l'argent si les valeurs *continuaient* à baisser.

PAGE 110

Petit à petit les arbres se **desserrèrent** et un vent pur et frais **vint** à la rencontre du promeneur. Des fraisiers posaient dans l'herbe plus pâle leurs fines fleurs nacrées comme de minuscules anémones. Enfin les arbres **lâchèrent** prise et il ne **resta** plus qu'une prairie où s'inscrivaient, éclatantes et royales, les gentianes bleues… Hans s'**assit** quelques instants sur l'herbe courte, recevant avec bonheur la coulée tiède du soleil sur son visage. Une cloche **sonna**, venue de très loin. Puis un ronronnement **rompit** la paix de ce haut lieu. Il **crut** apercevoir l'éclat métallique d'un avion, au même instant, des prairies **monta** le tintement de grelots de brebis prises de panique. Tout **redevint** calme, aérien; invisibles, les oiseaux **reprirent** leurs chants.

PAGE 112

1. André a **cru** que Cécile allait le retrouver à la gare, mais quand il y est arrivé, elle n'était pas là.

2. Anne a été obligée de s'absenter. Elle a **dû** retourner chez elle.

3. C'est dimanche et je m'ennuie. J'ai **lu** tous les journaux et il n'y a rien à faire.

4. Martin va manquer le train. Il a **mis** son passeport quelque part, et il ne le trouve plus.

5. J'ai **vécu** dans plusieurs grandes villes, mais c'est Paris qui me plaît le plus.

PAGE 114, EXERCICE A

1. J'ai cherché les diskettes et je les ai trouvé**es** dans le tiroir du bureau.

2. J'ai préparé les papiers qu'il fallait et je les ai passé**s** à mon chef.

3. Combien de billets a-t-on vendu**s**?

4. Quels livres de Giscard d'Estaing avez-vous lu**s**?

5. Que pensez-vous des photos que l'on a vu**es** aujourd'hui?

PAGE 115, EXERCICE B

1. Pierre a lu la lettre qu'il avait reçu**e** ce matin-là.

2. L'ambassadeur n'a pas pu accepter les conditions que lui ont offert**es** les autorités.

3. Combien de logiciels a-t-il acheté**s**?

4. Quelles raisons a-t-on donné**es**?

5. Mes enfants m'avaient demandé les nouveaux vidéos Disney et je les leur ai acheté**s**.

PAGE 115, EXERCICE C

1. Non.

2. Oui: Les nouvelles que je lui avais **données** n'étaient pas très agréables.

3. Non.

4. Oui: Combien de femmes avait-on **attendues** pour le congrès sur le féminisme au 21e siècle?

5. Oui: Quels livres avez-vous **lus** sur les philosophes comme Foucault?

6. Oui: Michel m'avait demandé mes notes sur l'Ancien Régime et je les lui ai **prêtées**.

PAGE 116, EXERCICE A

1. Sylvie s'est lev**é**e et est sortie.

2. La même situation s'est reprodui**te** deux mois plus tard.

3. Les deux armées se sont attaqu**ées**.

4. Les dames se sont mis**es** en route.

5. La directrice s'est montr**é**e favorable au projet.

La prononciation change dans les phrases 2 et 4.

PAGE 117, EXERCICE B

1. Les deux leaders se sont rencontr**és** au congrès de Paris.

2. Le président et le chancelier allemand se sont parlé au sujet des dettes du Tiers-Monde.

3. Charlotte et Guy se sont envoyé des e-mail.

4. Juliette s'est décid**é**e à abandonner ses études à l'Université de Strasbourg.

5. Anne et Fatima se sont pris**es** de bec.

6. Après la boum, les gars ne se sont lev**és** qu'à midi.

7. «J'étais si fatiguée que je me suis couchée de très bonne heure hier soir», a dit Sylvie.

8. Lorsque Mme Martin s'est retrouvée dans sa ville natale, elle ne s'attendait pas à y rencontrer son ancien fiancé.

PAGE 118

1. Non, ils sont déjà arrivés.

2. Non, il est déjà parti.

3. Non, elles sont déjà descendues dans les rues.

4. Non, il est déjà passé.

5. Non, ils y sont déjà retournés.

6. Non, elles sont déjà venues me voir.

PAGE 119, EXERCICE DE CONSOLIDATION

Cet incident **s'est produit** sur les locaux d'une boîte à Lille. Quand Roger Constant et sa femme y **sont arrivés** vers neuf heures du soir, ils **ont vu** un groupe de jeunes devant la porte d'entrée. L'un des jeunes **a demandé** du feu à M. Constant. Celui-ci lui en **a offert**, et à ce moment-là, l'un des autres garçons **a saisi** le sac à main de Mme Constant et **a essayé** de s'enfuir. M. Constant **a** vite **réagi** et **a fait** un croche-pied au petit voyou, qui **est tombé** sur le trottoir, se fracturant le bras. Les autres, voyant le sort de leur ami, **se sont sauvés** à toutes jambes. Le manager de la boîte **a appelé** la police. Trop choqués pour jouir d'une soirée en boîte, M. et Mme Constant **sont rentrés** à la maison.

PAGE 121

Exemple:

Selon l'agent de police, l'incident **s'était produit** sur les locaux du Perroquet Bleu, rue de la Huchette. M. et Mme Constant y **étaient arrivés** vers 2100 heures. Ils **avaient vu** un groupe de quatre ou cinq jeunes devant la porte d'entrée. Un des jeunes **avait demandé** du feu à M. Constant. Celui-ci lui en **avait offert**. Un des autres suspects **avait saisi** le sac à main de Mme Constant et **avait essayé** de s'enfuir. M. Constant **avait** vite **réagi** et **avait fait** un croche-pied au suspect qui **était tombé** sur le trottoir, se fracturant le bras. Les autres **s'étaient sauvés**. Le manager de la boîte, M. Martin, **avait appelé** la police. Trop choqués pour jouir d'une soirée en boîte, M. et Mme Constant **étaient rentrés** à la maison.

PAGE 122, EXERCICE A

1. Quand M. Dufour **aura fini** le manuscrit de son livre, il le remettra à la maison d'édition.

2. Quand nous **aurons lu** toutes les lettres de candidature, nous dresserons une liste des candidats à interviewer.

3. Quand le groupe **aura enregistré** une douzaine de chansons, ils mixeront le tout dans leur studio suisse.

4. Quand j'**aurai fini** de faire cette traduction, je la faxerai au client.

5. Quand j'**aurai réussi** mon examen de conduite, mon père m'achètera une voiture.

PAGE 123, EXERCICE B

Exemples:

a Quand je serai rentré, je téléphonerai à mon père.

b Quand j'aurai visité les monuments principaux, je reviendrai.

c Quand j'aurai fini ce livre, je vous le donnerai.

d Quand j'aurai payé ma voiture, je m'achèterai un nouvel ordinateur.

e Quand j'aurai eu des nouvelles de Jean, je vous écrirai.

PAGE 124, EXERCICE A

1. Si les ministres *avaient discuté* de tous ces dossiers, ils **auraient compris** les problèmes qui en résulteraient.

2. Si ma copine *avait eu* le temps, elle **serait allée** en ville.

3. Nous **aurions pu** nous baigner, s'il *avait fait* plus chaud.

4. Je me **serais acheté** une nouvelle maison, si j'*avais gagné* le Gros Lot.

5. Si Nicolas *avait passé* plus de temps en Grèce, il **aurait visité** Delphi.

PAGE 124, EXERCICE B

1. Si Alexander Fleming n'avait pas découvert la pénicilline, on n'aurait pas eu d'antibiotiques.

2. Si Saddam Hussein n'avait pas enhavi le Koweit, la guerre du Golfe n'aurait pas eu lieu.

3. Si Neil Armstrong n'avait jamais aluni, on aurait eu moins d'informations sur la structure de la lune.

4. Si l'Internet n'avait pas été inventé, on n'aurait pas pu se mailer.

5. Si Nelson Mandela n'avait pas été libéré, l'Afrique du Sud ne se serait pas libérée.

6. Si John F. Kennedy n'avait pas été assassiné, l'histoire des États-Unis aurait été tout à fait différente.

7. Si Mère Thérèse n'était pas née, les pauvres de Calcutta n'auraient pas eu de patronne.

8. Si l'URSS ne s'était pas effondrée, la Guerre Froide se serait poursuivie.

PAGE 126, EXERCICE A

ayant – buvant – disant – devant – étant – faisant – mettant – pouvant – prenant – sachant – voulant

PAGE 126, EXERCICE B

1. = 12

2. = 5

3. = 4

4. = 3

5. = 6

6. = 7

PAGE 127, EXERCICE C

1. Travailler avec Eleanor était très difficile.

2. Elle avait perdu son poste en se querellant avec son patron.

3. Ayant commis cette erreur, elle a cherché un autre poste.

4. En feuilletant le journal, elle a vu une annonce.

5. Elle a téléphoné au bureau, tout en faisant une petite prière.

6. En parlant au manager, elle s'est rendu compte qu'elle le connaissait.

PAGE 128, EXERCICE A

1. les maltraitées

2. les hôspitalisés

3. les abusés

4. les blessés

5. un élu

6. un inconnu

7. les nouveaux-morts

8. les retraitées

PAGE 129, EXERCICE B

1. Arrivés

2. Perché

3. Montés

4. Couchée

5. Assises

PAGE 131, EXERCICE A

1. Plusieurs milliers d'hectares de bananiers **ont été** détruits par l'ouragan.

2. Si ce vent terrible avait continué de souffler, les maisons des habitants des îles **auraient été** emportées.

3. Des centaines de travailleurs **auront été** dépourvus de travail.

4. Les autorités **avaient été** averties de l'approche du cyclone.

5. Les survivants **sont** actuellement **logés** dans des écoles et des collèges.

PAGE 131, EXERCICE B

1. Les villages limitrophes de la frontière **ont été attaqués** par des troupes ennemies.

2. Les nouveaux ordinateurs **seront installés** la semaine prochaine par la société Computo-Tec.

3. La ligne ferroviaire **a été fermée** par les agents de police en raison d'une alerte à la bombe.

4. Les défenseurs de la ville **ont été entourés** par l'armée ennemie.

5. Selon les rapports qu'on a reçus, toute cette région **aurait été dévastée** par l'ouragan.

PAGE 131, EXERCICE C

La nouvelle ligne R.E.R. a été ouverte.

Une nouvelle centrale nucléaire a été installée.

L'impôt sur le revenu a été augmenté.

Les cadeaux ont été distribués aux pauvres.

Une croissance économique a été prévue.

PAGE 132

1. On a exclu l'Irak des pourparlers internationaux.

2. La musique traditionnelle anglaise s'entend rarement à la radio aujourd'hui.

3. Un nouveau ministre se verra nommé cet après-midi.

4. On a distribué tous les documents aux avocats ce matin.

5. On a déjà abordé votre cas.

PAGE 134, EXERCICE A

C = Corrosif

Xi = Irritant

O = Comburant

N = Dangereux pour l'environnement

T – T+ = Toxique –Très Toxique

E = Explosif

F – F+ = Inflammable – Très inflammable

Xn = Nocif

PAGE 135, EXERCICE B

1. Les jeunes de la ville pensent **pouvoir** trouver les moyens de faire construire un terrain de jeux.

2. Les habitants de la cité de Sarcelles disent **avoir** moins peur de sortir qu'il y a quelques années.

3. Je ne crois pas **pouvoir** convaincre le directeur de ce qui s'est passé.

PAGE 141

1. Après avoir fait du racket dans ce petit quartier, les gangsters se sont installés en plein Paris.

2. Après avoir pris des photos de la voiture écrasée, les paperazzi se sont enfuis.

3. Après s'être installé à son compte, Pierre a fait fortune.

4. Après être tombée dans l'escalier, ma mère a décidé d'acheter un petit bungalow.

5. Après s'être installés dans les locaux du journal, les manifestants ont invité le rédacteur à venir leur parler de la situation.

PAGE 141, EXERCICE DE CONSOLIDATION

1. Past historic

2. Future

3. Future perfect

4. Pluperfect; conditional perfect

5. Imperfect

6. Perfect; conditional

7. Present

8. Past anterior; past historic

9. Passé surcomposé (double perfect); perfect

10. Present; future

PAGE 142

1. There will certainly be repercussions.

2. It is essential that parents should accept their responsibility in school matters.

3. It is high time that this problem should be resolved.

4. It's best to say nothing about it.

5. It will be a question of managing as best one can.

PAGE 145

il aille, nous allions – il attende, nous attendions – il ait, nous ayons – il conduise, nous conduisions – il doive, nous devions – il dise, nous disions – il soit, nous soyons – il fasse, nous fassions – il finisse, nous finissions – il mette, nous mettions – il suive, nous suivions – il vienne, nous venions – il vive, nous vivions

PAGE 149

a Verbes réguliers

1. Ma mère ne veut pas que nos parents **arrivent** la veille des noces.

2. Mon fils n'aime pas que sa petite sœur **se couche** à la même heure que lui.

3. Je préférerais que mes enfants ne **regardent** pas les émisions de télévision qui contiennent des éléments violents.

4. Céline préfère que sa fille **finisse** toutes ses corvées de ménage avant de sortir.

5. A vrai dire, je souhaiterais que vous me **rendiez** tout ce que je vous ai prêté.

b Verbes irréguliers

1. Je déteste qu'on me **fasse** attendre chez le dentiste.

2. Vous préféreriez que votre fils n'**ait** pas accès à l'Internet.

3. Les teenagers n'aiment pas que les parents **soient** là quand on fait une boum.

4. On est ravi que la princesse de Monaco **puisse** assister au festival de Cannes.

5. Nous nous étonnons que la municipalité ne **soit** pas en mesure de résoudre ce problème.

PAGE 150

1. Je crains que nous (ne) **soyons** en retard.

2. Je crains que le train (ne) **soit** déjà parti.

3. Je crains qu'on (n') **ait** perdu nos bagages.

4. Je crains que Jean ne nous **attende** pas.

5. Je crains que les autorités (ne) **puissent** refuser notre demande.

PAGE 151

1. L'ONU a exigé que le général rebelle **rende** tous ses armes aux forces de l'ordre…

2. Les autorités ont interdit que les camions transportant la nourriture aux rescapés de la violence **franchissent** la frontière.

3. La dévastation a empêché que les œuvres de secours se poursuivent.

4. Les soldats envahisseurs ont commandé que les villageois **quittent** la région en moins de 24 heures.

5. Le commandant des forces a permis que chaque individu **prenne** un seul sac et de la nourriture.

PAGE 151, EXERCICE A

1. Tu t'attends à ce que ton amie **vienne** aujourd'hui?

2. Je compte qu'il y **ait** assez de place pour tout le monde.

3. Vous avez l'intention que le groupe **parte** à midi?

4. Je ne m'attends pas à ce que ce poste vous **soit** proposé.

5. Frédéric ne compte pas que ses collègues **sachent** les détails de cette affaire.

PAGE 151, EXERCICE B

1. Je m'attends à ce que tout le monde soit là.

2. On s'attend à ce que vous assistiez à la réunion.

3. Je compte qu'on sache la vérité.

4. Tu t'attends à ce que Stéphane vienne?

5. Je compte qu'il vienne en tout cas.

PAGE 153

1. Moi, je doute que les résultats soient tout à fait prévisibles.

2. Moi, je doute que Laforgue ait de grandes ambitions.

3. Moi, je doute qu'il puisse renouveler la politique du parti.

4. Moi, je doute qu'il veuille devenir député à l'Assemblée Nationale.

5. Moi, je doute qu'il sache manipuler les idéologues du parti.

PAGE 155

1. **Il n'est pas vrai** que la population de la France soit plus importante que celle de l'Angleterre.

2. **Il faut** que nous fassions de notre mieux pour réduire la pollution.

3. **Il est peu probable** que le conflit entre les protestants et les catholiques en Irlande du Nord puisse se résoudre de notre vivant.

4. Je n'en suis pas sûr, mais **il semble** que le directeur soit sur le point de démissionner.

5. **Il est impossible** qu'un homme puisse survivre sur Vénus à cause de la gravité et de l'atmosphère d'acide sulphurique.

PAGE 157, EXERCICE A

1. Je dois verser de l'argent à mon compte en banque **pour que** je ne sois pas à découvert.

2. Il faut que tout soit prêt **avant que** le maire et les notables arrivent.

3. L'ONU continuera avec ses pourparlers **jusqu'à ce qu'**on en arrive à une solution.

4. **Supposons que** tous les conseillers démissionnent. Qui va les remplacer?

5. Nous pourrons payer le loyer de salle polyvalente, **à condition que** toutes les places soient vendues ce soir.

PAGE 158, EXERCICE B

1. Dans les institutions éducatives, il y a de plus en plus de paperasse, bien qu'il n'y ait pas suffisamment de fonds pour qu'on achète les livres dont on a besoin.

2. Bien que les CD ne coûtent presque rien à produire, les fabricants font un énorme bénéfice avec eux.

3. Bien qu'on ait à soutenir un fils en fac, on ne bénéficie d'aucune baisse d'impôts.

4. En Europe on mange bien, bien que le Tiers-Monde meure de faim.

5. Bien que la littérature du dix-neuvième siècle se lise de moins en moins, elle a encore un message à transmettre à notre société de consommation.

PAGE 160

1. Si vous pouvez venir – et si vous **voulez** venir – téléphonez-moi le plus tôt possible.

2. Si André arrive à temps à Londres et qu'il **ait** réservé une chambre d'hôtel, il n'aura pas de problèmes.

3. Moi, je vais réserver deux places pour le congrès, de sorte que nous **puissions** être sûrs de pouvoir y assister.

4. Tout s'est bien déroulé, de telle manière que nous **avons** décidé de répéter cette expérience.

5. Les portes du théâtre sont barrées de manière à ce que les fans ne **puissent** pas entrer pendant le concert.

PAGE 162

1. Whether young people are aware of it or not, the danger represented by the abuse of drugs and alcohol is always there.

2. Whatever you think of Angélique, she is really well-intentioned.

3. Wherever you find abuses of this type, you must report them to the police.

4. Whatever reasons may have been given, the one thing that is certain is that people are trying to hide this affair.

5. The fact that the director denied everything is not at all important.

6. Whatever allegations may have been made against her, Margot is innocent.

PAGE 163

Molière est le seul des trois grands dramaturges classiques	qui n'ait pas été membre de l'Académie Française.
Le Général Charles de Gaulle	était le plus brillant soldat qui ait vécu.
La Renault Twingo	est le seul véhicule moderne qui me plaise.
Paris	est la seule grande ville où je puisse vivre.
Les peintures de Picasso	sont les dernières qui aient vraiment choqué le monde.
La musique de Jean-Michel Jarre	est la seule qui me donne des frissons quand je l'entends.

PAGE 165

1. Nous avons embauché une secrétaire qui **est** forte en informatique.

2. Nous voulons embaucher un cadre qui **connaisse** l'Europe.

3. J'ai trouvé une maison qui **correspond** exactement à mes souhaits.

4. Mon père cherche un emploi qui ne **soit** pas si exigeant.

5. Ma mère a un emploi qui lui **convient** parfaitement.

6   Adverbs

PAGE 170

Alternative positions for the adverbial expresions are given in brackets.

1. (**Demain**) Nous comptons partir (**demain**).

2. (**La veille,**) Marianne et les autres étaient sortis (**la veille**).

3. On a dû attendre une heure, mais (**enfin**) Céline est **enfin** descendue de sa chambre.

4. On m'a dit que Beauchamp était arrivé **la veille au soir**.

5. (**Ce matin-là,**) Il ne se passait rien de spécial (**ce matin-là**),

6. (**Autrefois**) Les femmes n'avaient pas la possibilité d'aller en fac (**autrefois**).

7. Paul était sorti à dix heures du matin. (**Douze heures plus tard**) Il n'était pas encore rentré (**douze heures plus tard**).

8. Il est revenu **tard**.

9. C'était 1940. On n'avait pas **alors** beaucoup à manger.

10. On a **longtemps** attendu l'arrivée du nouveau prêtre.

PAGE 177, EXERCICE A

activement – difficilement – malheureusement – impoliment – aveuglément – profondément – couramment – violemment

PAGE 177, EXERCICE B

1. Jacques Chirac parle **couramment** l'anglais.

2. Mon mari n'a pas pu assister au concert. **Malheureusement**, il était malade.

3. J'ai toujours du mal à réveiller mon fils – il dort **profondément**.

4. Sans savoir exactement où il allait, Jean continua à pénétrer **aveuglément** dans la jungle.

5. Il faut décourager **activement** ce genre de conduite.

PAGE 178

1. Henri a **violemment** réagi OR Henri a réagi **violemment**.

2. On serait **facilement** tenté de croire que la société va s'écrouler.

3. Hier soir, je me suis **beaucoup** amusé.

4. Anne est **complètement** captivée par le charme de ce jeune homme.

5. Je ne cesse d'être **constamment** étonné par les découvertes de la science.

PAGE 182, EXERCICE DE CONSOLIDATION

1. – Cette émission commence à 7 heures?
   – Oui.

2. – Ta radio ne marche pas, non?
   – Si.

3. Si tu veux quitter le foyer familial, soit.

4. Peut-être que le train est en retard/Le train est peut-être en retard.

5. Sans doute pourrons-nous trouver un hôtel.

PAGE 186

1. Nous **n'avons pas pu** attendre l'arrivée de Jules pour commencer.

2. Les exclus **ne peuvent pas** s'offrir des vacances.

3. Nous avons décidé de **ne pas acheter** la maison que nous avons vue la semaine dernière.

4. J'ai toujours regretté de **ne pas avoir assisté**/de **n'avoir pas assisté** à cette série de conférences.

5. Dans ce collège-là, les élèves semblent **ne pas devoir** être obéissants.

PAGE 188, EXERCICE DE CONSOLIDATION

Exemples:

1. Maintenant on ne voyage plus comme ça. On voyage en auto, en avion à réaction et en vaisseau spatial.

2. Maintenant on ne les respecte plus. On parle même d'un monde républicain.

3. Maintenant on n'écoute plus le jazz, qui a été remplacé par le rock.

4. Maintenant on ne va plus souvent au cinéma. On a la télévision, les vidéos et l'Internet.

5. Maintenant ils ne se conduisent plus bien. Il y a de plus en plus de chahuteurs.

PAGE 189

Exemples:

1. Jusqu'à maintenant, les astronautes n'ont jamais exploré les autres planètes du système solaire.

2. Jusqu'à maintenant, les hommes politiques n'ont jamais pu tenir leurs promesses.

3. Jusqu'à maintenant, les mères n'ont jamais réussi à avoir un salaire de ménagère.

4. Jusqu'à maintenant, les hommes n'ont jamais pu avoir un bébé!

5. Jusqu'à maintenant, les ordinateurs n'ont jamais fait preuve d'une intelligence comparable à celle de l'être humain.

PAGE 192, EXERCICE DE CONSOLIDATION

1. Non, il n'a été vu de personne.

2. Non, je ne l'aime pas.

3. Non, elle n'y va plus.

4. Non, ils n'ont jamais rien vu qui puisse les convaincre de leur existence.

5. Non, personne ne m'attendait.

6. Non, il n'y a rien à manger dans le placard.

PAGE 198

1. … il n'est plus jamais revenu.

2. … je n'ai plus rien trouvé.

3. Je ne vais plus jamais essayer des sauts de ce genre!

4. … je n'ai vu plus personne.

5. On n'a plus rien trouvé.

PAGE 198, EXERCICE DE CONSOLIDATION

1. Hakim lives not far from the bakery where he works.

2. The government was certainly not aware of this matter.

3. We no longer believe that science can resolve all our problems.

4. Never was a flood more devastating.

5. There is nothing more terrible than the death of a loved one.

6. Nobody is ready to take responsibility.

7. The woman who was pulled out of the ruins was scarcely aware of what was happening.

8. I hadn't seen André anywhere.

9. There was neither radio nor television in the house.

10. We wanted to play football, but we had only ten players.

7   *Prepositions*

PAGE 200

1. Alors, vous voyez là la boulangerie et le café? Eh bien, l'entrée de l'appartement est située **entre** les deux.

2. J'ai été très soulagé de revoir Delphine, car elle avait été absente **pendant** plus de trois heures.

3. **Dès** le début, j'ai su que ce métier me plairait.

4. Quelle émotion peut-on éprouver **devant** un homme de ce genre?

5. Évidemment le directeur était en colère, et il est sorti **sans** mot dire.

6. **Malgré** tous les efforts des chirurgiens, on n'a pas pu sauver la vie à cette victime.

7. **Depuis** 1997, Aurélie habite rue d'Anvers.

8. Tous mes amis étaient à la boum, **sauf** Karen, qui était malade ce jour-là.

9. **Selon** les tabloïdes, le ministre des affaires étrangères aurait eu une affaire de cœur avec sa secrétaire.

10. **Dans** dix ans, tous ceux qui se sont battus à la première guerre mondiale seront morts.

PAGE 201

1. Maria voulait savoir ce qu'il y avait **au-delà** des montagnes qui fermaient la vue de la maison.

2. **Au lieu** d'aller en prison, il a pu payer une amende.

3. **Faute d'**argent, nous n'avons pas pu aller en vacances.

4. Vous continuez **jusqu'au** carrefour, et là il faut prendre à gauche.

5. Tous les ministres ont assisté à cette réunion extraordinaire, **à l'exception** de M. Lenoir, qui était en Russie à ce moment-là.

6. Tu as bien raté le coup. Ta note est **au-dessous** de la moyenne.

7. Tout l'après-midi, nous avons marché **le long du** canal, et vers le soir on est arrivés à l'écluse qu'on cherchait.

8. Mon fils a pu assister au cours **grâce à** sa grand'mère qui a payé ses frais.

9. **A force de** travailler, nous avons pu nous procurer plus de trente mille francs.

10. **Lors de** la Révolution, notre ville n'était qu'un tout petit hameau.

PAGE 203

1. Après le concert, tout le monde est rentré.

2. Le petit déjeuner sera servi de sept heures à dix heures.

3. Ici, c'est très calme pendant la journée.

4. Les magasins ont commencé à fermer vers une heure.

5. La délégation sera en Russie pour deux semaines.

6. Attendez jusqu'à lundi.

7. Je serai là entre midi et deux heures.

8. Durant l'hiver, la maison est vide.

9. Les pompiers sont arrivés en moins de cinq minutes.

10. A partir de ce moment, il n'y avait plus d'espoir.

PAGE 205, EXERCICE A

Le salon est en face de la salle à manger. Dans le salon il y a un canapé qui est situé entre deux fauteuils. Il y a une lampe derrière le canapé. Le téléviseur se trouve dans le coin derrière le porte.

La salle à manger est située à côté de la chambre. Il y a cinq chaises autour d'une table. Il y a un buffet dans le coin, derrière le porte.

La cuisine est à côté du salon et en face de la chambre. Au milieu, il y a une grande table. L'évier est sous la fenêtre. Il y a un placard contre le mur, et le frigo se trouve derrière le porte.

La chambre est située en face de la cuisine. Il y a un lit, table et un téléviseur. La table se trouve entre le lit et le téléviseur. Dans le coin, il y a un lavabo.

PAGE 206, EXERCICE B

1. Compared with Nice, Marseilles is unattractive.

2. Is it possible to choose between one's husband and one's children?

3. Faced with the massed forces of NATO, the dictator had to yield.

4. This hideous conurbation stretches from the mountains to the sea.

5. Politicians can see nothing beyond their term of office.

PAGE 207, EXERCICE A

1. Deux pompiers ont été brûlés **par** les flammes.

2. Mère Thérèse était adorée **de** tout le monde.

3. Mon père a terrassé le cambrioleur **d'**un coup de poing.

4. Toute la cuisine était pleine **de** boue.

5. Le directeur de la banque avait été rattaché **avec** une corde.

PAGE 207, EXERCICE B

1. Le maire est sorti, suivi des conseillers.

2. La table était couverte de plats délicieux.

3. Les Zoulous avaient été repoussés à coups de feu.

4. Charles fut surpris par cette admission.

5. Emma était vêtue d'une robe bleue.

8   *Conjunctions*

PAGE 211

1. Celui qui avait volé la voiture est entré dans la rue Paradis; **or**, cette rue est une impasse, et on a eu vite fait de l'arrêter.

2. Le ministre des affaires étrangères **et** son homologue britannique sont en pourparlers depuis quelques heures, **mais**, jusqu'ici, sans issue.

3. On a nommé le nouveau chef de la Banque de France, **à savoir** M. André Dutour.

4. Mes parents iront en Irlande **ou** en Angleterre. Ça dépendra de la situation politique.

5. Laforge a été déclaré coupable du meurtre de sa fiancée; **cependant**, les preuves ne sont pas tout à fait claires.

PAGE 215, EXERCICE A

1. On a téléphoné **mais** il n'y avait personne.

2. On soupçonnait Lefèvre d'avoir commis ces vols. **En effet,** il n'avait pas d'alibi.

3. Mon mari a oublié d'aller à la banque. **Par conséquent**, il n'avait pas d'argent.

4. La vieille Nancy vivait toute seule. **Or**, sa nièce habitait en Nouvelle-Zélande à cette époque-là.

5. La plupart des scientifiques s'enthousiasment pour ce projet. **Cependant**, il y a toujours des sceptiques.

6. On ne peut pas continuer avec ces recherches **parce qu'**il n'y a pas suffisamment de fonds.

7. **Bien que** Josyanne veuille se marier, Stéphane ne veut pas renoncer à sa liberté.

8. On sortira demain, **pourvu que** j'aie fini mon travail.

9. Jeanne a allumé la télé **dès qu'**on est rentrés.

10. Hélène a rougi **comme si** elle était coupable.

PAGE 216, EXERCICE B

Exemples:

1. Le gouvernement doit augmenter le nombre de professeurs dans les lycées **parce que** l'enseignement national est en crise.

2. Il faudra installer plus de bancs dans la salle polyvalente **pour que** tout le monde puisse assister au spectacle.

3. On ouvrira les portes **aussitôt que** le maire arrivera.

4. Tout se passera bien, **à moins que** Philippe ne soit malade.

5. On ne paie pas suffisamment les employés, **si bien que** les syndicats comptent se mettre en grève.

6. Cet auteur continue d'écrire, **bien qu'**il soit presque aveugle.

7. Matthieu a cessé de jouer au foot **depuis qu'**il s'est cassé la cheville.

8. Nous viendrons te voir **quand** tu iras mieux.

Irregular verb tables

Aller

INDICATIVE MOOD

Present	
je	vais
tu	vas
il	
elle	va
on	
nous	allons
vous	allez
ils	vont
elles	

Future
j'irai
etc.

Conditional
j'irais
etc.

Past historic
j'allai
etc.

Imperfect
j'allais
etc.

Perfect
je suis allé(e)
etc.

Future perfect
je serai allé(e)
etc.

Pluperfect
j'étais allé(e)
etc.

Conditional perfect
je serais allé(e)
etc.

SUBJUNCTIVE MOOD

Present	
j'	aille
tu	ailles
il	
elle	aille
on	
nous	allions
vous	alliez
ils	aillent
elles	

Perfect
je sois allé(e)
etc.

1. The principal meaning of *aller* is 'to go'.
2. The verb is irregular only in the present indicative and the present subjunctive. While its future and conditional stems are irregular, all the endings of these tenses follow the regular patterns.
3. *Aller* is used to form the tense known as the immediate future. No preposition is required between *aller* and the following infinitive – *Qu'est-ce que tu vas faire?* – *Moi, je vais lire le journal* (What are you going to do? – I'm going to read the paper). Note the use of the imperfect of *aller* with an infinitive – *J'allais prendre ma voiture, mais j'ai décidé d'y aller par le train* (I was going to take my car, but I've decided to go by train).
4. *S'en aller* is a reflexive verb meaning 'to go away'. Note the imperatives: *Va-t'en! Allez-vous-en!*

Idioms
Cela va sans dire – That goes without saying
Cette robe te va bien – That dress suits you
aller chercher le médecin – to fetch the doctor
aller à tâtons – to grope one's way along

Avoir

INDICATIVE MOOD

Present		Future	Past historic
j'	ai	j'aurai	j'eus
tu	as	etc.	etc.

il		
elle }	a	
on		

		Conditional	Imperfect
nous	avons	j'aurais	j'avais
vous	avez	etc.	etc.

ils }	ont	
elles		

Perfect	Future perfect	Pluperfect
j'ai eu	j'aurai eu	j'avais eu
etc.	etc.	etc.

Conditional perfect
j'aurais eu
etc.

SUBJUNCTIVE MOOD

Present		Perfect
j'	aie	j'aie eu
tu	aies	etc.

il	
elle }	ait
on	
nous	ayons
vous	ayez
ils }	aient
elles	

1. The commonest meaning of *avoir* is 'to have'. In other uses it can mean 'to be' (*avoir seize ans*), 'to receive' (*avoir un coup de téléphone*), 'to suffer from' (*avoir un rhume*), 'to feel' (*avoir froid*), 'to be obliged to' (*avoir à téléphoner à quelqu'un*), 'to give (a smile)' (*avoir un sourire*), 'to make (remarks)' (*avoir des remarques*).

2. *Avoir* is the auxiliary verb in compound tenses for most French verbs. See **5.15**.

Idioms
en avoir à/après/contre quelqu'un – to have something against someone (R1/R2 usage)
J'en ai pour dix minutes – It'll take me ten minutes
J'en ai marre/plein le dos/ras-le-bol/plein les bottes – I'm fed up with it
avoir affaire à quelqu'un – to have dealings with someone

Devoir

INDICATIVE MOOD

Present		Future	Past historic
je	dois	je devrai	je dus
tu	dois	etc.	etc.
il			
elle }	doit		
on		**Conditional**	**Imperfect**
nous	devons	je devrais	je devais
vous	devez	etc.	etc.
ils }	doivent		
elles			

Perfect	Future perfect	Pluperfect
j'ai dû	j'aurai dû	j'avais dû
etc.	etc.	etc.

Conditional perfect

j'aurais dû
etc.

SUBJUNCTIVE MOOD

Present		Perfect
je	doive	j'aie dû
tu	doives	etc.
il		
elle }	doive	
on		
nous	devions	
vous	deviez	
ils }	doivent	
elles		

1. The commonest meaning of *devoir* is 'to have to', although its basic meaning is 'to owe'.
2. No preposition is required before an infinitive: *Je dois parler à Babette*.
3. The conditional is often used with the sense of 'ought to': *Je devrais aller plus souvent voir mes parents*. There is a sense of moral obligation in this use which is not present in *il faudrait*.
4. The conditional perfect is used with the sense of 'ought to have' – *J'aurais dû l'en prévenir*. Again, there is a sense of moral obligation which is lacking in *il aurait fallu*.
5. *Devoir* is used to express probability or certainty: *Il devait être là = Il était probablement là/Il était certainement là*. To decide which tense of *devoir* to use in such instances, choose the same tense of *devoir* which the other verb would have had if *devoir* had not been there: *Il a eu une idée géniale* becomes *Il a dû avoir une idée géniale* – He must have had a brilliant idea.

Idioms
Je dois à ma femme d'avoir réussi – I owe my success to my wife
devoir une fière chandelle à quelqu'un – to owe someone a debt of gratitude

Être

INDICATIVE MOOD

Present		Future	Past historic
je	suis	je serai	je fus
tu	es	etc.	etc.
il			
elle	est		
on		**Conditional**	**Imperfect**
nous	sommes	je serais	j'étais
vous	êtes	etc.	etc.
ils			
elles	sont		

Perfect	Future perfect	Pluperfect
j'ai été	j'aurai été	j'avais été
etc.	etc.	etc.

Conditional perfect

j'aurais été
etc.

SUBJUNCTIVE MOOD

Present		Perfect
je	sois	j'aie été
tu	sois	etc.
il		
elle	soit	
on		
nous	soyons	
vous	soyez	
ils		
elles	soient	

1. The commonest meaning of *être* is 'to be'.
2. It may be used to indicate a fact: *Il est médecin*; to indicate the date: *Nous sommes le 24 mai*; to indicate position: *Sa maison est rue Victor Hugo*; to indicate possession: *C'est à qui? – C'est à moi*; to indicate what is to happen: *Cette maison est à vendre*; to indicate what is happening: *Il est à travailler/en train de travailler*; to indicate time: *Il est onze heures*; to add emphasis: *C'est elle qui a fait cela*.
3. *Être* is the auxiliary verb in compound tenses for **all** reflexive verbs and for **many** verbs of motion. See **5.17**.
4. It is used to form all tenses of the passive. *Il a été renversé par un camion*. See **5.27 – 5.28**.

Idioms
Pauvreté n'est pas vice – It's no sin to be poor
être à l'article de la mort – to be at death's door
être en mesure de/à même de faire quelque chose – to be able to do something

Faire

INDICATIVE MOOD

Present			Future		Past historic	
je	fais		je ferai		je fis	
tu	fais		etc.		etc.	
il						
elle	} fait					
on						
nous	faisons		**Conditional**		**Imperfect**	
vous	faites		je ferais		je faisais	
ils	} font		etc.		etc.	
elles						

Perfect	Future perfect	Pluperfect
j'ai fait	j'aurai fait	j'avais fait
etc.	etc.	etc.

Conditional perfect

j'aurais fait
etc.

SUBJUNCTIVE MOOD

Present		Perfect
je	fasse	j'aie fait
tu	fasses	etc.
il		
elle	} fasse	
on		
nous	fassions	
vous	fassiez	
ils	} fassent	
elles		

1. The principal meaning of *faire* is 'to do' or 'to make'.
2. *Faire* is often used in impersonal expressions concerning the weather: *il fait beau, il fait chaud, il fait froid, il fait du brouillard, il fait du vent*, etc.
3. *Faire* is used to form causative expressions. No preposition is required between *faire* and the following infinitive: *Je me suis fait couper les cheveux* = I had my hair cut; *On a fait venir le médecin* = The doctor was sent for (i.e. They caused the doctor to come); *Fais voir!* = Show me! (i.e. Cause me to see)
4. **Note:** *Cela la fait sourire* = That makes her smile **but** *Cela la rend triste* = That makes her sad. *Rendre* is used to translate 'make' when an adjective follows.

Idioms
Cela ne fait rien – It doesn't matter
C'est bien fait – It serves you/him/her right
faire la part de – to make allowances for
Faites comme chez vous – Make yourself at home
Il faisait noir comme dans un four – It was pitch-black

Mettre

INDICATIVE MOOD

Present

je	mets
tu	mets
il	
elle	met
on	
nous	mettons
vous	mettez
ils	
elles	mettent

Future

je mettrai
etc.

Conditional

je mettrais
etc.

Past historic

je mis
etc.

Imperfect

je mettais
etc.

Perfect

j'ai mis
etc.

Future perfect

j'aurai mis
etc.

Pluperfect

j'avais mis
etc.

Conditional perfect

j'aurais mis
etc.

SUBJUNCTIVE MOOD

Present

je	mette
tu	mettes
il	
elle	mette
on	
nous	mettions
vous	mettiez
ils	
elles	mettent

Perfect

j'aie mis
etc.

1. The principal meaning of *mettre* is 'to put'. With reference to clothing, it means 'to put on'.
2. Verbs based on *mettre* include *admettre* (to admit), *commettre* (to commit), *compromettre* (to compromise), *émettre* (to emit, publish), *omettre* (to omit), *permettre* (to permit, allow), *promettre* (to promise), *soumettre* (to submit) and *transmettre* (to transmit, pass on). All these verbs are identical in conjugation to *mettre*.
3. Note these senses of *mettre*: to add (*mettre du sucre dans son thé*); to place in a situation (*mettre un enfant à l'école*); to switch on (*J'ai mis la radio*); to install (*On vient de mettre l'eau et l'électricité dans sa maison*); to write (*Il met (dans sa lettre) qu'il ne peut pas venir*); to suppose (*Mettons que vous avez/ayez raison*).

Idioms
se mettre à faire quelque chose – to start to do something
y mettre du sien – to pull one's weight: *Il faut que tu y mettes du tien!*
J'ai mis deux heures à le faire – I took two hours to do it
se mettre dans un beau pétrin – to get into a right mess
Je m'en mettrais la main au feu – I'd swear to it

Pouvoir

INDICATIVE MOOD

Present		**Future**	**Past historic**
je	peux	je pourrai	je pus
tu		etc.	etc.
il			
elle	peut		
on		**Conditional**	**Imperfect**
nous	pouvons	je pourrais	je pouvais
vous	pouvez	etc.	etc.
ils	peuvent		
elles			

Perfecr	**Future perfect**	**Pluperfect**
j'ai pu	j'aurai pu	j'avais pu
etc.	etc.	etc.

Conditional perfect

j'aurais pu
etc.

SUBJUNCTIVE MOOD

Present		**Perfect**
je	puisse	j'aie pu
tu	puisses	etc.
il		
elle	puisse	
on		
nous	puissions	
vous	puissiez	
ils	puissent	
elles		

1. The commonest meaning of *pouvoir* is 'to be able to', but the verb is also used to express possibility, suggestion and the fact of being allowed to do something.
2. No preposition is required before an infinitive: *Je peux sortir maintenant.*
3. The conditional is often used with the sense of 'might': *Elle pourrait peut-être téléphoner à ses amis.*
4. When inverted, *je peux* becomes *puis-je?*
5. In higher registers and in idioms, *pouvoir* used negatively is sometimes found without its *pas* – *Elle n'en pouvait mais* – There was nothing she could do about it.

Idioms

Je n'en peux plus – I can't take any more
Je n'y peux rien – There's nothing I can do about it
Il se peut que... (+ subjunctive) – It's possible that...
Cela se pourrait bien – That may well be the case

Prendre

INDICATIVE MOOD

Present		Future	Past historic
je	prends	je prendrai	je pris
tu	prends	etc.	etc.
il			
elle	prend		
on		Conditional	Imperfect
nous	prenons	je prendrais	je prenais
vous	prenez	etc.	etc.
ils	prennent		
elles			

Perfect	Future perfect	Pluperfect
j'ai pris	j'aurai pris	j'avais pris
etc.	etc.	etc.

Conditional perfect

j'aurais pris
etc.

SUBJUNCTIVE MOOD

Present		Perfect
je	prenne	j'aie pris
tu	prennes	etc.
il		
elle	prenne	
on		
nous	prenions	
vous	preniez	
ils	prennent	
elles		

1. The principal meaning of *prendre* is 'to take'.
2. Verbs based on *prendre* include *apprendre* (to learn), *comprendre* (to understand), *entreprendre* (to undertake), *s'éprendre* (to fall in love – particularly in 17th century Classical texts), *se méprendre* (to make a mistake), *surprendre* (to surprise). All of this group are identical in conjugation to *prendre*.

Idioms
s'en prendre à quelqu'un de quelque chose – to blame someone for something
prendre le dessus sur quelqu'un – to get the better of someone
en prendre son parti – to make up one's mind
prendre le parti de quelqu'un – to take sides with somebody

Savoir

INDICATIVE MOOD

Present		Future	Past historic
je	sais	je saurai	je sus
tu	sais	etc.	etc.
il			
elle	sait		
on		**Conditional**	**Imperfect**
nous	savons	je saurais	je savais
vous	savez	etc.	etc.
ils	savent		
elles			

Perfect	Future perfect	Pluperfect
j'ai su	j'aurai su	j'avais su
etc.	etc.	etc.

Conditional perfect

j'aurais su
etc.

SUBJUNCTIVE MOOD

Present		Perfect
je	sache	j'aie su
tu	saches	etc.
il		
elle	sache	
on		
nous	sachions	
vous	sachiez	
ils	sachent	
elles		

1. The commonest meaning of *savoir* is 'to know', but it is also used to express ideas of *ability* and *realisation*.
2. No preposition is required before an infinitive: *Je sais nager*. Note that this use expresses the *skill* of being able to swim, not the physical ability.
3. *Il sait bien que ce n'est pas vrai* = He is well aware that it's not true. This use expresses *awareness* or *realisation*.
4. The use of *savoir* as a reflexive may avoid the necessity of a subordinate clause: *Elle se savait incapable de le faire* = She knew she was unable to do it.
5. In higher registers and in idioms, *savoir* used negatively is sometimes found without *pas*: *Il ne savait que faire* = He didn't know what to do.

Idioms

… et que sais-je encore – … and I don't know what else
pas que je sache – not that I know/am aware
autant que je sache – as far as I know/am aware
vous n'êtes pas sans savoir… – you are well aware…
Je ne savais à quel saint me vouer – I didn't know which way to turn (Note omission of *pas*)

Venir

INDICATIVE MOOD

Present

je	viens
tu	viens
il	
elle	} vient
on	
nous	venons
vous	venez
ils	} viennent
elles	

Future

je viendrai
etc.

Conditional

je viendrais
etc.

Past historic

je vins
etc.

Imperfect

je venais
etc.

Perfect

Je suis venu(e)
etc.

Future perfect

je serai venu(e)
etc.

Pluperfect

j'étais venu(e)
etc.

Conditional perfect

je serais venu(e)
etc.

SUBJUNCTIVE MOOD

Present

je	vienne
tu	viennes
il	
elle	} vienne
on	
nous	venions
vous	veniez
ils	} viennent
elles	

Perfect

je sois venu(e)
etc.

1. The main meaning of *venir* is 'to come'.
2. It is the root of *revenir* – to come back, *devenir* – to become, *advenir* – to happen and *survenir* – to happen. Like *venir*, these verbs all require *être* as the auxiliary in compound tenses.
3. The verb *tenir* and its compounds follow the pattern of *venir*, but most require *avoir* as an auxiliary in compound tenses, unless used reflexively. The group includes *s'abstenir* – to refrain, *contenir* – to contain, *maintenir* – to maintain, *obtenir* – to obtain, *soutenir* – to support.
4. When used with an infinitive, *venir* does not require any preposition: *Alain est venu voir mon père* – Alain came to see my father.

Idioms

venir de faire quelque chose – to have just done something
Notre projet vient bien – Our plan is coming along nicely
venir au monde – to be born

Vouloir

INDICATIVE MOOD

Present		Future	Past historic
je	veux	je voudrai	je voulus
tu	veux	etc.	etc.
il			
elle	veut		
on		**Conditional**	**Imperfect**
nous	voulons	je voudrais	je voulais
vous	voulez	etc.	etc.
ils	veulent		
elles			

Perfect	Future perfect	Pluperfect
j'ai voulu	j'aurai voulu	j'avais voulu
etc.	etc.	etc.

Conditional perfect

j'aurais voulu
etc.

SUBJUNCTIVE MOOD

Present		Perfect
je	veuille	j'aie voulu
tu	veuilles	etc.
il		
elle	veuille	
on		
nous	voulions	
vous	vouliez	
ils	veuillent	
elles		

1. The commonest meaning of *vouloir* is 'to want (to)'.
2. No preposition is required before an infinitive: *Je veux aller en Espagne.*
3. *Vouloir* is used to make requests: *Veux-tu fermer la porte? Voulez-vous signer là, s'il vous plaît?*
4. Note the special form to close a formal letter: *Veuillez agréer, Monsieur/Madame, l'expression de mes sentiments distingués.*

Idioms

en vouloir à quelqu'un – to hold it against someone, to blame
Que voulez-vous? – What do you expect?
vouloir dire – to mean, e.g. *Que veut dire 'phagocyter'?* – What does 'phagocyter' mean?

IRREGULAR VERBS

In the table of irregular verbs, note the following conventions:

- The table is divided into **simple tenses**, **compound tenses** and **subjunctive forms**.
- Verbs whose *je* form ends in -*s* follow the pattern -*s*, -*s*, -*t*.
- Verbs whose *je* form ends in -*x* follow the pattern -*x*, -*x*, -*t*.
- Verbs of the *cueillir* type have -*er* conjugation endings in the singular: -*e*, -*es*, -*e*.
- Unless otherwise stated, the *vous* and *ils* forms follow on logically from the *nous* form.

Infinitive	SIMPLE TENSES			COMPOUND TENSES		SUBJUNCTIVE		SIMILAR VERBS
	Present	Future / Conditional	Past historic / Imperfect	Perfect / Pluperfect	Future perfect / Conditional perfect	Present	Perfect	
acquérir (to acquire)	j'acquiers, il acquiert, nous acquérons, ils acquièrent	j'acquerrai / -ais	j'acquis j'acquérais	j'ai acquis j'avais acquis	j'aurai acquis j'aurais acquis	j'acquière, nous acquérions	j'aie acquis	conquérir, s'enquérir, requérir
aller (to go)	je vais, tu vas, il va, nous allons, vous allez, ils vont	j'irai / -ais	j'allai j'allais	je suis allé(e) j'étais allé(e)	je serai allé(e) je serais allé(e)	j'aille	je sois allé(e)	
s'asseoir (to sit down)	je m'assieds, il s'assied, nous nous asseyons	je m'assiérai / -ais	je m'assis je m'asseyais	je me suis assis(e) je m'étais assis(e)	je me serai assis(e) je me serais assis(e)	je m'asseye	je me sois assis(e)	seoir (il and ils forms only) – not found in compound tenses
avoir (to have)	j'ai, tu as, il a, nous avons, vous avez, ils ont	j'aurai / -ais	j'eus j'avais	j'ai eu j'avais eu	j'aurai eu j'aurais eu	j'aie, tu aies, il ait, nous ayons, vous ayez, ils aient	j'aie eu	
battre (to beat)	je bats, il bat, nous battons	je battrai / -ais	je battis je battais	j'ai battu j'avais battu	j'aurai battu j'aurais battu	je batte	j'aie battu	abattre, combattre, débattre
boire (to drink)	je bois, il boit, nous buvons, ils boivent	je boirai / -ais	je bus je buvais	j'ai bu j'avais bu	j'aurai bu j'aurais bu	je boive, nous buvions	j'aie bu	

Infinitive	Present	Future / Conditional	Passé simple / Imparfait	Passé composé / Plus-que-parfait	Futur antérieur / Conditionnel passé	Subjonctif	Passé du subjonctif	Similar verbs
conduire (to drive)	je conduis, il conduit, nous conduisons	je conduirai / -ais	je conduisis je conduisais	j'ai conduit j'avais conduit	j'aurai conduit j'aurais conduit	je conduise	j'aie conduit	construire, déduire, détruire, instruire
connaître (to know)	je connais, il connaît, nous connaissons	je connaîtrai / -ais	je connus je connaissais	j'ai connu j'avais connu	j'aurai connu j'aurais connu	je connaisse	j'aie connu	reconnaître
courir (to run)	je cours, il court, nous courons	je courrai / -ais	je courus je courais	j'ai couru j'avais couru	j'aurai couru j'aurais couru	je coure	j'aie couru	accourir
craindre (to fear)	je crains, il craint, nous craignons	je craindrai / -ais	je craignis je craignais	j'ai craint j'avais craint	j'aurai craint j'aurais craint	je craigne	j'aie craint	
croire (to believe)	je crois, il croit, nous croyons, ils croient	je croirai / -ais	je crus je croyais	j'ai cru j'avais cru	j'aurai cru j'aurais cru	je croie	j'aie cru	
croître (to grow)	je croîs, il croît, nous croissons	je croîtrai / -ais	je crûs je croissais	j'ai crû j'avais crû	j'aurai crû j'aurais crû	je croisse	j'aie crû	(s') accroître
cueillir (to pick)	je cueille	je cueillerai / -ais	je cueillis je cueillais	j'ai cueilli j'avais cueilli	j'aurai cueilli j'aurais cueilli	je cueille	j'aie cueilli	accueillir, recueillir
devoir (to have to)	je dois, il doit, nous devons, ils doivent	je devrai / -ais	je dus je devais	j'ai dû j'avais dû	j'aurai dû j'aurais dû	je doive, nous devions, ils doivent	j'aie dû	
dire (to say, to tell)	je dis, il dit, nous disons, vous dites, ils disent	je dirai / -ais	je dis je disais	j'ai dit j'avais dit	j'aurai dit j'aurais dit	je dise	j'aie dit	interdire
écrire (to write)	j'écris, il écrit, nous écrivons	j'écrirai / -ais	j'écrivis j'écrivais	j'ai écrit j'avais écrit	j'aurai écrit j'aurais écrit	j'écrive	j'aie écrit	décrire, inscrire

Infinitive	SIMPLE TENSES			COMPOUND TENSES		SUBJUNCTIVE		SIMILAR VERBS
	Present	Future / Conditional	Past historic / Imperfect	Perfect / Pluperfect	Future perfect / Conditional perfect	Present	Perfect	
envoyer (*to send*)	j'envoie, nous envoyons, ils envoient	j'enverrai / -ais	j'envoyai / j'envoyais	j'ai envoyé / j'avais envoyé	j'aurai envoyé / j'aurais envoyé	j'envoie	j'aie envoyé	renvoyer
être (*to be*)	je suis, tu es, il est, nous sommes, vous êtes, ils sont	je serai / -ais	je fus / j'étais	j'ai été / j'avais été	j'aurai été / j'aurais été	je sois, tu sois, il soit, nous soyons, vous soyez, ils soient	j'aie été	
faire (*to do, to make*)	je fais, tu fais, il fait, nous faisons, vous faites, ils font	je ferai / -ais	je fis / je faisais	j'ai fait / j'avais fait	j'aurai fait / j'aurais fait	je fasse	j'aie fait	refaire
falloir (*to be necessary*)	il faut	il faudra / -ait	il fallut / il fallait	il a fallu / il avait fallu	il aura fallu / il aurait fallu	il faille	il ait fallu	
fuir (*to flee*)	je fuis, nous fuyons, ils fuient	je fuirai / -ais	je fuis / je fuyais	j'ai fui / j'avais fui	j'aurai fui / j'aurais fui	je fuie	j'aie fui	s'enfuir
lire (*to read*)	je lis, il lit, nous lisons	je lirai / -ais	je lus / je lisais	j'ai lu / j'avais lu	j'aurai lu / j'aurais lu	je lise	j'aie lu	élire
mettre (*to put*)	je mets, il met, nous mettons	je mettrai / -ais	je mis / je mettais	j'ai mis / j'avais mis	j'aurai mis / j'aurais mis	je mette	j'aie mis	admettre, permettre, promettre, soumettre

Infinitive	Present	Future / Conditional	Past historic / Imperfect	Perfect / Pluperfect	Future perfect / Conditional perfect	Present subjunctive	Perfect subjunctive	Related verbs
mourir (to die)	je meurs, il meurt, nous mourons, ils meurent	je mourrai / -ais	(je mourus) / je mourais	(je suis mort(e)) / (j'étais mort(e))	je serai mort(e) / je serais mort(e)	je meure, nous mourions	je sois mort	
mouvoir (to move)	je meus, il meut, nous mouvons, ils meuvent	je mouvrai / -ais	je mus / je mouvais	j'ai mû / j'avais mû	j'aurai mû / j'aurais mû	je meuve, nous mouvions	j'aie mû	émouvoir (p.p. ému), promouvoir (p.p. promu)
naître (to be born)	je nais, il naît, nous naissons	je naîtrai / -ais	je naquis / je naissais	je suis né(e) / j'étais né(e)	je serai né(e) / je serais né(e)	je naisse	je sois né(e)	renaître
plaire (to please)	je plais, il plaît, nous plaisons	je plairai / -ais	je plus / je plaisais	j'ai plu / j'avais plu	j'aurai plu / j'aurais plu	je plaise	j'aie plu	déplaire
pleuvoir (to rain)	il pleut	il pleuvra / -ait	il plut / il pleuvait	il a plu / il avait plu	il aura plu / il aurait plu	il pleuve	il ait plu	
pouvoir (to be able)	je peux, il peut, nous pouvons, ils peuvent	je pourrai / -ais	je pus / je pouvais	j'ai pu / j'avais pu	j'aurai pu / j'aurais pu	je puisse	j'aie pu	
prendre (to take)	je prends, il prend, nous prenons, vous prenez, ils prennent	je prendrai / -ais	je pris / je prenais	j'ai pris / j'avais pris	j'aurai pris / j'aurais pris	je prenne, nous prenions	j'aie pris	apprendre, comprendre, surprendre
recevoir (to receive)	je reçois, il reçoit, nous recevons, ils reçoivent	je recevrai / -ais	je reçus / je recevais	j'ai reçu / j'avais reçu	j'aurai reçu / j'aurais reçu	je reçoive, nous recevions	j'aie reçu	(s') apercevoir, concevoir, décevoir, percevoir
résoudre (to resolve)	je résous, il résout, nous résolvons	je résoudrai / -ais	je résolus / je résolvais	j'ai résolu / j'avais résolu	j'aurai résolu / j'aurais résolu	je résolve	j'aie résolu	absoudre (p.p. absous), dissoudre (p.p. dissous)

Infinitive	SIMPLE TENSES			COMPOUND TENSES		SUBJUNCTIVE		SIMILAR VERBS
	Present	Future/ Conditional	Past historic / Imperfect	Perfect / Pluperfect	Future perfect / Conditional perfect	Present	Perfect	
rire (to laugh)	je ris, il rit, nous rions	je rirai / -ais	je ris je riais	j'ai ri j'avais ri	j'aurai ri j'aurais ri	je rie	j'aie ri	sourire
rompre (to break)	je romps, il rompt, nous rompons	je romprai / -ais	je rompis je rompais	j'ai rompu j'avais rompu	j'aurai rompu j'aurais rompu	je rompe	j'aie rompu	corrompre, interrompre
savoir (to know)	je sais, il sait, nous savons	je saurai / -ais	je sus je savais	j'ai su j'avais su	j'aurai su j'aurais su	je sache	j'aie su	
suffire (to suffice, to be enough)	je suffis, il suffit, nous suffisons	je suffirai / -ais	je suffis je suffisais	j'ai suffi j'avais suffi	j'aurai suffi j'aurais suffi	je suffise	j'aie suffi	
suivre (to follow)	je suis, tu suis, il suit, nous suivons	je suivrai / -ais	je suivis je suivais	j'ai suivi j'avais suivi	j'aurai suivi j'aurais suivi	je suive	j'aie suivi	poursuivre
se taire (to say nothing)	je me tais, il se tait, nous taisons	je me tairai / -ais	je me tus je me taisais	je me suis tu(e) je m'étais tu(e)	je me serai tu(e) je me serais tu(e)	je me taise	je me sois tu(e)	
tenir (to hold)	je tiens, il tient, nous tenons, ils tiennent	je tiendrai / -ais	je tins je tenais	j'ai tenu j'avais tenu	j'aurai tenu j'aurais tenu	je tienne, nous tenions	j'aie tenu	(s')abstenir, maintenir, soutenir, retenir
vaincre (to defeat)	je vaincs, tu vaincs, il vainc, nous vainquons	je vaincrai / -ais	je vainquis je vainquais	j'ai vaincu j'avais vaincu	j'aurai vaincu j'aurais vaincu	je vainque	j'aie vaincu	convaincre

	il vaut, ils valent	il vaudra / -ait	il valut / il valait	il a valu / il avait valu	il aura valu / il aurait valu	il vaille	il ait valu	prévaloir, revaloir
valoir (to be worth)	il vaut, ils valent	il vaudra / -ait	il valut / il valait	il a valu / il avait valu	il aura valu / il aurait valu	il vaille	il ait valu	prévaloir, revaloir
venir (to come)	je viens, il vient, nous venons, ils viennent	je viendrai / -ais	je vins / je venais	je suis venu(e) / j'étais venu(e)	je serai venu(e) / je serais venu(e)	je vienne, nous venions	je sois venu(e)	advenir, devenir, revenir, (se) souvenir
vivre (to live)	je vis, il vit, nous vivons	je vivrai	je vécus / je vivais	j'ai vécu / j'avais vécu	j'aurai vécu / j'aurais vécu	je vive	j'aie vécu	revivre, survivre
voir (to see)	je vois, nous voyons, ils voient	je verrai / -ais	je vis / je voyais	j'ai vu / j'avais vu	j'aurai vu / j'aurais vu	je voie, nous voyions	j'aie vu	entrevoir, pourvoir (*fut.* pourvoirai, *past hist.* pourvus), prévoir (*fut.* prévoirai), revoir
vouloir (to want)	je veux, il veut, nous voulons, ils veulent	je voudrai / -ais	je voulus / je voulais	j'ai voulu / j'avais voulu	j'aurai voulu / j'aurais voulu	je veuille, nous voulions	j'aie voulu	

Index

The references are to page numbers.